BUILDING VALUE WITH CAPITAL-STRUCTURE STRATEGIES

Henry A. Davis
Henry A. Davis & Co.

William W. Sihler
Darden Graduate School of Business Administration
University of Virginia

A publication of Financial Executives Research Foundation, Inc.

Financial Executives Research Foundation, Inc.
10 Madison Avenue
P.O. Box 1938
Morristown, NJ 07962-1938
(973) 898-4608

International Standard Book Number 1-885065-11-6
Library of Congress Catalog Card Number 97-77704
Printed in the United States of America

First Printing

Financial Executives Research Foundation, Inc. (FERF™) is the research affiliate of Financial Executives Institute. The basic purpose of the Foundation is to sponsor research and publish informative material in the field of business management, with particular emphasis on the practice of financial management and its evolving role in the management of business.

FERF publications can be ordered by calling 1-800-680-FERF
(U.S. and Canada only; international orders, please call 770-751-1986).
Quantity discounts are available.

ADVISORY COMMITTEE

Arthur V. Neis (Chairman)
Vice President, Treasurer and Chief Financial Officer
Life Care Services Corporation

Roderick N. Dolan
Vice President
Piper Jaffray Inc.

James M. Drinkwater
Vice President and Treasurer
TELUS Corporation

Kathryn E. Falberg
Vice President and Chief Financial Officer
Amgen Inc.

Gracie F. Hemphill
Project Manager
Financial Executives Research Foundation, Inc.

J. Scott Kamsler
Senior Vice President, Finance and Chief Financial Officer
SymmetriCom, Inc.

J. James Lewis
Executive Vice President
Financial Executives Research Foundation, Inc.

John F. McGovern
Executive Vice President and Chief Financial Officer
Georgia-Pacific Corporation

Rhona L. Ferling
Publications Manager
Financial Executives Research Foundation, Inc.

CONTENTS

APPENDICES

A

INTRODUCTION

A company's financial structure is an essential concern of every chief financial officer (CFO) and treasurer and is an integral part of a company's strategy to build shareholder value. Policies on capital structure and dividends vary considerably. They are partly a matter of management choice, but are also influenced by the nature of the company's business and current circumstances. For example, many companies increased their leverage in the 1980s, but many decreased it in the 1990s. Despite the importance of financial structure, relatively few articles in the business press recently address it directly and comprehensively. Corporate finance textbooks and academic journal articles provide useful theoretical background, statistical research, and case studies. This research project was commissioned to document, based on interviews, how a selected group of CFOs and treasurers make their decisions about capital structure, dividends, and related issues, and to compare those findings with financial theory.

For this project, the authors interviewed 13 companies: Amgen Inc.; General Electric Company (GE); Georgia-Pacific Corporation; The Home Depot, Inc.; Marriott International, Inc., and Host Marriott-Corporation; Monsanto Company; Oracle Corporation; Paychex, Inc.; Sheplers, Inc.; SymmetriCom, Inc.; TELUS Corporation; and Vermeer Manufacturing Company. The authors used a standard interview protocol, contained in appendix A. The order of topics in the case studies and summary chapters follows the order of the interview protocol.

Two of the variables used in recent academic studies to differentiate policies on capital structure and dividends are growth patterns and asset types. To ensure that the case-study companies would represent a variety of industries with different financial characteristics, the researchers developed a model to group the companies into four quadrants referred to as the "quadrant model," depending on whether their industries tended to have secular (i.e., more long term) or have volatile (i.e., cyclical) growth patterns and primarily fixed or intangible assets. Drawing on previous studies, the financial press, and other public information about industry and company characteristics, the researchers developed a prospect list of companies spread across the four quadrants. The Financial Executives Research Foundation, Inc. (FERF) sent invitation letters to participate in the study to Financial Executives Institute (FEI) members in the target companies. In reaching agreement with companies willing to participate, the researchers and FERF ensured that the case-study companies were spread evenly across the four quadrants. The researchers conducted interviews with senior financial management. Because the case-study companies had a preponderance of low debt, the researchers did a literature review to summarize recent studies of highly leveraged companies for comparison.

Table 1 displays the 13 case-study companies according to the quadrant model. While the model is useful for comparisons, not every company fits perfectly into any one quadrant. For example, the researchers characterize retailing and hotel management as volatile industries, but Home Depot and Marriott International are fast-growing companies.

How to Use This Book

A discussion of capital-structure theories, found in chapter 1, highlights the principal trends of academic thinking on capital structure and dividend policy. Chapter 2 compares the interview findings across all the case-study companies. The individual case studies follow in chapters 3 through 14. Chapter 15 summarizes recent studies of highly leveraged companies. The interview protocol is contained in Appendix A, followed by the bibliography in Appendix B, the glossary in Appendix C,

Table 1
Case-Study Companies

	Secular Growth	Volatile Growth
Fixed Assets	General Electric (M,I)	Georgia-Pacific (S,I)
	SymmetriCom (S,D)	Monsanto (M,I)
	TELUS (S,I)	Vermeer Manufacturing (S,I)
		Host Marriott (S,I)
Intangible Assets	Oracle (S,I)	Marriott International (S,I)
	Amgen (S,I)	Home Depot (S,D)
	Paychex (S,D)	Sheplers (S,D)

(S = single business, M = multibusiness, D = domestic, I = international)

and a statistical comparison of industry financials in Appendix D. Technical terms in the glossary appear in boldface type the first time they appear in the text.

Capital-Structure Theories

he brilliant economist and successful investor, the late J. Maynard Keynes, wrote in his *General Theory of Employment*, "Practical men, who believe themselves to be quite exempt from any intellectual influences, are usually the slaves of some defunct economist." In the case of capital-structure decisions, innovating academics like Franco Modigliani and Merton H. Miller are still very much alive and can enjoy seeing the influence their works have on finance decision makers. A few academics have even left the ivory tower to help put their theories into practice, as Keynes did.

This chapter will review briefly the major theoretical threads woven into the fabric of capital structure decisions in the last half century. In addition to serving as a refresher for the reader, this review of academic insights will facilitate comparisons between the actions financial managers take about capital structure and what the conceptual frameworks suggest should be the practice in order to maximize shareholder value.

Background

Joel Dean's *Managerial Economics*[1] text started capital-investment analysis on its analytical course in the early 1950s. He suggested classifying capital-expenditure projects into four categories, each with a different hurdle rate reflecting its risk. After nearly 50 years of academic discourse that flirted enthusiastically with single hurdle rates, the conceptual guidance has returned to Dean's basic model. It again concludes that each investment should have a hurdle rate that relates to its own risk characteristics.

Conceptual guidelines for capital-structure decisions have followed a similar route, which this chapter will describe. The guidelines moved from an emphasis on managerial judgment in selecting the proper balance of debt and equity to a rigid prescription of the proper balance.

These certainties were subsequently eroded as questions arose about dimensions that the rigid concepts had assumed away. The conceptual frameworks have now returned the decision to the arena of judgment. They provide suggestions and insights about what should be considered, but managerial judgment is again the principal player in balancing the conflicting risks and rewards of the capital-structure decision.

It is therefore an opportune time for a field study of how today's managers make their capital-structure decisions. An extensive field study was last done more than 35 years ago by Gordon Donaldson.[2] This new study will not replicate Donaldson's work, but it shares the purpose of identifying and reporting current practices, approaches, and analytical methods used by practitioners. These techniques can then be compared with the guidelines provided by the academic literature to explore the congruence of the practices and the conceptual frameworks. It also will be possible to see if significant changes in managerial approach have occurred in the past 35 years.

The following two sections set up a basic framework for discussing and evaluating approaches to the capital-structure decision. They will provide baskets in which the academic works can be placed, so apples are compared with apples and oranges with oranges. The first section outlines the basic components of the capital-structure decision, allowing the more theoretical concepts to be placed against a common background. The second section briefly classifies the literature into four types, which is useful in considering the validity of the material discussed. The remainder of the chapter is devoted to reviewing the concepts themselves.

Components of Capital-Structure Decisions

Financial decisions are very simple in structure—the judgments get complex. The capital-structure decision is no exception to this rule.[3] It has four components, as illustrated in figure 1.1: asset selection, debt-equity proportion, new equity issuance, and dividend payout. Current theory specifies that the decisions should be made simultaneously in order to optimize a firm's financial value; the order in which the decisions are made is irrelevant. In practice, however, it is seldom possible to address all four decisions concurrently. Because capital-structure

Figure 1.1
Components of the Capital-Structure Decision

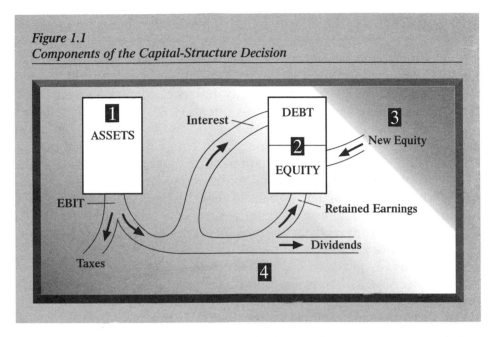

theory focuses on the three latter decisions, it usually presumed that tentative decisions have been made about the firm's assets. The *asset decision* is therefore designated as decision 1.

This approach is consistent with the simplifying concepts theorists have developed. Much of the capital-structure conceptual framework has been based on the assumption that the nature of the available assets did not depend on the capital structure. The extreme assumption was that all investments offered the same risk-adjusted return and were equally available to all investors in unlimited quantity. The assets—the opportunities for investment—were there, waiting for the investor with capital to seize them.

Assets, once predominantly physical but now increasingly of an intellectual nature, generate the stream of cash that attracts investment. Assuming that depreciation must be reinvested to maintain that stream, the earnings before interest and taxes (EBIT) are distributed to the government as taxes, to the creditors as interest, and to the holders of the equity. The *capital-structure decision*, decision 2 in figure 1.1, establishes the proportions of the capital to be raised from the debt and equity markets, which determines how the earnings before interest and after taxes (EBIAT) are to be divided. The debt-equity ratio selected should be the one that maximizes the entity's market capitalization.

Decision 3, the *new equity decision*, is whether to issue additional equity to finance the firm if necessary to maintain both the selected investment schedule and the debt-equity balance. Many conceptualizations presume that the answer to this question is "yes," as long as the additional assets generate a positive net present value. For many economic enterprises, particularly closely held companies, the answer may be "no." One reason for this decision may be that existing stockholders place a very high imputed value on maintaining control. Another may be that the owners or managers believe that the stock is underpriced. As a result, the additional assets do not return as much as they appear to because the existing owners' returns are eroded by the unfavorable price at which new shares will be sold.

If the answer to the new equity decision is "no," then the *dividend decision*, decision 4—the proportion of the profits to be paid to the equity owners as dividends—is also determined. In a four-decision system, if any three decisions are made, the fourth is made by default. Thus, given the flows to the equity holders, which are determined by the asset and the capital-structure decisions, and the decision not to raise new equity, the amount of equity the firm must retain is set.

For example, if assets generate an EBIT of $100 and $25 is left as profits after taxes, and if attractive investments of $40 have been selected (the asset decision), then a management that believes a debt-equity ratio of 1:1 is optimal (but does not wish to issue new equity) must raise $20 of debt and retain $20 of profit. Only $5 is left for distribution as dividends. The dividend is truly the plug figure in this instance. John Lintner has even defined the investor's true profits as the dividends that can be paid out when the firm has an optimal debt-equity proportion and has the ability to pay those dividends in the future.[4] Dividends more than this amount are, in essence, a return of capital that must be replaced by new equity.

On the other hand, if the entity is willing to raise new equity, the new equity and the dividend decisions become more complex. Suppose, in the example sketched in the previous paragraph, management decided to pay out more than $5 as dividends, returning some capital to the owners. In this case, to maintain its ability to generate cash and grow while maintaining its desired capital-structure ratio, the firm must then raise new equity exactly equal to the amount by which the dividends exceed the $5 maximum. The new equity dilutes the ownership proportion of the existing investors and slows the growth in their future earnings and dividends. The issue in this instance is whether the marketplace values dividends today at the cost of slower dividend growth in the future.

Many conceptualizations dismiss this tradeoff as irrelevant to the creation of value. The presumption is that an investor must reinvest in the firm any capital returned to maintain the investor's existing proportionate ownership and growth. Given existing institutional arrangements, however, in some cases the tradeoff between dividends and new equity is a decision that can influence value. For instance, the individuals who invested in stable, slowly growing companies, as electric utilities were for many decades, were believed to be the elderly, who were looking for stability of cash flow in their retirement years. These individuals were often not only living off their income, but were also presumed to be gradually consuming their capital. Thus, existing owners would be unlikely to reinvest the return of capital in the firm, preferring to dilute their future returns by allowing new investors to provide necessary new capital.

The conceptual alternative would be for the firm to avoid issuing new equity, retain the funds, and allow the stock price to rise more than it would if diluted by new investors. Investors wishing to withdraw their capital could sell the appropriate proportion of their now more highly priced investment to gain the return of capital on which they need to live.

The problem with this scenario is that the transaction costs for the individual investor to liquidate a small portion of an investment are usually far higher than for the firm to issue new stock. The elderly investor may thus prefer investing in a firm that makes it as inexpensive as possible to withdraw capital. If this preference applies to a sufficiently large group, the price-earnings ratio of the firm that provides this service should be higher than of a firm that does not.

This section has outlined the relationships of the four components of the capital-structure decision. In assessing a theoretical approach, it is important to identify which of the four decisions is being discussed and what assumptions are made about the effect that decision has on the other decisions. To illustrate briefly with the dividend decision, the tradeoff between the new equity decision and the dividend decision results in more cash for the investor today but less over the longer term. A high dividend payout also can be funded by allowing the debt-equity ratio to change as the dividend is financed by borrowing. This option is clearly not sustainable in the longer run, but it has often been the route taken in a period of brief adversity or when a firm's initial debt position is very low compared to the target level. A high dividend also can be maintained by reducing the investment in assets. This approach, too, presents difficulties in the longer run because the firm will lose market share and probably its strategic position.

Analytical Frameworks

Analytical frameworks, largely developed by economists and academics in related fields, can be divided into four main categories: conceptual, empirical, anecdotal,[5] and institutional. The practitioners in each area tend to view alternative approaches with some skepticism. The differences among these perspectives will be briefly indicated as background for discussing the evolution of the theories of capital structure. It is not appropriate, for example, to use the same standard in evaluating a conceptual study and an empirical one. As an illustration, consider F. Scott Fitzgerald's proposition that "The rich are different from us."

After reflecting on this proposition, the conceptualist would develop a set of internally consistent relationships relating changes in the consumption of goods (say, potatoes) and services to changes in wealth and to one another, usually based on some generally accepted but abstracted assumptions about the world. The equations would probably show that as wealth increased, the consumption of more attractive but more costly goods would increase relative to the base case. The conceptualist would thus conclude that based on the relative consumption of potatoes, the rich are different.

The empirical analyst, perhaps building on the conceptualist's suggestions, would gather data on the consumption habits of several thousand individuals, selected in a manner suitable to the desired validity of the research. The consumption habits would be studied mathematically as functions of wealth.[6] The conclusion would be that there is only a slight chance the relationship showing the consumption of potatoes as an inverse function of the level of wealth is random. Therefore, it is likely that the rich are different. In most empirical studies in finance, although the relationships are probably not random, they are not precise enough for useful forecasting. Furthermore, on most important conceptual issues in the capital-structure area, the empirical studies come down on both sides of the question.[7]

The anecdotal analyst would approach the question by identifying a number of wealthy and less wealthy individuals and interviewing them about their culinary preferences. The analyst might visit restaurants in various price ranges to ask the chefs about the proportion of potatoes to other food the restaurants serve. The conclusion would state that in general the rich might be different because potatoes do not appear to form as significant a proportion of their diet, except at clambakes on Martha's Vineyard. Because of the limited sample size, however, it would not be possible to make statements about the probability that the observed relationships were not random.

The institutional analyst would describe the types of potatoes, their cultivation and harvesting, the packaging and marketing techniques involved, any impediments to their consumption, and the situations in which they might be served. The analyst would provide a vast amount of data without offering a strong conclusion except, perhaps, to mention that more advertisements for potatoes appeared in publications aimed at the less wealthy. In an excellent nontechnical article surveying academic approaches to capital-structure decisions, Michael J. Brennan refers to the "detailed institutional fussiness of the previous era of financial research, represented by Dewing and other institutionalists."[8]

The Early Frameworks

Although Brennan is a bit harsh about the institutionalists, it is true that Dewing's work, reputedly the first published financial text, contained little about how the capital-structure decision should be made. The implication, even in his later editions, is that quality companies and investors prefer debt. Equities, except perhaps preferred shares, are much more speculative. In contrast to his reticence about selecting the proportions of debt and equity, he does offer entertaining advice about the use of convertible securities.[9]

John F. Childs, in his time a mainstay of the financial-consulting function at Irving Trust Company in New York City, was an institutionalist with a prescriptive message.[10] He advocated that a company should borrow no more than it could while keeping the highest possible debt rating for which it could qualify, considering such factors as its industry and size. This policy, Childs argued, would give the firm fast access to capital in an emergency when an absence of financial resources could lead to the firm's failure. The debt-equity decision was thus assigned to the analysts at the rating agencies.

Donaldson's monograph was viewed, at the time it was published, as restoring decisions about capital structure to financial officers. His extensive field study of how capital-structure decisions were being made identified eight rules financial managers followed to craft their firms' debt-equity proportions. These decision rules were as follows:

1. Incur no long-term debt under any circumstances.

2. Borrow the maximum available.

3. Borrow the maximum available "at the prime rate."

4. Borrow the maximum available consistent with an "A" rating.

5. Limit the principal amount of (long-term) debt to "X" percent of total capitalization.

6. Borrow until a minimum ratio of earnings to debt burden (interest plus debt repayment) is reached.

7. Borrow the amount that can be serviced by the cash flow from the asset (such as an acquisition) that the debt will be used to purchase.

8. Borrow only in a favorable part of the business cycle and only to the extent the borrowed amount can be repaid before the cycle turns unfavorable.[11]

In addition to his anecdotal discoveries, Donaldson offered a new conceptual framework for the capital-structure decision. He suggested that the critical variables were not balance-sheet or coverage ratios but the ability of a firm in adverse conditions to service obligations from operating cash flow. This led to the popularity of recessionary-cash-flow analysis in measuring debt-servicing ability. It also may have contributed to the change in the bankruptcy law that established the failure to meet current obligations as a condition for a firm's being able to seek protection in the bankruptcy courts.

The margin of safety a firm keeps, in Donaldson's concept, should depend on the willingness of the management and owners to accept the risk of default in exchange for the cash-flow benefits of leverage in good times. The decision is comparable to the purchase of insurance. Just as few individuals can afford to postpone enough consumption to insure the present value of their lifetime worth, few companies can have sufficient resources to be competitive if they only finance with equity. This policy implies management is subordinating the asset decision to the capital-structure decision: The volume of assets is limited to the amount that can be financed by internal equity sources.

How much debt management accepts depends, in Donaldson's concept, on how comfortable management is with the risks the company faces. The implication of his work is that companies should keep enough debt and cash-flow capacity to take care of the likely risks and one or two of the most devastating ones.

At the time Donaldson was working on his book, there was interest in how his approach conflicted with Childs' approach. A visit by Childs to the Harvard Business School to participate with Donaldson in a discussion of financial policy was eagerly awaited as an opportunity for the two authorities to expound on the differences in their theories. Those expecting a confrontation were apparently disappointed when the event took place in a cordial atmosphere.

It is easier, in retrospect, to see that Childs and Donaldson were operating on complementary rather than conflicting paths. Donaldson's cash-flow analysis addressed the short-term financial problem that can be cured by converting assets to cash to meet debt service. This pattern is characteristic of the response to a recession: Sales drop, inventories are run down, receivables are collected, and the cash generated (usually considerably more than profits) is used to service the debt. Once the crisis has passed, funds flow back to the company to allow it to restore its assets to the level needed for continued operations. This pattern has been termed a response to "risk."[12]

Childs, in contrast, was more concerned with a response to a "flexibility" problem. Unlike risk circumstances, which are usually self-correcting, a flexibility problem is created by an unfavorable permanent change in the environment. For example, the development of inexpensive calculators and computers had a devastating effect on slide-rule producers and publishers of bond tables. These changes cannot be dealt with by a temporary contraction of assets and their conversion into cash. The resolution, or at least an effort to survive such an assault, requires access to cash in periods of uncertainty. Although the arrival of a flexibility event will usually reduce a firm's credit, the firm that has more credit in the first place should have more after the hit—other things being equal.[13]

In the long run, therefore, a company must pass both the Donaldson and the Childs tests. If a company has so much debt that it cannot survive the occasional risk event, there will be no long run to worry about. If it does not have the resources to deal with a flexibility problem, the first serious flexibility problem could kill it off.

Enter Normative Prescriptions: Thou Shalt Borrow

The movement to a more analytical approach was pioneered by David Durand's conceptual article about the controversy over valuation.[14] Although he did not take sides in the debate, he defined the front lines. One position argued that equity was valued by the market independently of the amount of debt a company had (within reason). This approach emphasized the profit after tax and the earnings per share. It held that the same price-earnings ratio would be applied to the earnings per share as long as the interest deduction was not too great. Its conclusion was that there were great value-creating advantages to debt.

This approach is illustrated in figure 1.2. As long as debt dilutes the earnings per share less than the equity it replaces, the earnings per share will rise. (Because debt is cheaper than equity, adding debt to the capital structure will lower the weighted average cost of capital. Therefore, when a company is valued by the discounted-cash-flow method, using the weighted average cost of capital as the discount rate, the value of the company increases. See **capital asset pricing model**, **discounted cash flow valuation**, and **weighted average cost of capital** in the glossary for an explanation of cost-of-capital calculations.) As long as the price-earnings ratio does not fall faster than the earnings per share rises, the market price of a common share will increase.

As the proportion of debt becomes greater, the marginal cost of debt will rise, slowing earnings-per-share growth. As the market be-

Figure 1.2
Market Price Influenced by Capital Structure

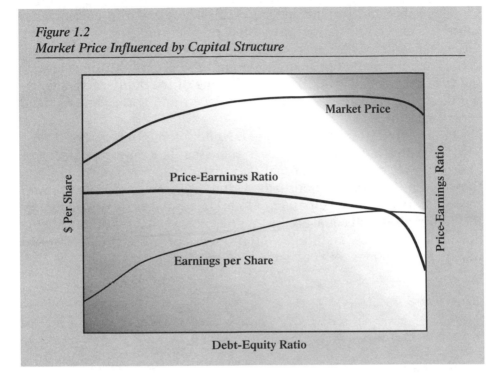

comes concerned about the financial risk created by the high proportion of debt, the price-earnings ratio starts to fall. The fall may be slow
at first, further slowing the growth in the market price that is already responding to the slower earnings-per-share growth. Eventually, the market becomes so concerned that the price-earnings ratio drops more
rapidly than the earnings per share increases. At this point, the market
price of the shares starts to fall. The optimal capital structure is at the
debt-equity ratio at the point just before the decline starts in the market
price.

The other position was that equity would be continuously discounted as debt was added to the capital structure because a firm's value depended on its EBIT, not on how the EBIT was divided. This group held
that the price-earnings ratio would therefore drop as the risk increased
because of debt's prior claim on the cash flows. Earnings per share
might rise but would not be translated into a comparably increased
market price.

This approach is shown in figure 1.3. The growth in earnings per share is mirrored by the decline in the price-earnings ratio, reflecting the market's immediate response to the risk created by the additional debt. Thus, the market price of the common stock and the total value of the firm are constant, with the market value of the debt exactly matching the market value of the stock it replaces, and there is no optimal capital structure.

Franco Modigliani and Merton H. Miller (commonly referred to as MM) delivered a definitive answer to the issue. In a powerful conceptual article, they developed internally consistent support for the position that—given their assumptions—the value of a firm does not vary with its capital structure.[15] Their assumptions stated that all players had perfect information and equal access to limitless investments and financing at comparable rates, that there were no taxes or transaction costs, and that all decision makers were value-maximizers.[16]

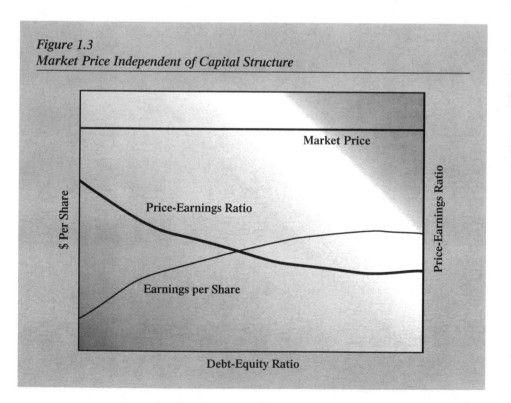

Figure 1.3
Market Price Independent of Capital Structure

Dealing only with the capital-structure decision (decision 2), Modigliani and Miller proved that as companies substitute lower cost debt for higher cost equity, the extra risk to the equity holder will cause the price-earnings ratio to go down by the same proportion the earnings per share go up. This is the effect illustrated in figure 1.3. Thus, the market price of the stock will not vary, and the total value of the firm will remain the same. Regardless of the amount of debt taken on, the cost of capital is always the same as the cost of capital for an all-equity firm.

The MM conclusions are illustrated in figure 1.4. As the proportion of debt reaches 100 percent of the firm's value, it becomes equivalent to the value of a 100-percent-equity firm because the debt has become the equity.

The MM conclusions might be described as the "Alfred E. Neuman" approach to finance: Why worry about the capital-structure decision if it makes no difference? Needless to say, neither practitioners nor academics found this conclusion satisfying, despite its conceptual elegance. Given the propensity of academics to think otherwise, the MM propositions set off an explosion of empirical studies to determine whether capital-market behavior validated the concepts. A second line of investigation was aimed at determining the effects on the conclusions if the assumptions changed.

In a later article, MM noted that if tax treatments differ for the various types of securities, then the form with the highest tax benefit should be used to the greatest extent possible—thus putting the capital structure decision back into the hands of the credit suppliers.[17] Because in the United States interest can be deducted from income in calculating taxable income but equity costs cannot, MM's conclusion is that companies should use as much debt as possible. This conclusion was a normative prescription—given their assumptions, MM specified *the* way to maximize value.

Finally, MM addressed the question of the optimal dividend policy.[18] Looking strictly at the dividend decision, they showed that under their perfect-market assumptions, the dividend decision was immaterial, regardless of the asset, capital-structure, and new-equity decisions. Because MM assumed a limitless quantity of assets providing a return at the cost of capital, any funds a company did not pay out could be reinvested. These new assets would generate a net present value of

Figure 1.4
Modigliani-Miller Concept of Capital Structure and Firm Value

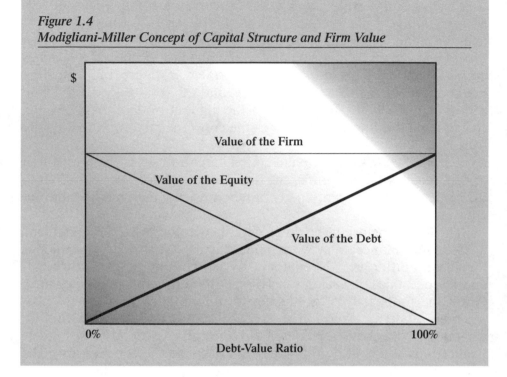

exactly the amount retained. The market value of the company would rise by the amount of the funds reinvested. The wealth of the equity holder would thus be precisely the same, regardless of whether (1) the company paid dividends and the investor held equity of a lower value plus cash received from the dividend, or (2) if the cash was retained and the value of the investor's equity rose by exactly that amount.

Unlike the MM assumption of infinite investment alternatives returning the cost of capital, most companies found investment schedules whose projects offered lower returns as the level of spending increased, at least in the short term. Investments in assets returning less than their capital costs result in an erosion of value compared with paying out those funds as dividends to the shareholders.

Nevertheless, MM's approach appeared to prescribe making the investment decision first, getting as much debt as possible second, and then either paying out the balance of funds if there was an excess of cash or paying no dividend and raising new equity if there was a cash shortage. The new-equity and dividend decisions were thus the plug figures, determined by the asset and capital-structure decisions.

When the definitive economic history of the 1980s is written, the conceptual foundation for the enthusiasm for leveraged buyouts is likely to be attributed to the MM theory. First, MM provided a strong normative justification for using debt to the maximum a firm could persuade the creditors to lend. Second, they provided a normative justification for terminating dividends and reinvesting all profits, particularly if the alternative was to raise new equity and incur the transaction costs that make raising new equity expensive. The first action was mandated by the MM concepts. The second did no harm, provided the assets were returning more than the capital costs. In the sense of the word "normative" as setting the standard, MM set the standard for capital structure and dividend decisions.

Challenges to MM: It Can't Be That Simple

MM's work was almost entirely conceptual, although in their first article they made an effort to show empirically that their formulation reflected reality. No one reports having replicated their empirical conclusions, and later efforts to support or disprove the theory by recourse to empirical studies have been notably lacking in success. Because of the stringent provisions within which the MM formulations hold (and which depart from the reality of the marketplace), it is easy to understand why validation has been so disappointing.

It was not long, however, before efforts were being made to introduce more realistic elements into the conceptual framework to see how the normative prescriptions might change under more real-world assumptions. Would they continue to be unvarying in their message to the financial manager, or would judgment be found to have a useful role in the capital-structure decision?

One of the first challenges to MM attacked the assumption that investors could arrange the same financing for themselves that corporations could. This assumption is central to the MM theory because it allowed investors to create for themselves any capital structure that a corporation could create. The challenge has never been successfully resolved, partly because its resolution depends on empirical studies that have been inconclusive. For large markets such as those in the United

States, academics appear to have stopped attacking this assumption. They seem to have accepted the proposition that enough investors exist who can fund themselves comparably to any corporate borrower that the MM assumption holds. It may not hold, however, in less well-developed markets.

Another early attack on the MM position was based on the insight that bankruptcy costs are first borne by equity holders. In theory, if far from always in practice, the debtholders are only impaired after the equity has been eliminated.[19] When enough debt is added to the balance sheet that the risks of bankruptcy become serious, returns to the stockholders no longer grow proportionately with risk. Therefore, the price-earnings ratio falls faster than earnings per share rise; the market price of the common stock and the total value of the firm begin to fall. An optimal debt-equity ratio should thus exist that would maximize the value of the common stock and minimize the cost of capital.

This conceptual development launched the usual torrent of empirical studies attempting to confirm or reject the theory. As usual, the results were not conclusive. It appears that although bankruptcy costs are large in relation to the bankrupt estate, they are not large prospectively as a portion of the assets of an ongoing firm.[20]

A third major line of conceptual attack was based on the differential taxes assessed on investors' earnings from debt and from equity (as when capital gains are taxed at a different rate from interest and dividends). As Miller pointed out, however, this challenge is not useful in developing capital-structure decision guides for the managers of individual corporations.[21] He agreed that corporations could offer investors a higher return on their debt in this situation than they would have to if the tax rates were equal. As long as the company can save more on its taxes by using debt than it must offer to induce investors to sell its stock and buy its debt, both those that trade and those that remain will have enhanced value. If personal tax rates are so progressive that the personal tax on interest becomes higher than the corporate tax rate, there will be no economic way for the company to attract investors in those higher tax brackets to shift into the company's debt. The optimal debt ratio therefore occurs when all the lower-taxed investors have exchanged their equity for debt.

Once all lower-taxed investors have moved to bonds, however, Miller argued there would be no further advantage to any particular company of being either higher or lower than the economy-wide ratio. Firms that first enticed the lower-taxed investors would have a permanent advantage. No other firm could economically offer investors enough to attract them to change. Of course, if the relative tax rates changed, the economy-wide optimal level of debt would change, which could give a firm an opportunity to take advantage of lowering its capital cost.

The tax-rate differentials that exist in the real world are generally far less than those Miller used in his conceptual structure. This discrepancy was particularly true after the 1986 changes in the personal income tax in the United States. Furthermore, because companies only benefit from the tax-savings effect to the extent they are reporting taxable income, it is possible corporations could run out of taxable income before they have cleared the market of lower-taxed investors. In that case, the rate of interest paid would be less than the equilibrium level, because firms would not be willing to use as much debt as the market would want to provide. This condition would create a true benefit to the equity holders from the use of debt.[22]

Behavioral Challenges: Incentives Count

In contrast to the indeterminant results of the conceptual and related empirical challenges to the MM capital-market assumptions, behavioral challenges have made considerable conceptual inroads. They have challenged the MM assumption that the schedule of investments is independent of the capital structure. For example, the threat of bankruptcy has the potential to create behavior that may be more expensive than the bankruptcy costs. On the one hand, as the firm gets into deeper and deeper trouble, a management truly representing the stockholders may begin to speculate with the assets that properly belong to the debtholders. Any loss will decrease the debtholders' wealth; any gain will enhance the equity holders' position. This moral hazard behavior was particularly evident in the savings and loan industry debacle.

On the other hand, however, is the situation in which the management of a firm facing troubled times believes the debtholders might agree to compromise their position. Management may defer profitable investments until the debtholders have given ground, thus capturing more of the profits for the equity holders than they should receive.

Information Content of
Capital-Structure Decisions

A major behavioral issue was raised about how capital-structure decisions might convey information to the public that would normally have been kept within the senior management of the firm.[23] This process is known as signaling. It has long been argued that equity owners benefit if equity is issued when it is overpriced.[24] If management knows that proposed investments have significant net present values, it will finance with debt. Conversely, an issue of equity should be favored over debt if the company's outlook is risky. If prospective investments are less profitable, management will raise equity. Why take the risk of debt if it has little to gain? Therefore, management's decision about a company's capital structure is closely linked to its assessment of future capital-investment prospects. This violates MM's assumption of the independence of the asset and capital-structure decisions.

Whether this managerial propensity actually creates value for the shareholder is not certain. If investors are aware of management's bias, they will discount a new equity issue to compensate for its unfavorable implications.

Richard A. Brealey and Stewart C. Myers conclude that the size of the discount required for a new equity issue averages 3 percent of the capital value of the existing stock.[25] This cost can be significant when charged against the amount of money a small issue raises. It also suggests management should seek extraordinary returns from investments that require the use of equity, which is contrary to the behavioral assumptions. In any event, the possibility that the investment schedule and the financial structure are even slightly interrelated erodes the independence MM hypothesized.

Dividend policy has also been suggested as a way management communicates a company's prospects to the market. To the extent dividends serve as signals, the dividend decision can no longer be considered a residual one but must be balanced against the asset and the new-equity decisions. It may be possible to increase stockholders' value more by paying a dividend than by investing in assets. Likewise, dividends may increase the value of the equity by enough to offset the effect of issuing new common stock to replace the funds disbursed.

Debt's Effects on Agency Costs

A second conceptual challenge to the independence of the two sides of the balance sheet was first raised in another context by Adolph A. Berle and Gardiner C. Means. They wrote about the effects of separating power and property.[26] The contemporary concern with the subject, termed moral hazard or agency costs, was initiated by Michael L. Jensen and William H. Meckling.[27] They addressed the potential conflicts between management's self-interest and its obligation to its equity holders, known as agency conflicts. For example, because shareholders have the ability to diversify risks by portfolio structure, they may want the individual company's management to seek high-return investments even if they have high risk or to increase their returns with additional leverage. But management is motivated to seek protection of its employment and may prefer lower-risk projects and lower leverage. Management has no "employment portfolio" over which to spread its risk.

Similarly, when the company's set of attractive investments begins to run out, generating surplus cash not required for reinvestment, management may be tempted to make its job more comfortable rather than passing along the cash to the shareholders. For example, management can use the cash to reduce debt below optimal levels because this action reduces the firm's risk. As already noted in the discussion of financial failure, it is possible that management's efforts to thwart the creditors' interests also may result in suboptimal investment decisions. Naturally, these conceptual propositions have spawned a vast school of empirical studies, most of which are inconclusive or contradictory.

One suggestion is if the company is kept more highly leveraged, fewer spare funds will be available for management to exploit, and more investors will be watching to see that the firm is properly managed.[28] The same rationale has been advanced as a technique for moderating the demands of labor and the suppliers: Management would like to be more accommodating, but the high level of debt prevents it.[29]

When management and shareholder interests are aligned, the company avoids agency conflicts. Many ideas have been proposed to more closely identify management with shareholder interests. Compensation methods depending heavily on the performance of the stock and increased managerial ownership have been suggested. One frequently used measure, whose relevance is highly doubtful, is the proportion of a firm's stock held by senior managers. The relevant measure, which is harder to calculate from public information, is the proportion of a manager's net worth invested in the company's common stock. A manager does not need to own a large percentage of the company to identify with the stockholder if a large percentage of the manager's net worth is tied to the company's common stock performance.

An alternative approach to management behavior was suggested by Stewart C. Myers. He proposed that management decisions on capital structure follow a "pecking order."[30] Managers, in this concept, prefer to use internally generated funds first, debt second, and to avoid new equity issues until other sources have been exhausted. This idea appears to hark back to positions held in the 1950s that ascribed a zero cost to retained earnings. Myers, however, believes managers prefer internally generated equity (i.e., retained earnings) because this alternative involves little risk of mispricing caused by imperfectly distributed information.

Dividend policies, Myers observed, tend to be stable, following the pattern of increases lagging higher earnings and resistance to decline that Lintner identified.[31] Given volatility in earnings and uneven requirements for capital investments, the pecking-order concept holds that firms will save funds (or restore borrowing capacity) when enjoying cash surpluses and will draw funds down when the cash flow is negative.

Once the surplus cash is gone, according to the pecking-order theory, firms turn first to simple types of debt because they are the least risky way of obtaining external funds. Junior securities, such as high-yield debt or convertible-preferred stock, are the next preference. Straight common stock comes last. This conceptualization suggests that the reason highly profitable firms do not borrow is that they do not need to. Less profitable firms have no choice but to raise outside funds to take advantage of attractive investments, and they turn first to debt.

Although this description sounds as though the pecking order would lead management to actions that invite leveraged buyouts and to avoid capital-market discipline, conceptual arguments can be made to support the pecking-order approach as having rational economic support. For example, managers of companies in cyclical industries with risk rather than flexibility demands, such as forest products and machine tools, know that their firms will face periods of both generous and tight cash flows over a cycle. Considering the issue costs of new securities, it makes sense for this type of firm to follow the pecking-order concepts as a way of minimizing capital costs over the longer term. Occasional large issues in sequence are much less expensive than smaller simultaneous issues. Moreover, the pecking order raises funds from the lowest-cost sources first. Existing cash, for instance, is provided by the mix of capital. This mix should represent the lowest capital cost if the firm is optimally financed.

A completely different policy would be proper for a company with an expected negative cash flow during a sustained period of growth. To have a capital base that would allow easy access to the debt markets in a period when the equity markets might be closed to new issues, managers of this type of firm would access the equity market in good times. In both these examples, and indeed in its concept, a rational economic interpretation of the pecking-order approach depends on relaxing the conceptual separation between assets and capital structure.

Recent empirical studies by Michael J. Barclay, Clifford W. Smith, Jr., and Ross L. Watts[32] hark back to the pre-MM days by suggesting that the nature of the company's assets does in fact affect corporate capital structure. High debt may not be best for all companies. For example, Barclay and Smith report data suggesting that high-growth firms avoid debt because of the restrictions debt can place on growth. It is also possible, of course, that such firms tend to be overvalued by exuberant investors. If so, management is not faced with the danger of selling underpriced equity.

Because of the temptations the cash flows of mature firms have for the managers, higher debt and larger dividend payouts are appropriate as a discipline. In addition, these firms offer greater certainty that they can service their debt and thus can borrow more of their capital without paying penalty rates. Firms whose assets may be readily liquidated also qualify for higher leverage, although experience suggests that by the time such a firm gets into financial difficulty the assets may have lost much of their value or even disappeared. If the results of Barclay et al. are valid, either companies are drastically miscapitalized, a situation that even reasonably perfect markets should sort out, or investors look favorably on capital structure that reflects asset composition.

The Barclay et al. studies did not confirm that capital structure was being used to convey information to the markets, nor did they confirm that a company's lower tax rate was a factor in its capital structure.

Where Are We Now?

Barclay and Smith et al., although empirical rather than conceptual in nature, reinforce the erosion of the normative prescriptives of the early MM years. After 40 years, management again is told that judgment is important. Management must consider not only a firm's capital structure but also the mutual relationship between the capital structure and the assets in which the firm invests. Given a set of assets, in other words, a capital structure may be selected that maximizes the value of the firm. Given a capital structure, a set of assets may be selected that maximizes the value of the firm. The two must be considered together to select the proper combination.

To borrow an analogy from an unpublished paper by Robert S. Harris, the traditionalists in the pre-MM days believed the value of the asset pie depended on how it was packaged for sale to the market.[33] The higher the price, the lower the capital cost and the more assets that could be acquired. MM rejected both assertions. They proved, given their assumptions (which included that the nature of the pie was independent of the way it was financed), that the value of the pie was constant regardless of how it was packaged. The first attacks on MM challenged the valuation propositions. The second set of attacks questioned the static relationship between the composition of the pie and the way it is cut into pieces and sold. Depending on the way the pie is financed, its size and composition will change. The problem again, as in the pre-MM period, is to find the combination of assets and financing that creates the biggest risk-adjusted pie for the existing shareholder.

In the following chapter, the information gained from the field research will be compared to the conceptual frameworks and insights outlined in this chapter to assess the present state of capital-market decision making. The case studies, which come after the comparative chapter, provide detailed information about the guidelines practicing managers use to make capital-structure decisions.

Endnotes

1. Dean, Joel. *Managerial Economics*. Englewood Cliffs, N.J.: Prentice-Hall, 1951.

2. Donaldson, Gordon. *Corporate Debt Capacity*. Boston: Harvard Business School, 1961.

3. Sihler, William W. "Framework for Financial Decisions." *Harvard Business Review* (March–April 1971): 123–135.

4. Lintner, John. "Normative Criteria for Dividends Payouts in Large Corporations." *Abstract Econometrica* (October 1958): 603.

5. Professor Karen H. Wruck, of the Harvard Business School, used the term "discipline-based clinical research" in the title of a recent case-based working paper.

6. In disciplines more conducive to experimentation, the empirical researcher might develop experiments to test the effect being studied.

7. See, for instance, Harris, Milton, and Arthur Raviv. "The Theory of Capital Structure." *Journal of Finance* (March 1991): 297–355, especially 337–349. This is a comprehensive capital-structure survey article, one of a number written in the 1988–1991 period. It is excellent but on the technical side.

8. Brennan, Michael J. "Corporate Finance Over the Past 25 Years." *Financial Management* 24, no. 2 (Summer 1995): 9–22. His reference is to Arthur Stone Dewing. *The Financial Policy of Corporations*. New York, N.Y.: The Ronald Press, in various editions beginning in 1920. Dewing himself was a practitioner of financial arts as well as a professor at the Harvard Business School. He developed a very rewarding skill, fussy though he may have been, in consolidating waterworks and then taking them public.

9. "…the corporation may quite probably receive more for this composite security, consisting of a combination of the obligation

and the gamble on future earnings, than the strict combined value of the two would seem to justify. Broadly speaking, the demand for any security comes from three groups of human beings—and the groups shade imperceptibly into one another. There is the so-called investor. He wants security and a reasonably assured income return. There is the businessman, a term sometimes applied to the individual who is willing and is able, because of large reserve income, to take considerable chances in a single security purchase. He expects income; and he hopes, in addition, for enhancement of principal. He trusts, by spreading his risks over many purchases, that the law of averages will yield him an excess of gains over losses. Finally, there is the speculator. He purchases a security in order to obtain a profit arising from increase in market value. He buys a gamble. The convertible security, particularly the convertible bond, appeals to all three of these classes. The bond alone would appeal, if at all, only to the first class. The conversion privilege alone would appeal, if at all, only to the third class. The combination, by looking both ways at the same time, appeals to the businessman investor. By combining the two elements in a single investment, all these classes of buyers are brought within the scope of its appeal. Price, in the things we buy and sell, is increased by an increase in the demand. The investor and the speculator bid against each other, and offer to pay a price for something neither wants; and the businessman investor is lured into paying a competitive price for a composite value which he can neither appraise nor understand. Surely in such a game the corporation has much to gain and little to lose." Dewing, *op. cit.*, 5th ed. (1953): 270–271.

10. Childs, John F. *Long-term Financing*. Englewood Cliffs, N.J.: Prentice-Hall, 1961. The acquisition of The Irving Trust Company by The Bank of New York occurred long after Childs had retired.

11. See Donaldson, *op. cit.*: 93–120.

12. For a more extensive discussion defining "risk" and "flexibility," see Sihler, *loc. cit.*

13. There is also the argument that having borrowed a large amount presents the lender with a problem and may help a firm obtain support in a flexibility crisis. Although this may have been true in the past, the present tendency of lenders to sell off their bad loans to someone who wants to gain control of the company may make institutional support less likely in the future.

14. Durand, David. "Costs of Debt and Equity Funds for Business: Trends and Problems of Measurement." *Conference on Research in Business Finance.* New York: National Bureau of Economic Research (1952).

15. Modigliani, Franco, and Merton H. Miller. "The Cost of Capital, Corporate Finance, and the Theory of Investment." *American Economic Review* (June 1958): 261–297.

16. These assumptions appear to erode the differences between debt and equity that are found in the real world, which helps to explain why the MM conceptualization was so intellectually unassailable.

17. Modigliani, Franco, and Merton H. Miller. "Corporate Income Tax Shields and the Cost of Capital: A Correction." *American Economic Review* (June 1963): 433–443.

18. Miller, Merton H., and Franco Modigliani. "Dividend Policy, Growth, and the Valuation of Shares." *Journal of Business* (October 1961): 411–433.

19. An early article introducing this subject was written by Stiglitz, Joseph E. "Some Aspects of the Pure Theory of Corporate Finance: Bankruptcies and Take-overs." *Bell Journal of Economics and Managerial Science* (Autumn 1972): 458–482.

20. Warner, Jerold B. "Bankruptcy Costs: Some Evidence." *Journal of Finance* (May 1977): 337–347.

21. Merton H. Miller, half of the MM team, responded to these challenges in "Debt and Taxes." *Journal of Finance* (May 1977): 261–276.

22. See Ross, Stephen A., Randolph W. Westerfield, and Jeffrey Jaffe. *Corporate Finance*, 4th ed. Chicago: 1996, 434–438.

23. Ross, Stephen A. "The Determination of Financial Structure: The Incentive-Signaling Approach." *Bell Journal of Economics* (Spring 1977): 23–40. This approach also challenges the perfect-markets concept that inside information does not exist for more than a very brief time, too brief for it to be of value.

24. Myers, Stewart C., and Nicholas S. Majluf. "Corporate Financing and Investment Decisions When Firms Have Information that Investors Do Not Have." *Journal of Financial Economics* 13, no. 2: 187–221, were among the first to explore the effects of imperfect information on various parties to the capital-structure decision.

25. Brealey, Richard A., and Stewart C. Myers. *Principles of Corporate Finance*, 4th ed. New York: McGraw-Hill, 1991, p. 349 and n. 21. Although Asqueth, Paul, and David Mullins. "Equity Issues and Offering Dilution." *Journal of Financial Economics.* (January-February 1986): 61–90, report that the size of the discount is related to the size of the offering, other empirical studies fail to support this effect. This calls the nature of the effect into some question. See also Smith, Clifford W., Jr. "Investment Banking and the Capital Acquisition Process." *Journal of Financial Economics* 15, no. 1/2: 3–29, who reports no unfavorable effect on the equity price from an issue of debt.

26. Berle, Adolph A., and Gardiner C. Means. *The Modern Corporation and Private Property.* New York: Macmillan, 1932.

27. Jensen, Michael C., and William H. Meckling. "Theory of the Firm: Managerial Behavior, Agency Costs and Ownership Structure." *Journal of Financial Economics* (October 1976): 305–360.

28. Harris, Milton, and Arthur Raviv. "Capital Structure and the Information Role of Debt." *Journal of Finance* 45, no. 2: 321–349, point out that the contractual terms of debt instruments are important in giving debtholders influence to protect

themselves as a company develops financial stress. In reality, the vagaries of the bankruptcy process can violate the debtholders' position.

29. Although this possibility has been mentioned in passing, apparently there has been no serious study of it.

30. Myers, Stewart C. "The Capital Structure Puzzle." *Journal of Finance* (July 1994): 575–592. This article probably best fits into the "institutional" category, a surprise coming from an authority who is well known for his excellent conceptual and empirical work. Its roots can be found quite early in articles such as Solomon, Ezra. "Measuring a Company's Cost of Capital." *Journal of Business* (October 1955): 240–252.

31. Lintner, John. "Distribution of Income of Corporations among Dividends, Retained Earnings, and Taxes." *American Economic Review* (May 1956): 97–113.

32. Barclay, Michael J., Clifford W. Smith, Jr., and Ross L. Watts. "The Determinants of Corporate Leverage and Dividend Policy." *Journal of Applied Corporate Finance.* (Winter 1995): 4–19. Barclay, Michael J., and Clifford W. Smith, Jr. "On Financial Architecture: Leverage, Maturity, and Priority." *Journal of Applied Corporate Finance.* (Winter 1996): 4–17, summarizes and extends a series of articles including Barclay and Smith. "The Maturity Structure of Corporate Debt." *Journal of Finance.* (June 1995): 609–631, and "The Priority Structure of Corporate Liabilities." *Journal of Finance.* (July 1995): 899–917.

33. Harris, Robert S. "A Note on Elements of Capital Structure Theory." Unpublished paper, The Darden Graduate School of Business Administration, University of Virginia, 1996. This concept is certainly familiar to those marketing consumer goods. Apartment dwellers are willing to pay a premium to buy their soap powder in small packets convenient to taking to the laundry in the building's basement. Those living in the suburbs with large families prefer to buy in bulk and enjoy the savings that offers.

Comparison of Capital-Structure and Dividend Policies

This chapter compares and contrasts financial-structure policies of the 13 case-study companies. It starts with a summary of principal findings and lessons learned. In the summary and the remainder of the chapter, the order of topics follows the interview protocol. The comparison of capital-structure and dividend policies is followed by a discussion of how companies develop and approve policies, which financial instruments and tactics have been particularly useful in implementing those policies, and how companies communicate their financial-structure policies to the markets. The chapter concludes with a discussion of the relationship between investment and financing decisions, the valuation methods used most frequently by corporate financial officers and investors, and the sources of information on capital-structure and dividend policy that CFOs and treasurers find most useful.

Principal Findings and Lessons Learned

This section is a brief summary of the principal findings and lessons learned in the study.

How Capital-Structure Policies Vary

Following the quadrant model described in table 1 of the Introduction, the majority of case-study companies with secular revenue growth have low debt, whereas the majority of companies with volatile revenue growth have moderate or high debt.

The majority of fixed-asset companies have moderate or high debt, whereas the majority of the intangible-asset companies have low debt. These characteristics support the theory that capital structure partly depends on asset selection. Conversely, asset selection may depend on capital structure, but to a more limited degree. For example, capital expenditures may be limited by a company's constraints on borrowing and unwillingness to sell new equity.

Low-Debt Policies

For seven case-study companies, the flexibility and risk protection provided by a conservative balance sheet is more important than the reduction in the cost of capital that would result from higher debt. With such low-debt policies, there are possible agency costs that make life easier for management at the expense of shareholders, who might prefer higher risks and returns.

Home Depot and Paychex, currently low-debt companies, are the two case-study companies with the highest price-earnings ratios. They do not believe that taking on more debt to reduce their weighted average costs of capital would increase their value. They believe their share prices are based mainly on growth.

Moderate-Debt Policies

Four case-study companies, Georgia-Pacific, Marriott International, Monsanto, and TELUS, maintain moderate levels of debt to lower their weighted average costs of capital and thereby theoretically increase their corporate values as calculated in a discounted cash-flow analysis.

High-Debt Policies

High debt, although not the norm for the majority of case-study companies, is appropriate for certain industries, such as hotel real estate investment, in the case of Host Marriott, and special situations, such as the management buy-out of Sheplers and the founding of Home Depot and Paychex. A number of other studies summarized in Chapter 15, The Role of High Debt, show that, for appropriate companies, management ownership combined with high leverage can provide both a carrot and a stick, resulting in superior financial performance. Many of the failures of highly leveraged companies in the late 1980s were caused by a combination of leverage carried too far and poor operating performance.

Private Companies
The two private case-study companies, Sheplers and Vermeer, realize that external capital could help them accelerate their growth but would require them to change their company cultures and cede at least some control to outside parties.

Fixed- and Floating-Rate Debt
In recent years, relatively low interest rates throughout the yield curve have encouraged companies to issue fixed-rate debt with the longest possible maturities. Some consider very-long-dated debt to have attractive pricing and equity-like characteristics.

Importance of Operating Performance
One of the overriding findings is that strong operating performance plays a larger role than capital structure in building shareholder value. Strong operating performance also allows a company wide latitude in deciding on the most appropriate capital structure. Georgia-Pacific's CFO expresses a view shared by financial officers of other case-study companies: Developing good projects that return more than the cost of capital is the first priority, and finding the appropriate financing follows suit.

Factors That Influence Capital-Structure Decisions

Internally Generated Cash
All 13 case-study companies generate sufficient operating cash flow for normal capital expenditures. However, two case-study companies finance their growth partly with new debt, and the majority would consider additional borrowing for a large, strategic acquisition.

Cash Reserves
Four case-study companies, Amgen, Oracle, Paychex, and Symmetri-Com, justify large cash reserves for risk protection and possible acquisitions. None of those cash balances are considered high enough to increase the company's vulnerability to hostile takeover. General Electric, on the other hand, has raised its stock price by repurchasing stock rather than keeping a cash reserve for possible acquisitions.

Credit Ratings
For the eight case-study companies that have rated debt, credit-rating guidelines play an important role in capital-structure policy. These companies, spread across all four quadrants of the model, all consider their current credit ratings to be appropriate. Credit-rating guidelines may put an upper limit on a company's debt, thereby putting an upper limit on capital expenditures. However, the treasurers of Amgen and Monsanto believe that moving from a single-A to a double-A credit rating would restrict their flexibility and save only a few basis points in borrowing costs.

Timing
Home Depot and TELUS take advantage of favorable markets to raise funds even when they are not needed for more than a year. On the other hand, Georgia-Pacific prefers to finance at current rates when it needs funds.

Tax Considerations
Tax considerations do not play an important role in the case-study companies' choice of equity and debt instruments. However, recent legislation will restrict future tax-free spin-offs.

Control
The public companies in the study seem more concerned with shareholder value than with control. With the private case-study companies, both control and shareholder value are high priorities.

Implementation Issues

Business-Unit Capital Structures
Except for finance subsidiaries, only one case-study company, TELUS, has different capital structures and hurdle rates for different business units. Although many in the academic community favor different capital structures and hurdle rates, the case-study companies generally think the complications of implementing such systems outweigh the benefits. For example, the calculations must constantly be changed and often are subject to dispute.

Stock Splits

Four case-study companies, General Electric, Home Depot, Monsanto, and Paychex, have done frequent stock splits. The most frequently cited reason is to make the company's stock more affordable to employees and retail investors. GE follows a common pattern of splitting its stock to return to the previous post-split price level.

Dividends and Share Repurchases

"Sticky" dividend policies continue to be widespread. These are policies of increasing dividends gradually and only to a level that can be sustained given a range of foreseeable circumstances, including temporary dips in earnings.

Companies are reluctant to break patterns of steadily increasing dividends for fear of adverse market reactions. Conversely, companies that pay no dividends realize that if they started, the market would expect them to continue and increase their payouts.

Several case-study companies are sensitive to the guidelines of institutional investors who buy only the stock of companies with records of dividend payments. Monsanto's treasurer believes a consistent dividend payout makes her company's stock attractive to yield investors, and this tends to set a floor on its stock price.

Findings in the study support the theory that companies with greater growth opportunities tend to pay less dividends as well as to assume less debt. Amgen, Host Marriott, Oracle, and SymmetriCom have never paid dividends and do not intend to in the near future.

There has been a recent corporate trend toward more stock repurchases. As the disparity between regular income and capital-gains tax rates widens, the incentive to substitute share repurchases for dividend payments should increase. Eight case-study companies have stock repurchase programs, two of them primarily to offset dilution from stock options exercised, four of them primarily to return cash to investors in a tax-efficient manner, and two to do both. One disadvantage of stock buybacks is that they restrict a company's ability to use pooling-of-interest accounting for acquisitions. On the other hand, reductions in the amount of stock repurchased are much less disturbing to the market than reductions in dividends, giving companies more flexibility in managing their cash flows.

Development and Approval of Policies

Companies generally develop capital-structure and dividend policies by a process of ongoing consensus among management and the board. The policies are often discussed with the board as part of the annual plan and budget process.

Only two case-study companies have written policies. Georgia-Pacific has a rather general one, and Monsanto prepares a book for annual rating-agency reviews that its board of directors also reviews.

Financial officers consider the test of their capital-structure and dividend policies to be how well the stock price performs, how well the company is able to carry out its strategy, and how well investors, lenders, and analysts receive the policies.

Instruments and Tactics

Financial managers appear to be skeptical about the more complex types of derivatives, convertibles, and other instruments developed by financial institutions, adopting them only occasionally to serve very specific needs.

Convertibles

Whether or not convertibles are appealing depends partly on a company's view of its own stock price. If a company believes its stock will not exceed the conversion price, convertible debentures offer low-cost financing. If the stock price is expected to rise above the conversion price, convertibles could result in selling equity too cheaply and creating unnecessary dilution.

Spin-Offs

The case-study companies include a recent spin-off (Marriott and Host Marriott), a spin-off in process (Monsanto), and a possible spin-off (SymmetriCom). After a spin-off, each surviving company can make investment and financing decisions and approach the capital markets in a way appropriate to its own asset structure, revenue sources, and business objectives. Recent tax legislation denies tax-free status to spin-offs that are deemed to be precursors to the sale of business units to other companies.

Targeted Stock

Targeted stock, tied to the performance of specific business units, has not suited the needs of Amgen, the former Marriott Corporation, or TELUS. However, Georgia-Pacific is creating targeted stock tied to its profitable and relatively stable timber business because it is more tax efficient than a spin-off and allows the company continued control of those operations.

Costless Collars

Amgen and Oracle have sold put warrants and used some of the proceeds to buy call options on their common stock. This combination, sometimes called a costless collar, allows a company to express a bullish view on its stock.

Real-Estate Ownership

Real-estate ownership provides Home Depot with flexibility in opening and closing stores and the benefit of its own low cost of capital. It offers Oracle the possibility of a bargain when land prices are low. General Electric, Paychex, and Sheplers, on the other hand, prefer the flexibility of leasing. GE's lessors have a relatively low cost of capital because of high leverage.

Communication with the Markets

Case-study companies generally believe that retail ownership helps stabilize their stock prices, but small shareholders are more costly to service.

Securities analysts pay little attention to capital structure unless there is a decline in earnings growth. This may reflect the good business climate and the low interest rates in recent years. Capital structure tends to be a topic of greater concern in less favorable economic environments.

Investment and Financing Decisions

At the overall company level, asset selection has a strong influence on capital-structure policy, and to a more limited degree, capital constraints may influence asset selection. But with a few exceptions, such as tax-exempt municipal financing and borrowing to buy back stock when both the borrowing rate and stock price are favorable, case-study companies make individual investment decisions and financing decisions independently.

Valuation Methods

Two case-study companies regularly compare internal discounted-cash-flow valuations with market prices of their stocks. Although buy-side securities analysts are becoming more cash-flow oriented, sell-side analysts still primarily use price-earnings ratios for valuation. Some sell-side analysts relate price-earnings ratios to growth rates. General Electric's treasurer observes that a company's price-earnings ratio tends to expand as its growth rate rises.

Detailed Comparison of Policies

The remainder of the chapter is a more detailed comparison of capital-structure, dividend, and related policies.

How Capital-Structure Policies Vary

The capital structures of the case-study companies, summarized in table 2.1, vary from low debt to high debt, depending on factors such as cash-generating capability, growth opportunities, asset structure, industry cyclicality, and management risk tolerance. For purposes of this analysis, low-, moderate-, and high-debt companies are classified based on long-term debt as a percentage of capitalization. Long-term debt is considered by the researchers to be less than 25 percent of capitalization for low-debt companies, 25 to 50 percent of capitalization for moderate-debt companies, and more than 50 percent of capitalization for high-debt companies. Seven of the case-study companies have policies of low or minimal debt. Four have policies of moderate debt within limits defined by their current credit ratings. Two are highly leveraged now or have been in the recent past.

When the quadrant model is used to analyze the debt levels of the case-study companies, it is clear that fixed-asset companies tend to have higher debt than intangible-asset companies and volatile-revenue-growth companies tend to have higher debt than secular-revenue-

Table 2.1
Debt Levels of Case-Study Companies

	Secular Growth	Volatile Growth
Fixed Assets	General Electric - LO	Georgia-Pacific - MOD
	SymmetriCom - LO	Monsanto - MOD
	TELUS - MOD	Vermeer Manufacturing - LO
		Host Marriott - HI
Intangible Assets	Oracle - LO	Marriott International - MOD
	Amgen - LO	Home Depot - LO
	Paychex - LO	Sheplers - HI

growth companies. Comparing the secular-revenue-growth to the volatile-revenue-growth companies, five of six secular-revenue-growth companies have low debt, and five of seven volatile-revenue-growth companies have moderate or high debt. Comparing the fixed-asset to the intangible-asset companies, four of seven fixed-asset companies have moderate or high debt, and four of six intangible-asset companies have low debt. This supports the theory that capital structure partly depends on asset selection.

Appropriate Level of Debt
Low-Debt Policies: For seven case-study companies, the flexibility and risk protection provided by a conservative balance sheet is more important than the reduction in the weighted average cost of capital that would result from higher debt. For example, General Electric is a conglomerate with heavy fixed assets and strong cash-generating capacity that maintains low debt to protect its flexibility and its triple-A credit rating. SymmetriCom is a small, growing high-technology manufacturer that chooses not to compound business risk with financial risk. Vermeer Manufacturing (agricultural and industrial equipment) is a family-owned company with a policy of very low debt to minimize risk and maintain control. Amgen (biotechnology), Oracle (software), and Paychex (payroll services) are relatively young companies with mostly

intangible assets that are able to fund their growth from internally generated cash. For these companies, a conservative balance sheet provides both risk protection and a reserve for possible acquisitions in the future.

Home Depot, the retailer, has financed its growth periodically with debt, but consistently high price-earnings ratios have allowed the company to issue new equity to pay down its debt and to force conversion of its convertible debt. From the time Home Depot went public in 1981, the company believes a strong balance sheet with low debt has given it an advantage over its competitors. The company has been able to be more aggressive because it does not have to worry about how a possible rise in interest rates might affect its income statement. With more debt, the company would have incurred higher interest expense, and its stock price might not have been so high. With a lower stock price, the company might have had less borrowing power today. (On the other hand, with fewer shares, the earnings per share would have been higher and growth faster. This might have offset the lower price-earnings ratio.)

Management's preference for low debt in these companies could be explained partly by agency theory, wherein a balance sheet with less debt places less external control on management but may be against the interests of shareholders looking for higher risk-adjusted returns. On the other hand, the case-study companies show that many managers consider the extra returns from high leverage to be of less value to shareholders than protecting the viability of the company so it can fulfill its business strategy over the long run.

Moderate-Debt Policies: Four case-study companies, Georgia-Pacific, Marriott International, Monsanto, and TELUS, maintain moderate levels of debt to lower their weighted average costs of capital while not jeopardizing their current credit ratings. For TELUS' telephone subsidiaries, equity has been limited historically by the Canadian Radio-television and Telecommunications Commission (CRTC) to 55 percent of capitalization to lower the cost of capital and telephone rates for the consumer. But this diversified telecommunications company has raised its overall target percentage of equity to 60 percent because of the changes and risks in the industry. The case-study companies generally support the theory that companies with higher business risk and growth opportunities tend to have less debt in their capital structures.

High-Debt Policies: Two case-study companies are highly leveraged now or have been in the recent past. Host Marriott's capital structure is designed to be consistent with its asset base. At the end of 1996, long-term debt was 70 percent of capitalization. Management believes the most prudent way to finance real estate, a long-life asset, is with equity and long-term, fixed-rate debt. The company is funding its growth with approximately 50-percent debt and 50-percent equity. More than half of the company's long-term debt is nonrecourse in the form of mortgages on individual properties.

For Sheplers, the retailer, high debt was a necessary tool for management to buy the company. Borrowing capacity was based on proven cash flow and the appraised value of real estate. Since then, management has been sufficiently confident in the company's strong operating performance and its ability to survive a worst-case recession scenario that it has paid down term debt on schedule but not ahead of time. Realistic financial forecasts allow the company to follow its capital-structure plan and warn its banks of possible problems several quarters ahead of time. The management team that bought Sheplers was able to avoid the pitfalls of many other leveraged buyouts (LBOs) done in the 1980s: paying too much and making unrealistic assumptions about assets that could be sold or spun off.

The story of Revco, a drugstore company whose LBO failed largely because of those pitfalls, is told in Chapter 15, The Role of High Debt. That chapter summarizes several studies of highly leveraged transactions, including LBOs and leveraged recapitalizations, and discusses the reasons some succeeded and others failed. In most successful LBOs, an ownership stake combined with high leverage motivates management to improve operating performance and shed unnecessary assets. Many of the leveraged recapitalizations that failed were defensive transactions motivated by hostile takeover attempts. Some notably successful leveraged recapitalizations, such as CUC International and Sealed Air Corporation, were undertaken for special reasons, such as sending a signal to the markets and motivating management.

Fixed- and Floating-Rate Debt

In recent years, relatively low interest rates throughout the yield curve have encouraged companies to issue long-term debt. This is a marked contrast to the early 1980s, when companies tended to fund short term in anticipation of declining rates. Long-term, fixed-rate debt is a funding source mainly available to large companies with investment-grade credit ratings. Since the mid-1980s, however, smaller companies that borrow mainly from commercial banks have been able to create fixed-rate debt synthetically with **interest-rate swaps**. Naturally, they pay a higher effective rate than investment-grade borrowers.

Georgia-Pacific, Host Marriott, Marriott International, and Monsanto favor high portions of long-term debt at fixed rates. Georgia-Pacific borrows mostly with fixed-rate public debt for the longest possible maturities, protecting itself with call provisions if it does not need the funds. John F. McGovern, Executive Vice President and Chief Financial Officer, believes a capital structure of mostly fixed-rate debt at reasonable rates allows more capacity for additional borrowing than does a similar capital structure with a higher portion of floating-rate debt.

As mentioned above, Host Marriott's management believes the most prudent way to finance real estate, a long-life asset, is with equity and long-term, fixed-rate debt. Marriott International's financial objectives include diversifying its financing sources and optimizing the mix and maturity of its long-term debt. Management favors debt in the 10-to-12-year range. Both Host Marriott and Marriott International have taken advantage of opportune rates in the last 18 months and locked in 95 percent of their debt at fixed rates.

Monsanto planned to issue 100-year debt at favorable rates in 1995, but decided not to go ahead when the U.S. Treasury Department proposed legislation that interest for bonds with weighted-average maturities greater than 40 years would no longer be deductible for tax purposes. Treasurer Juanita Hinshaw was disappointed because she believed that 100-year debt would have seemed like inexpensive equity. Later, after Congress postponed consideration of the proposed legislation, there were more opportunities to issue 100-year bonds, but the rates were higher than they had been in late 1995.

Although Monsanto does not have a firm policy on fixed- and floating-rate debt, its floating-rate debt tends to range from 30 to 50 percent of total debt as seasonal credit terms are offered to agricultural customers. A large part of the company's floating-rate debt is in the form of commercial paper. Depending on her view of the rates, Hinshaw may swap some of that debt into fixed rates.

Most of Home Depot's borrowing is through commercial paper at floating rates, which is refunded by convertible debenture offerings. The company is always aware of the opportunity to use interest-rate swaps to fix the rates. However, it is usually reluctant to use swaps because of the possibility that it will refund its debt with proceeds from an equity offering.

All of Sheplers' bank debt has been at floating rates. When the company had higher leverage, half of its bank debt was covered by an **interest-rate collar**. Given the decline in interest rates since then, such protection might seem in retrospect like a poor financial decision. Management, however, preferred to feel secure by eliminating its exposure to higher rates.

Although Vermeer does not have a policy on fixed- and floating-rate debt on its own balance sheet, it has in effect a fixed-rate-only policy for the interest subsidies it provides to dealers. Dealer financing programs are generally tied to the prime rate. Vermeer's subsidy to the dealers is not a percentage of total interest but just the top three percentage points. If the prime rate is 7 percent, the dealer pays 4 percent and Vermeer pays 3 percent. Even though the dealer's cost of financing may rise and fall, Vermeer's interest subsidy is fixed.

Management Judgment

Although the nature of a company's business is a determinant of its capital structure, management judgment plays an important role. Amgen, Oracle, and SymmetriCom are low-debt companies because they are in high-risk industries and have substantial growth opportunities. Host Marriott has high debt because that is the most appropriate way to finance real estate. Managements of most of the other case-study companies have considerable latitude in determining their capital structures, largely as a result of strong operating performance and cash flow. For example, while Monsanto always takes into account the riskiness of the business, industry norms, and market conditions, its capital structure is based primarily on what management considers suitable to the company's needs. The company has had sufficient cash flow for internal funding of capital expenditures, dividends, and a stock-repurchase program. With Monsanto, as well as TELUS, Georgia-Pacific, and Marriott International, management has made a trade-off between lowering the cost of capital and restricting the company's access to funds in determining an optimal capital structure. For Home Depot, Paychex, and Vermeer Manufacturing, low debt is largely a matter of management preference.

General Electric's Treasurer James Bunt believes it is difficult to calculate the optimal capital structure for such a diversified company because of the many variables and uncertainties. Management has to know the company's ability to generate cash flow over the next five years. It has to have a sense of how risky each business is, how much money it can lose, and how bad times could affect the ratios used by rating agencies. Then capital-structure decisions should be based on the amount of risk the company is willing to tolerate. This is consistent with Donaldson's proposition that the amount of debt management accepts depends on how comfortable it is with the risks the company faces.[1] (See Chapter 1, Capital-Structure Theories, page 5.) A conservative management would keep enough debt and cash-flow capacity to take care of the most likely risks and one or two of the most devastating ones. On occasion, this might require subordinating the asset decision to the capital-structure decision, limiting the volume of assets to the amount that can be financed with internally generated funds.

Importance of Operating Performance
Strong operating performance plays a larger role than capital structure in building shareholder value. It allows a company wide latitude in determining the most appropriate capital structure. For example, General Electric has doubled its stock price in the past three years through sustained growth and by constantly improving profit margins. It chooses to have low debt and would probably increase its debt only for an unusual strategic acquisition opportunity. Monsanto and TELUS have strong cash-generating capacity, which gives them the ability to increase debt temporarily for acquisitions and then return to their longer term debt-equity targets. Vermeer's leadership positions in its markets help it remain a low-debt, private company. For McGovern of Georgia-Pacific, developing good projects that return more than the cost of capital is the first priority, and then finding the appropriate financing follows suit. He says, "You cannot make bad projects look good with financing."

Cost of Capital and Shareholder Value

The case-study companies have different views about how the cost of capital affects shareholder value. Georgia-Pacific, Marriott International, and Monsanto use debt to lower their weighted average costs of capital and at least theoretically increase their corporate values as calculated by discounting future cash flows. But Home Depot and Paychex, the two case-study companies with the highest price-earnings ratios, do not believe that taking on debt to reduce their weighted average costs of capital would increase their stock prices. They believe their high share prices are based mainly on expectations for continued growth.

While Georgia-Pacific has a stated policy of using debt to optimize its weighted average cost of capital and thereby enhance shareholder value, McGovern warns against overstating the role of capital-structure policy. The mission of the treasury function at Georgia-Pacific is to maintain a solid liability structure and support the operating side of the business, not to make money independently.

John Morphy, Vice President and Chief Financial Officer of Paychex, also believes that a company's success or failure is determined not by its capital structure but by whether it is in a well-conceived business with the ability to generate a good return. In his opinion, too much attention to financial engineering can divert attention from growing the business. Morphy believes that whether or not a project clears the hurdle rate, however derived, is a secondary question. More important is whether the project can be implemented successfully and whether it can help the company in its strategy to grow profits.

Efficient Frontier: Once every year, an investment banking firm prepares an analysis to show Monsanto where its debt portfolio stands in relation to the **efficient frontier**. The efficient frontier is the point at which taking on more debt starts to increase rather than decrease a company's cost of capital. The analysis takes into consideration whether Monsanto should have more fixed-rate or floating-rate debt, longer or shorter maturities, or more foreign-currency borrowings. The purpose of the analysis is to develop an appropriate mix of debt, given the company's risk profile and objective of optimizing its weighted average cost of capital. After the most recent analysis, Monsanto was told the composition of its debt portfolio was close to optimal. Hinshaw comments that the company has been fortunate in being able to make adjustments to its debt portfolio on an opportunistic basis.

Internally Generated Cash

For companies with high business risk, cash reserves combined with low leverage are an important protective measure for survival through hard times. Examples range from fast-growing semiconductor and software companies that face a combination of technological and competitive risks to automobile companies that need large cash reserves to survive a recession. The substantial cash reserves that many companies hold today may partly reflect a long, prosperous business cycle. When carried too far, they also may reflect agency theory, in which management lowers the risk profile of the company and therefore could reduce stockholders' risk-adjusted returns.

All 13 of the case-study companies generate sufficient operating cash flow for normal capital expenditures to sustain current operations. However, two case-study companies borrow regularly to sustain their growth, and the majority would consider additional borrowing for a large, strategic acquisition. General Electric, Georgia-Pacific, Monsanto, and TELUS have borrowed in recent years to make acquisitions and used cash flow from operations to bring debt back to a long-term target level.

Amgen and Oracle, both high-growth, intangible-asset companies, generate more than enough cash to cover their reinvestment needs but borrow modest amounts to support their cash reserves and stock repurchases. For Amgen and the telecommunications-equipment business segment of SymmetriCom, investment for future growth is largely through research and development. Unlike plant and equipment investment, most R&D cannot be capitalized. This fact requires both companies to make trade-offs between current earnings and the development of products for the future. Neither company borrows to support its R&D expenditures.

In SymmetriCom's semiconductor business, "make-or-buy" decisions are required. Management has a choice between raising a large amount of capital to expand its wafer-fabrication plant or subcontracting a portion of its wafer fabrication to another company with excess capacity. By manufacturing its own wafers, the company would earn higher margins but also increase its risk in the event of an unsuccessful product or cyclical downturn.

Both Marriott International and Host Marriott require external capital to sustain their high growth rates. Marriott International's capital expenditures, financing for hotel properties, and corporate acquisitions are funded by a combination of operating cash flow and additions to debt within internal leverage guidelines. In the past three years, cash generated from operations has been more than twice the level of capital expenditures, leaving the company substantial cash flow and borrowing capacity for expansion. The company has no plans to issue new equity in the foreseeable future. Host Marriott recently has financed its growing portfolio of hotel properties with new equity as well as debt and internally generated funds.

The managements of the two private case-study companies, Sheplers and Vermeer Manufacturing, recognize that they could accelerate their growth with external capital but prefer to grow at a rate that can be supported with internally generated funds. They have chosen not to take on external financing because it would change their company cultures and cede at least some control to outside parties. Because the companies are private, their managements can make these decisions without agency conflicts.

Cash Reserves

As previously noted, the substantial cash reserves that many case-study companies are holding today may stem from the current phase of the business cycle. They may also be a manifestation of agency theory, in which management lowers the risk profile of the company at the possible expense of equity holders. Maintaining a substantial cash balance is an important part of capital-structure policy for four case-study companies. Amgen, Oracle, Paychex, and SymmetriCom justify large cash balances for risk protection and possible acquisitions. Amgen is subject to risks related to competing products, patent lawsuits, and having only two products. Management wants to have enough combined cash and borrowing capacity for a strategic acquisition. On the other hand, it does not want to hold too much cash because investors do not buy Amgen stock to participate in a bond portfolio. To help determine the appropriate level of cash, Kathryn E. Falberg, Vice President and Treasurer, compares Amgen to leading pharmaceutical and biotechnology companies using a ratio of cash to market capitalization. (Since the interviews for this study, Ms. Falberg has become Vice President and Controller of Amgen.)

Oracle maintains a substantial cash reserve to preserve its flexibility for opportunities such as acquiring other companies or real estate or re-purchasing stock when the price is unexpectedly low. Although the company's management has discussed the effect that debt could have on its cost of capital, the primary reason it plans a modest level of bor-rowing in the near future is to support that cash reserve. Oracle spends about half of the cash it generates on discretionary items such as stock repurchases, real estate, and cash acquisitions and the other half on in-creasing cash reserves.

Cash and short-term investments are currently about one-third of SymmetriCom's book assets. This gives management peace of mind, an opportunity to finance the company's growth internally, the ability to repurchase stock, and a reserve for possible acquisitions in the future. At the same time, management is aware of the risk of being taxed on ex-cessive retained earnings.

As mentioned above, when the managers of a company such as Sheplers are also the owners, the company can avoid agency conflicts. Sheplers' management is unwilling to bear the cost of cash reserves. The company maintains a no-cash policy it developed as a subsidiary of W. R. Grace with the help of a **zero-balance account** (ZBA) tied to a line of credit. Maintaining a cash balance would entail additional bor-rowing and a negative spread.

If cash and marketable securities are a significant percentage of a company's market capitalization, they may make the company vulnera-ble to takeover. The acquirer could use allegedly excess cash to reduce the purchase price. In this manner, the capital market reasserts itself over the agency inefficiencies. Despite the large absolute dollar cash balances of several of the case-study companies, none appears to be vul-nerable for this reason. In any event, cash and marketable securities as a percentage of market capitalization are approximately 17 percent for SymmetriCom, 6 percent for Amgen, and 3 percent for Oracle and Paychex.

Credit Ratings

Credit-rating guidelines play an important role in capital-structure policies for the eight case-study companies that are credit rated.[2] All of these companies consider their current credit ratings to be appropriate and consciously strive to maintain those ratings by adhering to suggested debt-level and coverage ratios and maintaining good communication with the rating agencies. The other five companies are private or do not have enough public debt to justify ratings. The most frequently assigned Moody's and Standard & Poor's ratings for the public debt of case-study companies are listed in table 2.2.

General Electric has sufficiently strong operating performance to justify a triple-A rating and chooses not to lower that rating by taking on more debt. Management would not want to see the company's triple-A credit rating change accidentally or unexpectedly. For both General Electric and Amgen, the only tolerable change would stem from a conscious decision to give up the current rating to finance a large, strategically important acquisition with debt. Although Amgen could tolerate a temporary downgrade for this purpose, it would not want to risk a rating below investment grade. If Amgen took on more debt, Falberg

Table 2.2
Credit Ratings of Case-Study Companies

	Moody's	Standard & Poor's	Canadian*
Amgen	A2	A	
General Electric	Aaa	AAA	
Georgia-Pacific	Baa2	BBB–	
Home Depot	A1	A+	
Host Marriott	Ba3	BB–	
Marriott International	Baa1	BBB+	
Monsanto	A1	A	
TELUS Communications			A

*Canadian Bond Rating Service (CBRS) and Dominion Bond Rating Service (DBRS)

believes analysts would be concerned primarily with how the proceeds would be used. She believes the company has more debt capacity within its current credit rating for a strategic acquisition than for stock repurchases.

Georgia-Pacific's policy is to maintain an investment-grade credit rating to preserve its access to capital. This puts an upper limit on debt, which in turn puts an upper limit on capital expenditures. By policy, Marriott International determines its debt capacity based on the amount and variability of its cash flows. The company manages its debt level so coverage and balance-sheet ratios stay well within the guidelines for a solid, investment-grade rating. Higher credit ratings would require lower debt levels than either Georgia-Pacific or Marriott International considers optimal.

Managements of both Amgen and Monsanto believe that moving up from a single-A to a double-A rating would restrict their flexibility and save only a few basis points in borrowing costs. The keystone of Monsanto's capital-structure policy is to maintain a single-A credit rating with a comfortable margin to ensure flexibility. The company tends to stay above the agencies' median cash-flow coverage ratios for a single-A rating, but the debt-to-capital ratio exceeds thresholds from time to time.

For both Monsanto and TELUS, debt tends to rise after an acquisition or a restructuring, and then it is managed down to its previous level. Jim Drinkwater, Vice President and Treasurer, considers a Canadian single-A rating to be the minimum acceptable for TELUS because even at the triple-B level, a borrower's access to the Canadian capital markets drops off noticeably.

Good communication helps both Monsanto and the rating agencies avoid unpleasant surprises. The company calls the agency analysts the day acquisitions are announced so they will be as knowledgeable as possible when talking to their rating committees. It has stated its policy of suspending share repurchases and repairing the balance sheet after acquisitions and then following through on its commitment.

Monsanto's management is currently planning the financial structures of the specialty-chemicals and life-sciences businesses after the spin-off it began in mid-1997.[3] Because of different risk profiles and capital-structure policies, the two new companies are likely to have different ratings after the spin-off. Management wants to structure the chemical company to have a triple-B rating because such a rating will allow the company to assume more debt and create greater shareholder value than a single-A rating would. The life-sciences company is expected to have a single-A rating, as Monsanto has now. Management believes that the life-sciences business has more business risk than the chemical business and more need for an equity cushion to provide the flexibility for growth.

Timing

Outguessing the markets is, of course, one of the most difficult financial tasks, and perfect timing is virtually impossible. Nonetheless, CFOs and treasurers of most of the case-study companies generally try to judge the markets and issue debt when conditions are most favorable. One exception is McGovern of Georgia-Pacific, who believes in financing at current market rates when funds are needed, rather than prefunding when rates look favorable.

Amgen bases both stock repurchases and related borrowing partly on its view of market conditions. In early 1997, the company issued 100-year bonds to buy back more stock because of its combined view that long-term rates were relatively low in their cycle and Amgen's stock was undervalued.

Most of Monsanto's debt issuance is opportunistic based on market conditions. There are occasional exceptions when it needs additional debt for a large acquisition, regardless of the markets. Having considered 100-year bonds in 1995, management decided not to issue them during another opportunity in 1997 because it did not consider the rates to be favorable.

Because of strong cash flow and a good credit rating, TELUS has considerable flexibility in the timing of its debt issues. Once, the company issued bonds several months before funds were required because the rate environment was expected to deteriorate. Another time, it refinanced a maturing bond issue with commercial paper with the expectation of issuing long-term debt later in the year in a more favorable rate environment. Home Depot is opportunistic in raising equity and convertible debt, sometimes keeping a cash reserve for future capital expenditures for a year or two after raising the funds.

Tax Considerations

Except for the obvious tax benefits of debt, tax considerations do not appear to affect the case-study companies' choice of debt and equity instruments. Six case-study companies repurchase stock partly to provide returns to investors in a more tax-efficient way than through dividends. In the interviews, the case-study companies mentioned a number of other tax issues indirectly related to capital structure and dividend policy.

For Amgen, Monsanto, and Oracle, minimizing the tax impact of dividends repatriated from overseas subsidiaries is an important tax issue. For SymmetriCom, the tax shield from stock options exercised recently has been an important source of cash. The company's options are generally granted at a price equal to the current market value, and therefore Accounting Principles Board (APB) Opinion 25 does not require the company to recognize any compensation expense. However, if the stock price rises and the option is exercised the same year it is granted, tax rules allow the company to deduct from the taxable income the difference between the option grant price and the exercise price. FASB Statement 123, which applies to financial statements for fiscal years beginning after December 15, 1995, allows a company either to recognize the compensation expense of options granted based on their fair value or to disclose the pro forma effect of that expense on net income and earnings per share in a footnote. The fair value is determined with an option pricing model, such as **Black-Scholes**.

Both Georgia-Pacific and Monsanto use tax-advantaged financing opportunistically. McGovern of Georgia-Pacific considers tax-free industrial revenue bonds to be more of a way to save taxes than to reduce the company's cost of capital. A tax specialist at Georgia-Pacific also periodically considers opportunities for structured financing including sales and leasebacks, cross-border leases, and tax arbitrage transactions.

Taxes are not a consideration in Home Depot's choice of equity and debt instruments, but are one of several considerations in the company's policy to own most of its real estate. Depreciation on real estate helps reduce the company's tax liability.

Paychex's primary tax considerations are related to its municipal investment portfolio. Because this tax-free investment portfolio is so large, the company's effective tax rate is about 28 percent.

For several years in the 1980s when cash flow was unusually strong, Vermeer elected **Subchapter S** status and paid out 100 percent of its profits in dividends. In 1993, Sheplers converted from a C corporation to an S corporation, which it remains today. Management wanted to pay increased dividends to the shareholders to help them diversify their portfolios rather than reinvest those funds in the company for faster growth. Because tax law restricts the number of shareholders in an S corporation to 35, a phantom stock plan was created for managers who could not be actual shareholders.

Recent Tax Legislation: In December 1995, the U.S. Treasury Department proposed that interest deductions be disallowed for debt instruments with weighted average maturities greater than 40 years. This was also part of the administration's revenue proposal for fiscal 1997. When the proposal was first issued, some corporations discontinued plans to issue 100-year bonds. Then Congress stated that it and not the Treasury Department would set the effective date for any legislation related to such long-term bonds, if indeed it passed such legislation at all. This proposal was also included in the fiscal 1998 revenue proposal issued by the administration in February 1997 with a revised effective date. During 1997, it became apparent that tax legislation related to bonds with very long maturities would be delayed, and perhaps not passed at all. Several companies saw a window of opportunity and issued 100-year bonds.

There was another administration proposal in the 1998 revenue package to defer interest deductions on zero-coupon convertible debt (described later in this chapter under "Instruments and Tactics— Convertibles") until interest is paid. One of the reasons zero-coupon convertibles have been popular is that they have allowed issuers to deduct interest for tax purposes while they are outstanding but not actually pay the interest until maturity.

The proposals related to bonds with very long maturities and zero-coupon convertible debt were not included in the Taxpayer Relief Act of 1997. It is unclear whether they will continue to be active proposals for future legislation.

However, the Taxpayer Relief Act of 1997 disallowed the deduction for interest or for original-issue discount payable in stock of the issuer. A debt instrument is treated as payable in stock if a substantial portion of the principal or interest is determined by reference to the value of the issuer's stock. The provision applies to debt securities that are mandatorily convertible or convertible at the issuer's option. Original issue discount on a debt instrument is the excess of the stated redemption price at maturity over the issue price of the instrument. An issuer of a debt instrument with original-issue discount generally accrues and deducts the discount as interest over the life of the instrument, even though interest may not be paid until the instrument matures. The holder of such a debt instrument generally includes the original-issue discount in income on an accrual basis.

The Taxpayer Relief Act of 1997 also tightened provisions relating to so-called **Morris Trusts** used in corporate spin-offs. The former Marriott Corporation and Monsanto were able to arrange tax-free spin-offs. Tax-free status for some types of spin-offs, however, may be more difficult to obtain under this legislation, especially those that are deemed to be simply precursors to the sale of business units to other companies. A corporation generally is required to recognize a gain on the distribution of property, including stock of a subsidiary, as if such property had been sold for its fair market value. The taxable gain is essentially the difference between book value and market value.

Section 355 of the Internal Revenue Code provides an exception to this rule for certain spin-off distributions of stock in controlled corporations (majority-owned subsidiaries). The code requires that the distributing corporation's shareholders own at least 80 percent of the stock in the controlled corporation before the spin-off. This exception was intended to apply when a corporation spins off a subsidiary as a special dividend to its shareholders, but not when it sells that subsidiary to another unrelated corporation.

The Taxpayer Relief Act of 1997 introduces additional restrictions under Section 355 in the case of a controlled corporation (subsidiary) that is spun off but then acquired by an unrelated corporation. The distributing corporation must recognize the amount of gain that it would have if it had simply sold the subsidiary for fair market value. The purpose of the legislation is to close, or at least tighten, the loophole that allows companies to use the spin-off mechanism to avoid recognizing a capital gains tax when they sell subsidiaries to other companies. A spin-off after which shareholders own two companies that were formerly combined generally continues to be tax free. Tax-free status for a corporation's sale of a subsidiary to another corporation is now more difficult to obtain.

Control

The issue of control is particularly important for a management or founders' group at three levels of ownership. The first is 100 percent. A desperate need for financing, because of either financial difficulty or very profitable opportunities, is usually required to overcome the owners' resistance to admitting outsiders. Once the control group's position has been diluted, there is generally little concern about further dilution until the control position approaches 50 percent. At this point, maintaining a voting majority is a key consideration in the capital-structure and investment decision. (The by-laws of some companies define specific supermajorities such as two-thirds or 85 percent that are required for specific decisions, such as the reponse to a takeover offer.) Once the majority control point has been passed, the next sensitive control point is in the vicinity of 25 percent. This level of ownership still almost ensures effective ownership of the company, particularly if the other shares are widely held. Below that level, control is often not a great concern.

The public companies in the study seem more concerned with shareholder value than with control. Control issues, such as management independence and borrowing covenants, were not frequently discussed in interviews with the public case-study companies. Except for the Marriott family's 20-percent interests in Marriott International and Host Marriott, the public companies did not mention any large shareholder blocks.

Control is a far more important issue with the two private case-study companies. John T. Mosley, Executive Vice President and Chief Financial Officer of Sheplers, Inc., comments that if a company is doing well, capital structure is under its control. If it is not doing well, capital structure is under the bank's control. Although going public has not been ruled out as a future possibility for Sheplers, Mosley observes the company would cede at least some control to outside investors, and Wall Street analysts would scrutinize quarterly performance. For now, Sheplers' owner-managers prefer the quality of life and control private ownership allows, even though external capital and public ownership could result in faster growth.

2

The Vermeer family has a stated policy of maintaining control of Vermeer Manufacturing and therefore rejects any financial decision that could cede any control to lenders or nonfamily investors. This policy, combined with the company's leadership position in its industry, creates a sense of security among employees.

External Influences
The case-study companies generally consider capital structure to be under their control. Aside from rating-agency guidelines for their credit ratings and possible legislation concerning instruments such as 100-year bonds, CFOs and treasurers interviewed mentioned little institutional and regulatory influence over their capital-structure policy. No discussions with institutional investors on capital structure were mentioned.

Implementation Issues

Why Capital Structure Varies
Corporations tend to set capital-structure policies that reflect their managements' perceptions of business needs and risks and what enhances shareholder value. Those policies may be reviewed with some frequency but tend not to change often. Temporary deviations occur, often because of large acquisitions that must be financed with temporary increases in debt, but they are usually repaired quickly to allow companies to return to their preferred policies. Sometimes a change in business circumstances leads to a change in capital-structure policies or even a spin-off, in which successor companies in different businesses pursue different capital-structure policies.

General Electric, Georgia-Pacific, and TELUS have increased their debt levels for large, strategic acquisitions and then used operating cash flow to reduce debt to its normal level. During the 1974 recession, GE's ratio of debt to capital reached a high of 39 percent. The company was able to maintain its triple-A credit rating throughout that period, but embarked on a six-month cash-conservation program to reduce the ratio to less than 30 percent. Property, plant, and equipment expenditures were reduced and collections were accelerated. Bunt observes that GE's corporate management has sufficient control to get everyone in the company focused on such a program and to make dramatic changes quickly. Since the mid-1970s, the most important variance in GE's capital structure has been the increase in debt related to the RCA acquisition in 1986. The company's debt was increased substantially at that time, and since then it has been steadily reduced.

In 1990, Georgia-Pacific used debt to finance a $5.4 billion takeover of Great Northern Nekoosa Corporation, raising long-term debt from 40 to 57 percent of capitalization. The debt load and the costs of integrating the acquired company placed Georgia-Pacific under significant stress during a subsequent downturn in the paper industry. Despite reporting negative net income for three years, Georgia-Pacific reduced long-term debt to 52 percent of capitalization during the following four years by deferring capital expenditures, selling nonstrategic assets, and not increasing its dividend. Management has stated that any similar acquisition in the future would be financed with a combination of debt and equity.

Both Home Depot and Paychex had relatively high debt when they were founded and then steadily paid it down as they grew. Sheplers' management team took the company private in an LBO in 1985 and then steadily reduced the company's leverage with the benefit of strong operating cash flow.

Chapter 15, The Role of High Debt, describes reasons that a number of companies decided to increase their leverage to a substantial degree in the 1980s. First, the growth of LBOs and leveraged recapitalizations was partly a result of the growth of the high-yield or "junk" bond market. Some of the most successful LBOs were former subsidiaries of large conglomerates in stable businesses with proven cash flows. LBOs gave the managements of these companies an ownership opportunity, and high leverage was a spur that encouraged cost control and the sale of unproductive assets. Second, a number of LBOs and leveraged recapitalizations were undertaken in response to hostile takeover attempts. Many of these companies were put in play because they were underperforming, but they did not perform well after they became highly leveraged. Finally, there have been some very specific reasons for leveraged recapitalizations, such as motivating management and providing signals to the capital markets, which are described in greater detail in chapter 15.

Business-Unit Capital Structures

Finance theory suggests that different divisional capital structures can help control adverse agency behavior; low debt could make management complacent or lead to overinvestment in businesses with excess cash flow but few growth opportunities. Some multibusiness companies internally ascribe different capital structures and costs of capital to each business unit, depending on the norms for independent companies in its industry. In this way, those companies can use different hurdle rates depending on the level of risk in each business. However, except for finance subsidiaries, joint ventures, and other affiliates, TELUS is the only case-study company that has different capital structures for different business units.

While TELUS follows a capital-structure guideline for the corporation as a whole, management has the flexibility to vary the capital structures of its subsidiaries considerably. In contrast to tax requirements in the United States, each subsidiary within a Canadian corporation such as TELUS files an individual tax return. Subsidiaries with higher effective tax rates are sometimes capitalized with higher levels of debt. The capital structures of the two telephone companies, TELUS Communications and TELUS Edmonton Holdings, are still regulated. For TELUS Communications, maintaining the current single-A credit rating is also a consideration.

General Electric considers all of its 12 component industrial businesses to have the same capital structure and the same cost of capital for the purposes of hurdle rates and capital budgeting analysis. Bunt believes that trying to figure out the appropriate capital structure and cost of capital for each component business would be excessively complicated. Plant and equipment may be new for one business and fully depreciated for another. A given business may be a consistent cash generator showing a relatively small net investment on the books. Another business may have done a recent acquisition or have required more recent capital investment. All of this has averaged out in the company's 100-year history.

The capital structures of GE's joint ventures and other affiliates vary considerably, driven by factors such as taxes and partners' objectives. If an affiliate has **net operating loss carry-forwards** (NOLs), there is no tax shield provided by debt, and a high percentage of equity capital is preferred. In high-tax countries, affiliates tend to have more debt.

60

Both the building-products and the paper and pulp side of Georgia-Pacific are considered to have the same capital structure and cost of capital. However, McGovern believes the building-products side probably could support more debt than paper and pulp because it has more stable cash flows.

Vice President and Corporate Treasurer Bruce M. Lange considers Oracle's capital structure to be appropriate for the entire company now. However, he can conceive of future parts of the business that might justify higher leverage than the parent company has—for example, a leasing subsidiary or a customer sales and support unit with very predictable income streams.

Allocating Capital among Business Units: Sometimes, having diverse businesses enhances a company's ability to support its growth with internally generated funds, regardless of whether different business units have different capital structures. Several case-study companies have businesses that generate excess cash and other businesses that need cash to grow. Their approaches differ considerably. Vermeer and SymmetriCom have established ways for each business to stand on its own financially. Monsanto is in the process of spinning off its specialty-chemicals and life-sciences businesses. SymmetriCom is considering a similar spin-off of its telecommunications and semiconductor businesses. General Electric has consistently strong cash flows from its 12 diversified component businesses. Management does not consciously use cash flow from one business to support cash needs of another, but rather thinks in terms of company-wide capital spending priorities.

Vermeer has always used cash generated from established product lines to develop new product lines, but in recent years the company has made the process more systematic, establishing an internal bank and requiring each business to stand on its own. Each division is allocated capital, on which it pays interest at an internally defined rate, such as prime. A business that needs capital for growth pays for additional funds at the internal rate; a business that generates excess cash reduces its capital charges. Division managers are compensated partly on the return on net assets they achieve.

SymmetriCom's telecommunications equipment business and semiconductor business are run as separate, unrelated entities under common corporate ownership, and may eventually become separate companies for improved access to the capital markets. If excess cash from the telecommunications business, a net cash generator, were used to fund plant and equipment expenditures for the semiconductor business, it would be an arm's-length transaction at current market rates.

Monsanto in recent years has funded the growth of its life-sciences business partly with cash generated from its specialty-chemicals business. Management believes that continuing this policy indefinitely could jeopardize the leading market positions of the chemicals business. Therefore, it plans to spin off the chemicals business as a separate company, able to determine its own investment priorities and financing strategies.

Stock Splits

Robert M. Conroy and Robert S. Harris note that two interrelated patterns in U.S. financial markets are not well explained by standard financial theory: (1) Companies routinely engage in stock splits; (2) the average price per share on the New York Stock Exchange has remained roughly the same for decades.[4] Over the past half century, the average price per share has remained in the range of $30 to $40, while the average adjusted price is 60 times the 1926 level. According to traditional financial theory, a stock-split decision should be a trade-off between minimizing the transaction costs of large investors and increasing the ability of small investors to trade in round lots. But this does not explain why average share prices have remained constant over such a long period. Traditional theory also suggests that management signals good news to the market by its willingness to drive up transaction costs by increasing the number of shares.

Data collected by Conroy and Harris provide evidence that managers split stocks primarily based on some firm-specific price level, often the absolute level of the lagged split price, the price level after the prior split. The data also provide strong evidence of investor "framing" around reference prices. In "framing," investors are reacting, at least in part, based on historical, firm-specific reference prices, even though those reference prices may be from the relatively distant past—more than seven years on average. Therefore, wealth gains around announcements of stock splits depend on price deviations from the lagged split price. When a stock splits to a level below its framing level or reference price, investors interpret such action as signaling managerial confidence in good prospects. Therefore, they tend to bid the price up to its traditional framing level.

General Electric, Home Depot, Monsanto, and Paychex have done regular stock splits. The most frequently cited reason is to make round lots, and even smaller blocks, more affordable to employee and retail investors. General Electric follows a pattern observed by Conroy and Harris in timing each two-for-one split to return the company's stock price to the previous post-split price of $50.

Home Depot has done one 4-for-3 and six 3-for-2 stock splits, which, compounded, are equal to a 60-for-1 split. The reason for a split is to allow more employees to own 100 shares. After each split, however, the company must earn a higher dollar amount for each penny per share. This can create difficulty for management in a quarter when the stock may miss Wall Street's expectations by a penny or two per share.

Monsanto recently split its stock 5-for-1 to make the price more compatible with employee-incentive plans. A lower price makes a psychological difference to Monsanto's business managers. Raising the price of a $30 stock through operating performance appears to be easier than raising the price of a $150 stock. Hinshaw believes the market has interpreted the stock split as evidence that management expects the stock to continue to rise. However, she believes companies that do such transactions deliberately to send signals to the market often encounter problems.

Paychex did six 3-for-2 stock splits between 1986 and 1996. The CEO has chosen to do 3-for-2 rather than 2-for-1 stock splits because that allows the company to do more of them.

Dividends and Stock Repurchases

So-called "sticky" dividend policies continue to be widespread. Sticky dividend policies follow a pattern observed by John Lintner in 1954: Companies increase their dividends gradually, lagging increases in earnings, only to a level they can sustain, given a range of foreseeable circumstances, including temporary dips in earnings. They are reluctant to break their established patterns for fear of adverse market reactions.[5] With the exception of Vermeer Manufacturing, a private company, none of the case-study companies mentioned formulas or other quantitative guidelines for their dividend-payout ratios. Several were sensitive to the investment guidelines of institutional investors that buy only the stock of companies with records of dividend payments.

Barclay, Smith, and Watts observe that companies with greater growth opportunities tend to pay fewer dividends and assume less debt.[6] Table 2.3, illustrating recent dividend-payout ratios of case-study companies, generally supports this proposition. Host Marriott, which pays no dividends, and Marriott International and Home Depot, which pay low dividends, are all fast-growing companies even though they are in what the researchers have defined as volatile-revenue-growth industries for the purpose of the quadrant model. TELUS's dividend-payout ratio is declining over time as it becomes more of a secular-growth company. General Electric is an exception because it generates enough cash to finance growth internally, buy back stock, and still maintain a substantial dividend payout. Another well-known example of a secular-growth company is Intel, which started paying dividends in 1992 because of its substantial cash flow.

A complication in interpreting dividend policy is how to allow for stock repurchase programs. To an increasing degree, financial officers are using these programs as a way to distribute value to the shareholders. A discussion of this tactic is provided in the next section of this chapter.

Table 2.3
Recent Dividend-Payout Ratios of Case-Study Companies

	Secular Growth	Volatile Growth
Fixed Assets	General Electric - 43%	Georgia-Pacific - 17–112%
	SymmetriCom - 0	Monsanto - 42%
	TELUS - 54%	Vermeer Manufacturing - formula
		Host Marriott - 0
Intangible Assets	Oracle - 0	Marriott International - 14%
	Amgen - 0	Home Depot - 12%
	Paychex - 28%	Sheplers - confidential

GE's dividend-payout ratio has been relatively constant in recent years at 40 to 45 percent of earnings. Its policy is determined largely by historical precedent, and also by what it perceives to be the interests of its investors. This is not always easy because different investors have different expectations. For example, some institutional investors have strict dividend-percent models. If GE had different capital requirements, its dividend policy might be different. Recently, its cash flow has been strong enough to maintain a steady dividend-payout ratio, to make sufficient capital expenditures to continue growing existing businesses, and to buy back stock. Bunt observes that the message the company conveys is just as important as the dividend policy itself. Investors want to know what the company's objectives are and what it plans to do with its cash.

Georgia-Pacific has raised the dollar amount of its dividend gradually over the past decade. The payout ratio has varied substantially because of cyclical earnings. When the company reported losses between 1991 and 1993, the dividend was held constant. Given the industry's cyclicality and limited long-term growth opportunities, McGovern believes a company like Georgia-Pacific should lean toward limiting capital expenditures and providing a cash return to its stockholders through dividends and stock repurchases. The investor relations staff believes that a portion of the company's shareholders considers dividends important and that cutting them would cause an adverse market reaction. Furthermore, the company would like its stock to be considered a qualified investment by as many institutions as possible, including those whose rules specify that common stock must pay dividends.

Home Depot's dividend policy is intuitive rather than a defined percentage of earnings. The company declared its first dividend of a penny a share in 1988 because many mutual-fund and pension-fund investors do not buy a stock if it pays no dividends. Since then, Home Depot has increased its dividends every year. Management has chosen to keep the dividend constant on a per-share basis after each stock split, thereby increasing the dividend payout as a percentage of earnings. In 1995, the dividend-payout ratio was 12 percent. As the company continues to do stock splits, Ronald M. Brill, Executive Vice President and Chief Administrative Officer, would like to guard against letting the dividend-payout ratio get too high, because Home Depot is still a growth company that needs cash. He notes that as long as the company continues to own real estate, it will continue to be a borrower. He can tolerate borrowing to pay dividends, but over the long term he would like to minimize the amount of equity sold to pay dividends, including the equity that originates as convertible debentures.

Monsanto has increased its dividends every year for 25 years and kept those increases ahead of inflation. Historically, management has wanted Monsanto to be considered a great company, and it has observed that great companies pay ever-increasing dividends. Monsanto has had sufficient funds to maintain a payout ratio of approximately 40 to 50 percent of earnings over the years and to keep dividend increases ahead of inflation. The company has tried to keep its dividend policy consistent with both the chemical industry and the pharmaceutical industry. Treasurer Juanita Hinshaw believes that a consistent dividend payout makes Monsanto's stock attractive to yield investors and thus tends to set a floor for the company's stock price.

Since Paychex started paying dividends in 1988, its payout ratio has risen from 14 to 29 percent. Because of the fast growth in earnings, dividends grew 50 percent per year between 1992 and 1996. With strong cash flow, management believes a reasonable level of dividends is appropriate and wants to continue sending a positive signal to the market. At the same time, it wants to retain flexibility by maintaining a substantial amount of cash on the balance sheet.

Vermeer's dividend policy is driven by a formula that starts with earnings and employee bonuses. There is a profit-sharing plan under which a defined percentage of each year's operating profit is allocated for employee bonuses and retirement funds. From the remainder of earnings after employee compensation, a percentage is paid to a charitable foundation. Then taxes are paid and dividends for the 35 shareholders are calculated as a defined percentage of what is left after taxes. The formula approach eliminates the need for year-by-year decisions on dividend policy. For several years in the mid-1980s, Vermeer elected Subchapter S status and paid out 100 percent of profits to its shareholders in dividends. This was after a period of rapid sales growth when cash flow remained strong.

TELUS deliberately has not articulated a dividend policy. The company started with a high payout to be consistent with the telephone industry and to ensure the success of its initial public offering. Now management wants to retain capital for reinvestment and does not want investors to expect a pattern of continually increasing dividends. Therefore, it has chosen to keep its dividend per share constant on a dollar basis as earnings rise.

In its three years as a separate company, Marriott International has paid dividends of only 10 to 20 percent of earnings. Its stated policy is to reinvest the major portion of its earnings in the business. Since the spin-off, Host Marriott has neither paid a dividend nor repurchased stock. Management believes investors are looking for a pure play in hotel real estate, not dividend income. It sees significant investment opportunities and believes it can serve investors better by reinvesting capital than by paying out dividends.

Three of the secular-growth case-study companies, Amgen, SymmetriCom, and Oracle, have never paid dividends. From the beginning, the managements of these relatively young, fast-growing companies have believed that investors expect them to reinvest cash generated from operations in the growth of the business. As they have begun to generate excess cash, they have considered stock repurchases to be a more tax-advantaged way to return some of that cash to shareholders.

Two reasons Amgen could consider paying dividends in the future are a desire to have more yield-oriented investors and to use pooling-of-interest accounting. Having more yield-oriented investors could stabilize the price of the company's stock. Because an excess of purchased over issued stock in a given 24-month period could restrict the company from using pooling-of-interest accounting in an acquisition, the company could decide to return cash to investors through dividends rather than stock buy-backs.

Stock Repurchases

There has been a recent trend toward more stock repurchases. According to Securities Data Corporation, U.S. corporations stated their intentions to purchase $176.7 billion of their own stock in 1996 and $87.3 billion in the first half of 1997. Some analysts see this as one of the causes of the current bull market. Others point out that much of the buyback activity is only to offset the shares issued through stock options. A report by Salomon Brothers notes that dividend yields, dividends paid as a percentage of stock prices, are at an all-time low of 1.7 percent for the S&P 500, and that even if the cash returned to investors through stock repurchases were added to the dividends paid, dividend yields would be only 2.2 percent, the lowest in 22 years.

In 1997, according McGee and Ip, several companies have announced increased borrowing to finance share repurchases.[7] Ipalco Enterprises, an Indianapolis utility holding company, cut its dividend 33 percent to repurchase 21 percent of its outstanding stock. It raised debt from 40 to 68 percent of capitalization, transforming itself from an income to a growth stock. Briggs & Stratton, OshKosh B'Gosh, and SPX Corp. announced share buyback programs financed with debt; SPX said it would suspend its dividend completely.

As the disparity between capital-gains tax rates and regular income-tax rates widens, the incentive to substitute share repurchase for dividend payments should increase. In addition, it is easier to vary a stock-repurchase program than to change a regular dividend. Thus, stock repurchase gives a company's financial management much more flexibility in balancing cash flows, investment decisions, and capital structure.

As shown in table 2.4, seven case-study companies have stock repurchase programs: two of them primarily to offset dilution from stock options exercised, three of them primarily to return cash to investors in a tax-efficient manner, and two to do both.

Marriott International, Monsanto, and Oracle repurchase stock when the price seems favorable to offset the dilution created by employee stock-option programs. The timing of Marriott International's

Table 2.4
Case-Study Companies That Have Repurchased Stock or Are Considering Doing So in the Future

	Secular Growth	Volatile Growth
Fixed Assets	General Electric	Georgia-Pacific
	SymmetriCom	Monsanto
	TELUS (considering)	
Intangible Assets	Oracle	Marriott International
	Amgen	Home Depot (considering)

stock repurchases is based on market conditions. For Monsanto, stock repurchases are also a method of capital-structure adjustment when the company has excess cash after R&D and capital expenditures. McGovern of Georgia-Pacific favors fewer dividends and more stock repurchases because they provide flexibility to the company and more favorable tax treatment for investors.

Amgen's stock repurchases have risen consistently over the past few years. Therefore, investors tend to think the pattern will continue. This is similar to precedents other companies establish with continuing dividend increases. If management decided to buy back less stock in a given year than it had the year before, it would make a particular effort to explain to investors how the company planned to use the extra cash.

Bunt believes General Electric has enhanced its share price by buying back stock rather than leaving cash on the balance sheet in case an acquisition opportunity comes up. As a result of the stock repurchased, earnings per share recently have grown about 2 percent faster than total earnings.

After its first priority of building a substantial cash reserve, Oracle prefers to use additional cash for stock repurchases rather than dividends, because they allow more flexibility than an established dividend policy and are more tax efficient for the investor. In recent years, Oracle has been buying back slightly less than the amount of stock required to offset the dilution from stock options granted to employees. Lange notes that the company's **overhang,** the number of shares on which there are stock options outstanding as a percentage of total shares issued, is currently about 6 percent, compared with 20 percent for a large competitor. As Oracle's stock price strengthens, it becomes more difficult to buy enough shares to keep dilution under 1 percent per year. Lange believes it is appropriate to use about $200 million per year generated from the exercise of stock options for related stock buy-backs, but may also put some debt on the balance sheet for that purpose.

Paychex does not buy back stock because it prefers to maintain a large cash reserve. Stock repurchases could prevent it from accounting for an acquisition as a pooling-of-interests accounting for three years. Also, buying back stock is dilutive to earnings per share when the stock is trading at a high price-earnings ratio. Morphy believes the only good reason for a company to repurchase its stock is a belief that it is undervalued.

TELUS has recently received $400 million in cash from the sale of its 50-percent interest in a British cable television company. Approximately one-half of that cash is expected to be used to buy back 5 percent of its shares under a normal-course issuer bid. The remaining 50 percent of the proceeds then will be available for investments or acquisitions.

Someday, if Home Depot starts to run out of attractive new store locations and slows down its real-estate acquisitions, it will start generating a large amount of excess cash. At that time, Brill expects Home Depot will start buying back its own stock. McGee and Ip quote a money manager who likes to see growth prospects as well as buyback activity in a stock and who avoids stocks where growth is beginning to plateau, even though prices are rising as a result of repurchases.[8] The money manager notes that buybacks have relatively less impact when a stock is trading at a high price-earnings ratio. He favors Home Depot, which he understands is not repurchasing its shares because it can put the capital to better use expanding its business.

Development and Approval of Policies

Capital-structure and dividend policies are developed by an informal process of ongoing consensus among management and the board in most of the case-study companies. The CFO and/or the treasurer generally make presentations to the board at least annually as part of the budget-review process. Only two case-study companies, Georgia-Pacific and Monsanto, have written policies; both are rather general. In addition, Monsanto prepares a comprehensive book each year for the rating-agency review process, which the board's finance committee also reviews.

When McGovern of Georgia-Pacific has specific proposals like the stock-repurchase program, he first discusses them with the board's finance committee. Then those policies are presented to the full board with the support of the finance committee. At Home Depot, the board's audit and executive committees review its financial structure and its external financing decisions.

For Amgen, the budgeting process triggers all the questions management needs to consider relevant to capital structure. How much cash should the company keep? How much stock should the company repurchase? Is the number of shares outstanding increasing or decreasing? What would be the impact of issuing debt and buying back more stock?

Marriott International's capital-structure and dividend policies are developed by the finance function as an integral part of the company's growth strategy. They are reviewed with the board as part of the annual budgeting process. The effectiveness of these policies is measured by the company's stock price and continuing ability to finance its growth.

As part of Oracle's annual budget review, Lange reviews with the board the expected dilution from employee stock options, cash forecasts, and how much cash he feels comfortable using to repurchase stock. He also reviews these issues and their expected effect on the balance sheet with the board's finance committee on a quarterly basis.

Because SymmetriCom is a relatively small company, financial policies can be developed informally among J. Scott Kamsler, Senior Vice President and Chief Financial Officer, the CEO, and the division heads. There is a mutual understanding of why the company does not pay dividends and how divisional performance results are affected by capital expenditures and increases in inventory and receivables.

Tests of Effectiveness

CFOs and treasurers of the case-study companies generally consider the effectiveness test of their capital-structure and dividend practices to be how well the stock price performs, how well the company is able to carry out its strategy, and how well investors, lenders, and analysts receive the policies. For example, management evaluates the effectiveness of TELUS' capital-structure and dividend policies based on several factors: the company's ability to finance its normal operations at reasonably favorable interest rates and to access other forms of debt when it wants to do acquisitions; stock price; and investor feedback, principally through securities analysts. It is also common for a company's financial management to compare the company on these dimensions with a group of peer companies, usually in the same industry. For such comparisons, they generally use the same ratios that security analysts and rating-agency analysts use. These ratios are identified later in this chapter.

Instruments and Tactics

Case-study companies were asked which derivatives and other financial instruments had been useful in implementing their capital-structure and dividend policies. In general, the larger companies are active users of interest-rate and currency derivatives such as simple purchased options and interest-rate swaps for their risk management programs, but are reluctant to use complex derivatives developed by financial institutions. The smaller public and the private case-study companies use derivatives less actively. Among the new instruments described in the financial press over the past couple of years are various types of convertible securities. Some case studies find convertible securities to be useful while others do not.

The following sections briefly summarize the financial instruments and techniques mentioned in the interviews with case-study companies, and how they are used.

Borrowing Instruments

Short-Term Debt: Short-term debt has been useful to GE in recent years because of its flexibility; it can be raised and lowered depending on cash needs. The company has been able to let long-term debt roll off and not replace it. Before the spin-off, Marriott Corporation was able to use short-term debt to finance real estate intended for sale to investors. Problems related to financing long-term assets with short-term debt in adverse market conditions led to the spin-off of Marriott International as the hotel services company. Now the remaining company, renamed Host Marriott, finances its real estate assets with equity and long-term debt.

Commercial Paper Classified Long Term: Both Home Depot and Marriott International carry commercial paper as long-term debt because it is backed by a revolving credit agreement rather than just a line of credit. This accounting treatment helps Home Depot's current ratio, which tends to be lowered by short-term borrowings and accounts payable that support store inventory. In 1995, a portion of Monsanto's short-term commercial paper, which was rolled over every 30 or 45 days, was classified as long term because it was used to finance the Kelco acquisition and because the company intended to replace it with longer term financing.

Put and Call Provisions: Monsanto has considered **put bonds** but has not found the right market conditions to use them. Treasurer Juanita Hinshaw comments, "They come and go the same way preferred stock does." Put bonds, also known as **puttable bonds**, and **put notes** have embedded features called early redemption (put) options, which permit the holders to sell the bonds back to the issuer or to a third party at par or close to par in the event interest rates rise and/or the quality of the issuer's credit declines.

Georgia-Pacific and Monsanto have included **call provisions** in their bond offerings when the price has seemed reasonable. McGovern believes the value of call provisions to Georgia-Pacific is higher than reflected in **option pricing models**. On the other hand, Marriott International does not foresee using a call provision to reduce its debt. If Michael A. Stein, Executive Vice President and Chief Financial Officer, wanted the ability to reprice the company's debt in six years, he would rather issue debt with a six-year maturity than longer term debt with a call provision.

Credit-Sensitive Notes: Credit-sensitive notes are securities with an adjustable coupon that is based on the issuer's credit rating. In the event of a rating upgrade, the coupon on the security is reduced. A rating downgrade, by contrast, leads to an increase in the coupon. Georgia-Pacific used credit-sensitive notes as part of the financing package for its acquisition of Great Northern Nekoosa Corporation in 1990 because the pricing was attractive compared with then-available bank financing.

Credit Subsidiaries: Although Vermeer has virtually no debt on its balance sheet, it has a credit subsidiary that has borrowed to support dealer floor-plan financing and loans to dealers' customers on several occasions. The parent company has securitized assets by selling off blocks of the credit subsidiary's receivables.

Sale of Receivables: The sale of receivables is generally more expensive than straight borrowing, but it can be useful in special circumstances. McGovern of Georgia-Pacific believes packaging of receivables is a particularly efficient way to lower the cost of debt when the company needs a large amount of financing for an acquisition. No matter where a company's credit rating is, it usually gets an excellent rating on the receivables. Georgia-Pacific does not continue to use accounts receivable financing today because it is more expensive than commercial paper.

When reducing debt to repair its balance sheet after an acquisition, Monsanto has considered selling receivables but, like Georgia-Pacific, found the cost to be too high compared with the company's commercial paper borrowing rate. Treasurer Juanita Hinshaw would consider the cost to be reasonable only if the company were beginning to run out of borrowing capacity within the guidelines for a single-A credit rating.

Recently Vermeer sold a $3-million tranche from the portfolio of its credit subsidiary to finance construction of a new plant. Borrowing the money would have been cheaper but against the company's policy of virtually no debt and complete control of its balance sheet.

Equity Instruments

Preferred Stock: Preferred stock accounts for only a small part of securities outstanding. It is generally treated as equity by the rating agencies, but it is nondilutive to the interests of common shareholders. Also, unlike the interest payments on debt, preferred dividends are not tax deductible. Under current tax law, when one corporation invests in the preferred stock of another, only 30 percent of dividends received are treated as taxable income. This tax benefit for the investor allows the issuer's preferred dividends to be lower than they would otherwise be; an issuer's coupon for preferred stock may be lower than the interest would be on comparable debt. Sometimes preferred stock offers advantageous financing rates for start-up companies that do not have the earnings to take advantage of interest tax shields but are still capable of attracting investors.

One case-study company, Host Marriott, has preferred stock outstanding, and two case-study companies, Oracle and TELUS, have authorized preferred stock. In 1996, Host Marriott issued $550 million company-obligated, mandatorily redeemable, convertible preferred securities of a subsidiary trust.

Monsanto's Hinshaw comments that the pricing for preferred stock looked good a couple of years ago but the company did not need long-term funds at the time.

Equity Put Warrants: Equity put warrants provide a company with premium income but also commit it, at least contingently, to buy a certain number of shares during a specified period. Monsanto has considered but rejected the use of equity put warrants because they could restrict its flexibility to stop buying back stock when it has cash needs.

Phantom Stock Plan: When Sheplers converted from a C corporation to an S corporation, it was required to reduce the number of its shareholders from 50 to 35. It created a phantom stock plan for managers who could not be stockholders. Holders of phantom stock received every shareholder's right except for a vote.

Spin-Offs: Wruck and Wruck note that a number of studies document recent attempts by corporations to sharpen the focus of their economic activities, in part by shedding operations not considered "core" businesses.[9] A variety of financial transactions are used to separate business units from their parent corporations, including asset sales and divestitures, equity carve-outs, and spin-offs. Parent stock prices have generally responded favorably to these transactions, but the authors note the fundamental sources of value creation remain a puzzle to both academics and practitioners. Hypotheses include improvements in operating efficiency, improved governance and incentives, improved access to capital markets, facilitation of the workings of the market for corporate control, the resolution of information problems, and the creation of tax-timing options. To date, no dominant explanation has emerged, and, as usual, the studies do not all agree.

Wruck and Wruck find evidence that spin-offs create value through operating efficiency. This is reflected, first, in the parent firms' positive stock-price performance at the time of announcement and, later, in the positive price performance of the spin-off firms associated with sales growth, increases in discretionary spending, and improvements in operating profitability. The authors find no evidence of spin-off transactions as "corporate cleansing" events. Instead, parent firms appear to invest in units to be spun off to make sure they are ready to operate as independent entities. The authors note that one of the important benefits of a spin-off is that the new entity has independent access to the capital markets. The discipline of and access to the capital markets replaces the parent's internal funding and resource allocation process and may thus reduce agency costs.

The case-study companies include a recent spin-off, a planned spin-off, and a possible spin-off. Two of the case-study companies, Marriott

International and Host Marriott, are the result of a spin-off in 1993. When interviews for this study were conducted, Monsanto was in the process of implementing a spin-off, which was completed by the end of 1997. SymmetriCom is a company composed of two separate business units, which may be separated in the future.

Marriott International was spun off in a special dividend to shareholders and Marriott Corporation was renamed Host Marriott in 1993. The purpose of the spin-off was to create two companies with different business strategies that would appeal to different investor objectives: Marriott International, with steady service revenues, and Host Marriott, with ownership positions in hotel real estate. The capital-structure and dividend policies of these two entities reflect their different asset structures, revenue sources, and business objectives.

During 1997, Monsanto separated its specialty-chemicals business, a heavy-fixed-asset, volatile-growth business, from its life-sciences business, an intangible-asset, secular-revenue-growth business. Although the different natures of the two businesses will lead to different capital structures, the primary reason for the spin-off is strategic: to give each business the ability to make investment and financing decisions independently.

SymmetriCom's telecommunications equipment and semiconductor businesses are run as two entirely separate companies under one corporate umbrella. In large investment banking and brokerage firms, the two industries usually are covered by different analysts. Many of those firms do not currently cover SymmetriCom because it is not big enough to justify the expense of coverage by two analysts. Management believes the two businesses would be valued more highly as separate companies, each with a separate, focused strategy and "story" to tell to the capital markets. After SymmetriCom's reemerging semiconductor business develops an earnings track record, it might be spun off as a separate company.

Targeted Stock: In recent years, a few large companies, including General Motors, Pittston, and U S West, have issued **targeted stock** to achieve some of the benefits of a spin-off, while retaining some of the benefits of different businesses within one corporation. The value of targeted stock theoretically depends on the performance of different business units. Therefore, the combined market values of the different classes of targeted stock could add up to more than the company's market capitalization as one entity.

In September 1997, Georgia-Pacific announced plans to create a separate class of common stock to allow shareholders to benefit from its profitable timber business. Timber represents a small fraction of sales but a relatively higher percentage of profits. Because earnings from the company's pulp, paper, and building-products businesses are highly cyclical, management believes Georgia-Pacific's stock trades at lower multiples of earnings and cash flow than that of companies with more predictable earnings. The two classes of common stock will allow each group to either retain cash flow for reinvestment in its business or return the cash directly to investors.

In contrast, despite proposals from investment bankers, neither Falberg of Amgen nor Drinkwater of TELUS has seen evidence to show that targeted stock would create value. More important, Falberg believes targeted stock would give Amgen's employees an incentive to focus on their own pieces of the business rather than working together as part of a company team. When Marriott Corporation announced a decision to split its hotel-management and real-estate-ownership operations in 1992, some dissatisfied bond investors suggested targeted stock instead. Stephen Bollenbach, then CFO of Marriott, commented that targeted stock would have been an accounting maneuver that did not represent real economic substance.[10]

Convertible Securities

Many of the new financial products offered recently by investment bankers to the case-study companies have been variants of convertibles. With convertible debt or preferred stock, the investor accepts a lower coupon for the ability to convert the security into common stock at a preset conversion price. Both the issuer and the investor take a view on the issuer's common stock price. If the issuer believes its stock will not exceed the conversion price, convertibles can offer low-cost financing. If the issuer's stock price is expected to rise above what the market would accept as a conversion price, a convertible could cause the issuer to sell equity too cheaply and create unnecessary dilution.

Among the case-study companies, there are disparate opinions about the use of convertibles. Home Depot, Host Marriott, and Marriott International have been regular users of convertibles. On the other hand, Amgen and Oracle prefer to express a view of their stock prices through costless collars (described later in this section). Oracle has used synthetic convertibles as well. Georgia-Pacific does not use convertibles. CFO Jack McGovern prefers to issue straight equity or debt, depending on the company's current cash and capital-structure needs.

Convertible Debt: Home Depot has been a regular issuer of **convertible debt securities** in recent years. They have appealed to the company because of the low coupon. In most cases, they also have resulted in the sale of equity at below-market prices, causing dilution in the equity interests of the original owners.

Amgen issued euroconvertible debt just before its first product, Epogen™, was introduced in 1989. It was converted almost immediately because the company's common stock price rose sharply when it launched Epogen.

McGovern of Georgia-Pacific does not like to mix borrowing with bets on where the company stock price is going. Therefore, the company has never issued debt linked in any way to the price of its stock. McGovern describes convertibles as expensive and "debt when you need equity and equity when you need debt."

Synthetic Convertibles: A synthetic convertible consists of the issuance of straight debt and the sale of equity call warrants at approximately the same time. Straight debt, having a higher coupon than convertible debt, provides greater tax shields. The warrant can be issued at a different time, depending on market conditions. Oracle's treasurer Bruce Lange finds synthetic convertible stock provides more flexibility and better tax benefits than actual convertible debentures.

Costless Collars: Both Amgen and Oracle have sold put warrants and used some of the proceeds to buy call options on their common stock. This combination is sometimes called a costless collar. It is a way to express a bullish view on the company's stock. If the stock price rises, the company can gain by using premium income from put warrants to buy calls on its stock. If the stock price falls, investors exercising their put warrants will force the company to buy back its stock at above-market prices.

Zero-Coupon Convertible Bonds: Zero-coupon convertible bonds are callable by the issuer and puttable by the investor. Like other zero-coupon bonds, they sell at a deep discount to their $1,000 face value and make a one-time, lump-sum interest payment at maturity—usually in 15 or 20 years. But like convertible bonds, they can also be exchanged for a fixed amount of the issuing company's stock, allowing investors to profit from a rise in share price. The issuer pays a lower rate on zero-coupon convertibles than on regular bonds in exchange for the conversion feature. Imputed interest is tax deductible each year, even though the issuer does not pay it until maturity. (Legislation was introduced to postpone the tax deduction until interest is actually paid at maturity, but was not included in the Taxpayer Relief Act of 1997.) If the securities are converted later, the issuer retains the tax benefits already realized up to the time of conversion.

Marriott International has found zero-coupon convertibles to be advantageous when rates appear low and conversion premiums appear to be relatively high. CFO Mike Stein notes they offer an attractive borrowing rate, the imputed or "PIK" (payment-in-kind) interest is currently deductible, and they are less costly than straight equity. Also, because they are convertible into a fixed number of shares, the conversion price rises at the interest rate. On the other hand, Treasurer Juanita Hinshaw of Monsanto has considered zero-coupon convertibles but not found them suitable to the company's needs. She has believed the company's stock price would rise above the implicit conversion price of the zero-coupon convertibles and, therefore, using those instruments would cause unnecessary dilution.

Derivatives: Financial managers in the case-study companies appear to be skeptical about the value of complex derivatives. They use derivatives cautiously to serve specific needs, mostly related to financial risk management. Monsanto, for example, is an active but conservative user of derivatives. The treasury staff is willing to look at new derivative products offered by bankers, no matter how complex they are, but generally does transactions customized to fit the company's needs. Monsanto regularly does interest-rate swaps, currency swaps, and swaptions.

SymmetriCom's only reason for using derivatives has been hedging foreign-currency-denominated accounts receivable. Most of its current overseas customers are willing to pay dollars, but Kamsler foresees the need in the future to bill in foreign currencies to stay competitive.

Off-Balance-Sheet Financing: To support continued growth while not incurring debt, Vermeer Manufacturing uses creative off-balance-sheet financing. The company provides its equipment dealers with interest subsidies to support inventory on their showroom floors. Rather than borrowing itself, Vermeer provides contingent support in the form of recourse arrangements for dealers that carry debt on their own balance sheets. Among the most important types of off-balance-sheet financing is leasing, which is discussed in the next section.

Real-Estate Ownership and Leasing: Real-estate ownership is the core of Host Marriott's business and dictates its capital structure. The financial strategies of both Home Depot and Oracle also include substantial real-estate ownership. Morphy of Paychex, on the other hand, regrets not buying real estate in several locations when prices were depressed.

Home Depot owns a high percentage of its stores. Real-estate ownership gives the company flexibility in opening and closing its stores and saves money because few landlords can match Home Depot's credit rating and cost of capital. One drawback that might cause the company to reduce the percentage of stores owned is the heavy capital requirement for continued expansion and the consequent need for external financing. As indicated below under "Leasing," Home Depot's management comes out directly opposite GE's management on the issue of capital costs and real-estate ownership.

Oracle buys real estate rather than leasing when the cost appears to provide good value. Sometimes, when real-estate prices in a given metropolitan region appear to be cheap, the company buys land and starts to create a campus, adjusting the rate of office construction to fit the company's needs. Wherever the company needs a substantial amount of space, it usually has to arrange to construct a suitable building, and the landlord usually wants a 10-year lease. Lange observes that signing a 10-year lease is not much different from owning the building.

Leasing: Rather than borrowing to finance additional real estate for new stores, Sheplers prefers to sign operating leases. The company has capital leases for two of its stores and operating leases for all the rest. The two capital leases are included in debt-coverage-ratio calculations, but Mosley comments that in substance, the capital leases are no different from the operating leases. To be conservative, Sheplers limits the term of its operating leases to five years and negotiates early-out clauses. In this way, a store that does not meet performance expectations can be closed quickly and at minimum cost.

Prior to the 1980s, General Electric's management had the view it was more economical to own land and buildings because the corporation's incremental cost of borrowings was lower than the implicit financing cost of a lease. During the 1980s, Chairman and CEO John F. Welch, Jr. and other top management concluded the economic value added for the shareholder arising from the ownership of warehouses and office buildings is simply a money-over-money return that provides adequate equity returns only to highly leveraged balance sheets. Thus, much of GE's real estate is leased because the underlying lessor can operate at much higher leverage than an industrial company can. Moreover, given the constant changes in the environment caused by global competition and technological advances, GE does not want to give up the flexibility of leasing.

Morphy of Paychex is approached often for capital leases on data-processing equipment but finds that owning the equipment is more economical. The company does not usually need leading-edge technology. It does not change software often and can generally use computer equipment for 5 to 10 years.

Phantom Leases: Some real estate is kept off Home Depot's balance sheet with a phantom-lease program. A trust owns the real estate, borrows in the commercial paper market with the benefit of the Home Depot credit rating, and leases the stores to Home Depot.

Real Estate Securitization: Home Depot has considered securitizing its real estate. However, management has found it easier to follow a well-established routine of convertible debenture issues that has been consistently successful and quick to implement.

Accounting Methods

Pooling of Interests: Despite a large cash balance, Paychex has taken advantage of its high price-earnings ratio to acquire other companies for stock. Pooling-of-interest accounting has been helpful to the company because it does not require the amortization of goodwill. The disadvantages of pooling are that the company cannot use any contingency or payout formulas related to the acquisition, it cannot use treasury stock for the acquisition, and it cannot repurchase stock. Morphy believes the pooling-of-interest method was designed primarily for the merger of similar-size companies where neither one is the acquiror. He wonders how long it will be allowed for large companies making relatively small acquisitions. In case the rules change some day, the large amount of cash on Paychex's balance sheet gives it the flexibility to make some acquisitions in the future for cash as well as stock.

One of the reasons SymmetriCom does not currently repurchase stock is that it would restrict the company's ability to use pooling-of-interest accounting for future acquisitions. In contrast, Amgen's management has made a conscious decision to live with the risk of "tainted" stock related to stock repurchases if it ever wanted to do a pooling. An excess of purchased stock over issued stock may be considered tainted unless the stock has been purchased in what accounting rules define as a systematic pattern. If the amount of a company's tainted stock exceeds 10 percent of the value of a merger, pooling-of-interest accounting is not allowed; the merger must be accounted for as a purchase.

Communication with the Markets

Managements of the case-study companies are concerned about maintaining good communication with and responding to the capital markets. Thus, they appear to be interested in minimizing agency costs by identifying their interests with those of the shareholders. Evidence from the case-study companies shows this takes place in two dimensions. First, security analysts communicate with management about the company's operating performance. These analysts are not particularly interested in the company's capital structure. This lack of concern may reflect the strong economy of recent years. However, it reinforces a conclusion of this study that operating results, evidenced by margins and growth, are most important, and financial engineering is secondary.

The second set of communications with the capital markets occurs through credit-rating-agency analysts. Because they are primarily interested in the ability of the company to service its debt, these analysts focus heavily on the company's capital structure. The ratios and other analytic tools they use help them determine how safe that structure is. Naturally, the credit ratings they assign are useful information for the security analysts.

Sell-side analysts communicate their concerns to Monsanto through telephone calls to the investor-relations staff and the treasurer. The analysts focus on strategic business issues and their effects on cash flow and earnings. They are interested in the stock buy-back program but do not pay much attention to capital structure. Treasurer Juanita Hinshaw believes this is largely because the capital structure has stayed so constant.

On any day that Monsanto announces a major event such as a planned acquisition, the investor-relations staff arranges a conference call with analysts early in the morning. Hinshaw invites the rating-agency analysts to participate. She generally explains the financial issues after investor relations has discussed the strategic issues.

Because Paychex's capital-structure and dividend policies have been simple and consistent, Morphy believes the market would react negatively to a change in those policies. Analysts tend not to ask questions about the company's capital structure or its large cash balance. One in ten might bring up dividends. The analysts are mainly interested in performance and earnings.

TELUS' management generally hears investor opinions through securities analysts. Capital structure is not an important issue for them. They are more concerned with how management will address changes in the technological, regulatory, and competitive environment. Occasionally, they ask questions about the dilution created by the company's dividend reinvestment and employee stock-purchase plans. Although the nature of the discussion does not vary to a significant degree between buy-side institutional investors and sell-side securities analysts, Drinkwater finds the institutional investors tend to take a longer term view.

Sheplers holds a shareholders' meeting every year to provide an in-depth review of results for the prior year, the budget for the coming year, and the five-year plan. The company does not share financial information with rating agencies. It provides financial information to outside parties such as vendors, banks, and landlords only when they have a need to know.

Anticipated Market Reactions

GE's dividend and financing decisions have been steady and predictable, in keeping with investor expectations. If earnings increase 15 percent, the company does not want to increase dividends only 10 percent just to save $100 million when it has ample borrowing capacity. Neither does it want to increase the dividend by 20 percent, restricting the stock buy-back program and creating a possibly false expectation that earnings are about to increase by 20 percent.

This outlook, explicitly stated by GE but implicit in the behavior of many other case-study financial officers, lends credence to the use of dividend policy as a signaling mechanism. The signaling content is another reason that repurchase of stock is important in many companies' capital-structure planning. Because it can be done without giving the same signals that a change in dividend policy might give, it is a flexible way to return temporary or volatile cash flows to stockholders without concern about the market's misinterpreting it as a policy change.

Satisfaction with Credit Rating

The seven case-study companies with rated public debt consider their current credit ratings to be appropriate and have policies in place designed to maintain those ratings. Falberg of Amgen and Hinshaw of Monsanto both believe that having double-A credit ratings rather than their companies' current single-A ratings would lower their companies' borrowing rates by only a few basis points at the cost of unacceptably restricting the amount of debt they could assume.

Amgen maintains ratios required for a double-A rating just to protect its single-A rating because it is in an industry considered risky by rating agencies. Falberg believes Amgen's ratios could move considerably without jeopardizing its single-A rating. If the company were to take on more debt, Falberg believes that the rating-agency analysts would look at the use of the proceeds, not just at the balance-sheet and coverage ratios. She believes Amgen has more debt capacity for a strategic or cash-positive acquisition than for buying back stock.

Hinshaw believes that a single-A rating is optimal for Monsanto and that either a higher or lower rating would restrict its flexibility. A double-A rating would require higher coverage ratios but would not substantially reduce the company's cost of borrowing. If the company decided to assume more debt to buy back more stock, thereby letting its rating slip to triple-B, it would lose some of the flexibility it has now to finance acquisitions with debt.

Home Depot is one of two retailers in the United States with a double-A credit rating; the other is Wal-Mart. Brill would not mind allowing Home Depot's rating to slip to a single-A if that was caused by higher leverage, which would make return on equity (ROE), economic value added, and earnings per share (not necessarily total earnings) higher.

Drinkwater considers single-A to be the minimum appropriate credit rating for TELUS Communications. He observes that the Canadian capital markets on the debt side are not as robust as those in the United States. Even at the triple-B level, there is a noticeable drop-off in the reliability of a company's access to the capital markets.

Although Vermeer has no public debt and therefore no agency rating, it is concerned with how banks score its credit internally. At one point, lack of audited financial statements was the only reason it did not have the highest internal bank rating. Since then, its statements have been audited by a Big-Six accounting firm.

How Companies Work with Rating Agencies

The core of Monsanto's discussion with the rating agencies is a confidential, two-year financial projection. Hinshaw explains assumptions for sales growth, profit margins, tax rates, and capital expenditures in the context of the company's business strategy.

During the time Georgia-Pacific increased its debt to acquire Great Northern Nekoosa and reported losses for three years, it was able to maintain its triple-B credit rating. This required good communication with the rating agencies. Management was able to demonstrate that historically the building-products and paper-and-pulp sides of the business do not reach the troughs of their cycles at the same time. In addition, it showed the company would generate sufficient cash for interest payments, taxes, dividends, and necessary capital expenditures under a worst-case scenario for both sides of the business.

Ratios and Analytic Tools

Jim Bunt of General Electric and Juanita Hinshaw of Monsanto comment that rating agencies consider debt coverage ratios at least equal to, if not more important than debt-equity ratios. Bunt notes that data from equally rated companies can be difficult to use for comparison because some of the numbers companies publish are not the same as the ones the rating agencies use for their decisions. In looking at ratios of similarly rated companies, Bunt finds some better and some worse than GE's with a couple of extreme outliers. He assumes that the undisclosed figures account for most of the significant differences and that a detailed knowledge of confidential data in the hands of the rating agencies would reveal a closer convergence.

Among the ratios used by investors, analysts, and rating agencies, Bunt considers free cash flow and operating margin to be most important. With the variance of accounting conventions across financial markets, it is likely more meaningful for analysts and investors to focus on cash flow than reported net income for comparative purposes. Bunt considers operating margin to be a fundamental measure of the value added that a company creates from its business activities. Operating margin also provides a useful measure of a company's ability to survive a downturn in the economy. A retail operation with low fixed costs and high volume has low operating leverage and can afford to operate with thin margins. Capital goods manufacturers such as GE have higher fixed costs and operating leverage and need to have relatively higher margins.

Monsanto's Hinshaw finds that the ratios most important to the rating agencies are the cash-flow ratio, interest coverage, and debt to capital. She notes that the agencies pay a lot of attention to the cash-flow statement but do not share every ratio they calculate with companies they are rating.

As mentioned under "Cash Reserves," treasurer Kathryn Falberg compares Amgen with leading pharmaceutical and biotechnology companies using a ratio of cash-to-market capitalization. She finds market value is more relevant than book value for such a ratio because the value of Amgen is in the intangibles that are not on the balance sheet. She believes most analysts also consider market valuation to be a more meaningful measure for biotechnology companies.

The most important financial measures for Sheplers are pretax profit, operating profit, direct store profit, gross profit, and inventory turnover. The company also calculates gross margin return on investment (GMROI) to measure the return on its inventory investment for merchandise classifications such as jeans, shirts, and boots. Mosley comments that the retail business is measured mostly by P&L because the most important asset is inventory. Sheplers also operates within a number of borrowing covenants, including minimum working capital and minimum debt-to-operating-cash-flow, debt-to-equity, cash-flow-to-fixed-charge, and current ratios.

Drinkwater of TELUS observes that the rating agencies in Canada are starting to look more at cash-flow-based ratios but that the interest-coverage ratio still appears to be most important to them. In comparing future debt maturities with underlying cash flow, the agencies usually look at the company's performance over the past five years and whether there are circumstances that may materially change future performance.

Debt-equity ratios are not relevant to Vermeer because it has virtually no debt. However, the company follows asset guidelines established by the founder. Each business is managed with targets of receivables at 10 percent of sales, inventory at 25 percent of sales, and fixed assets at 10 percent of sales. These three asset categories add up to 45 percent of sales, representing a two and one-half times asset turn. As the company has grown, it has been able to leverage its manufacturing capacity and achieve asset turns considerably above this benchmark. Management tries continually to improve inventory turns to provide cash for the company's growth. It reduces manufacturing cycle time through shop-floor controls and improved software.

Investor Mix

The estimated mix among institutional, retail, employee, and family shareholders for the publicly owned case-study companies is shown in table 2.5.

None of the participants interviewed expressed material dissatisfaction with their companies' current investor mix. There is general agreement that having more retail investors helps stabilize a company's stock price, but CFO Mike Stein of Marriott International notes that smaller investors are more costly for the shareholder relations function to process. Institutional investors can affect stock prices in different ways. Some fund managers are momentum investors who buy shares in anticipation of short-term price movements and sell when their targets are reached. Momentum investors contribute to price volatility. On the

Table 2.5
Ownership Distribution of Public Case-Study Companies (in percentages)

	Institutional	Retail	Employee	Family
Amgen	60	40		
General Electric	50	50		
Georgia-Pacific	80	20		
Home Depot	60	30	10	
Host Marriott	70	10		20
Marriott International	50	30		20
Monsanto	70	30		
Oracle	70	30		
Paychex	55	45		
SymmetriCom	20	80		
TELUS	60	40		

other hand, some portfolio managers have a long-term approach and therefore tend to stabilize stock prices.

Jack McGovern notes that Georgia-Pacific does not have many long-term investors because earnings are cyclical. The company's stock is mostly owned by momentum investors who make their money on volatility.

SymmetriCom's institutional ownership has declined from 40 to 20 percent in recent years because many of its original venture capital investors have sold their shares and its stock is now covered mainly by regional brokerage firms with a retail clientele. Scott Kamsler notes that retail shareholders tend to stay with a stock and ride the ups and downs. He thinks that if too much of the company's stock is held by institutional investors with a long-term perspective, the stock price could be hurt by lack of liquidity.

TELUS' initial public offering in 1990 was structured to give individuals in Alberta, Canada, the ability to buy their telephone company. Since then, the balance of ownership has shifted toward institutional ownership. As TELUS becomes less of a regulated telephone utility and more of a diversified telecommunications company, it becomes riskier and more complicated to follow. Institutional investors tend to be more capable of following such a stock than retail investors.

Related Issues

Investment and Financing Decisions

At the overall company level, asset selection has a strong influence on capital structure. The case-study companies, however, generally do not make a connection between individual asset investment and financing decisions. Typically, the weighted average cost of capital is used as a hurdle rate for investment decisions throughout the company, with some exceptions. Amgen borrows to repurchase its stock when the current combination of stock price and borrowing rates seems opportune. Oracle also plans to borrow to repurchase stock. It would also be conceivable for Oracle to compare the cost of borrowing to buy real estate with the cost of a 10-year lease.

Bunt of GE says, "Either it's a good investment or it isn't and there is a lot more that needs to be factored into that decision than discounting uncertain and unpredictable cash flows." Recently, all GE investments have been financed from free cash flow; however, a significant increase could be accommodated from the company's ample borrowing capacity. Monsanto and TELUS have also borrowed to make acquisitions based on the overall strength of their balance sheets.

Except for tax-exempt municipal plant financing, there is generally no connection between Georgia-Pacific's capital investment projects and the way they are financed. The company has not used project financing in the past because it had no desire to hide any of its debt, and off-balance-sheet financing tends to be more expensive. However, in one case it considered a project financing for a joint venture because it would be based primarily on the creditworthiness of that joint venture and only secondarily on the creditworthiness of the parent companies.

Valuation Methods

Two case-study companies do internal discounted-cash-flow valuations as part of their strategic planning and for comparison of their results with market prices. Although buy-side securities analysts are becoming more cash-flow oriented, sell-side analysts still primarily use price-earnings ratios for valuation. Some sell-side analysts relate price-earnings ratios to growth rates. (Buy-side analysts work with institutional investors. Sell-side analysts work with brokers who are selling stock.)

From time to time, a member of Amgen's treasury staff calculates a discounted-cash-flow valuation of the company using the 15-percent weighted average cost of capital as a discount rate. Falberg believes that many securities analysts take some sort of discounted-cash-flow approach to valuation. Some try to calculate break-up values for Amgen based on products on the market and still in the pipeline. Some try to make comparisons with other biotechnology companies in their effort to value the products in Amgen's pipeline.

Bunt of GE believes the most appropriate way to value GE is by a price-earnings multiple, using companies with comparable track records for comparison. He observes that a company's price-earnings ratio tends to expand as its projected earnings growth rate increases along with the degree of confidence and lower variability of those expectations. Neither Bunt nor Morphy of Paychex has seen many valuations of their companies based on future cash flows discounted at the then assumed weighted average cost of capital.

Hinshaw of Monsanto observes that what sell-side analysts write indicates they are primarily interested in earnings per share even though they profess to have a growing interest in cash flow over the longer term.

When Home Depot's earnings were growing at 25 percent per year, analysts appeared to be concerned primarily with price-earnings ratios. A couple of years ago, when earnings growth began to slow down, buy-side analysts started to focus on economic value added and discounted cash flow valuation.

Lange and his staff have done discounted-cash-flow valuations of Oracle, but the valuations they see in sell-side securities analysts' reports are mainly based on price-earnings ratios. Lange sometimes sees price-earnings ratios based on companies' growth rates and has difficulty seeing how the mathematics of such valuations work. The problem with discounted cash-flow valuations for a company such as Oracle is that the future growth rate is difficult to project. Extrapolating Oracle's recent growth rate 10 or 15 years into the future produces revenues, earnings, and valuations that are too high to believe, but the management of a fast-growing company is sometimes reluctant to forecast a slowing rate of growth.

SymmetriCom does not have a formal internal valuation process but periodically compares its semiconductor and telecommunications businesses with those of its peers, based on price-earnings ratios. When the semiconductor business was organized as a separate subsidiary, an appraiser valued the business using several methods, including discounted cash flow, to set a stock price for the purpose of granting stock options. Kamsler sometimes hears a rule of thumb that equates a company's compounded annual growth rate (CAGR) with the price-earnings ratio.

Most analysts appear to use price-earnings and market-to-book ratios in valuing TELUS, but Drinkwater can see a growing number using cash flow as well as earnings measures. When analysts talk to TELUS' management, one of their principal objectives is to identify anomalies and determine a normalized level of earnings to use as a base year in their projections. Then they use their own methods for valuation. They tend not to discuss assumptions like the weighted average cost of capital or the duration over which cash flows can be projected.

In its efforts to get the best possible return for the shareholder, TELUS' management cannot ignore the valuation methods used by the market. But it is trying to encourage analysts to look through the accounting and focus more on cash flows. Drinkwater points out that TELUS has higher depreciation rates than its Canadian peers, which management considers appropriate because technological change and competition have been reducing the useful life of telecommunications assets. As a result, the "quality" of TELUS' earnings is unusually strong.

On the two occasions when investment banking firms were hired to value Sheplers, their primary method was to use comparable companies' multiples of price compared with earnings, as well as price compared with earnings before interest, income taxes, depreciation, and amortization (EBITDA). Mosley is not aware of any valuations using projected free cash flow discounted at the weighted average cost of capital.

Vermeer's shareholders need to have their stock valued periodically for purposes such as estate planning and donations. A consulting firm helps management do both a discounted-cash-flow and price-earnings-multiple valuation. Vermeer is compared with competitors using ratios like book value to operating income and book value to earnings before interest and taxes (EBIT). A capital-asset-pricing model (CAPM) calculation is used, taking into account the risk-free rate, a market-risk premium, an assumed beta, a small-stock premium, and a specific-company-risk premium. Because Vermeer has no debt, its weighted average cost of capital is the cost of equity capital, which is estimated to be 17 percent. The resulting valuation is usually above book before subtracting 35 percent to account for the stock's limited marketability.

Steve Van Dusseldorp, Vice President-Finance, does not see very much connection between Vermeer's capital-structure and dividend policy and its valuation. Dividends are based strictly on book profits and could conceivably rise at the same time the company value falls.

Sources of Information

Peers in other companies, investment bankers, and commercial bankers are the sources of information finance professionals in the case-study companies considered most useful. Keeping up with the financial press is considered a necessity, but the technical accuracy and depth of the material varies. The periodicals considered most useful on capital-structure and dividend policy are the *Harvard Business Review* and the *Journal of Applied Corporate Finance.*

For one treasurer, the kind of judgment that comes from experience is more important than external sources of information such as studies or conferences. Another treasurer is particularly receptive to commercial and investment banks that can discuss transactions in countries throughout the world.

Findings and Theory

This section describes how the research findings, summarized earlier in the chapter, corroborate the finance theories explained in chapter 1.

Asset Selection and Capital Structure

In practice, the asset decision, decision 1, is considered the most important of the four principal financial decisions. Managements approve projects based first on their overall business strategies and second on whether the projects meet required hurdle rates. Success in asset selection and use generates the strong cash flow that creates value and opportunities. How those projects are financed and the corporate capital structure that results are secondary considerations but are not overlooked once the asset decisions are in place. Thus, the asset decision is independent of the capital-structure decision, but not the other way around.

Dividends

Dividend policies today vary among companies more than they did in the past. It is common practice for a growth company to pay no dividends at all. Stock repurchase programs have become widespread, because they provide a tax-advantaged way to return cash to investors and because they offer more flexibility than established dividend payout ratios. This trend runs counter to the importance of tax-free investors such as pension funds. However, it is consistent with individual investors using mutual funds as a preferred investment medium. Individual investors do not have to sell round lots of an underlying stock to realize their returns, but can obtain them in cash by drawing out the capital gains realized by their mutual funds.

Capital Markets and Corporate Life Cycle

Managements are very much aware of capital-market discipline and concerned with agency costs as they determine their capital-structure and dividend policies. A policy of low debt and substantial cash balances makes life secure for management, but when carried too far, it may produce suboptimal returns for investors. In companies with public debt, managements are concerned about maintaining credit ratings. The managements of several case-study companies believe their current, investment-grade credit ratings optimize the cost of debt, risk related to leverage, and access to capital. In companies with ample free cash flow, managements are concerned about overinvesting. Georgia-Pacific's management states explicitly that growth opportunities for a cyclical-revenue forest-products company do not exceed the growth of the economy as a whole, and that its policy is to return excess free cash flow to investors. In companies throughout the four quadrants of the model, there is concern about motivating value-creating behavior, as evidenced by the increasing use of value-based performance measures.

Company actions are consistent with corporate life-cycle concepts. Some companies finance their start-ups or management buyouts with debt because that is the only available source of funds. They then pay down their debt at the earliest opportunity. High-growth companies tend to use equity because they do not want to compound their inherent business risk with financial risk, and because they do not want pressure from lenders to interfere with investment decisions to grow their businesses. Firms with physical assets tend to use more debt because physical assets serve as a secondary source of collateral, although still less important than projected cash flow, and because many asset-intensive companies are in industries capable of servicing debt with well-established cash flows.

Pecking-Order Behavior
There is mixed evidence on pecking-order behavior. The case-study companies have a strong preference for financing their capital expenditures with internally generated funds before turning to outside sources. Some high-growth case-study companies with major cash-generation ability have developed large cash war chests. There is little consistent evidence that these companies used debt because it was easy to obtain.

Information Content
Evidence from the case study companies was contrary to the information-content hypothesis, which is that management favors debt when the outlook is favorable, and equity when the outlook is risky. In the case-study companies, debt was used not just to lower the cost of capital and signal management's confidence in the future. It was used more as a necessary tool for acquisitions, start-ups, and management buy-outs, even though managements recognized they would have to bear higher risk. Managements issued equity in good times even when they expected better times because they believed they could build shareholder value more effectively through continued growth supported by a strong balance sheet than through increased debt to lower the cost of capital.

Troubled Situations
The researchers did not consider companies that were currently in distress or that had recently recovered from troubled financial conditions as case-study companies. Therefore, they did not gain any direct insights regarding the behavior of managements in troubled situations.

Chapter 15, The Role of High Debt, provides some examples of highly leveraged companies that ran into financial difficulty.

Endnotes

1. Donaldson, Gordon. *Corporate Debt Capacity.* Boston: Harvard Business School, 1961, pp. 93–120.

2. Two thorough descriptions of the credit-rating analytical process are *Global Credit Analysis*, by Moody's Investor Service (London: IFR Publishing Ltd., 1991), and Standard & Poor's *Corporate Ratings Criteria* (New York: The McGraw-Hill Companies, 1996). See "credit rating" in the glossary.

3. Shortly before the interviews for this case study were conducted, Monsanto announced plans to spin off its specialty-chemicals business. The spin-off was completed September 1, 1997. The new chemical company is called Solutia, Inc. Since the spin-off, Monsanto has adopted a policy of lower dividends consistent with those of other growth companies.

4. Conroy, Robert M., and Robert S. Harris. "Stock Splits and Stock Prices in the U.S.: Why Do Share Prices Remain Constant?" Darden School Working Paper, Graduate School of Business Administration, University of Virginia, 1996.

5. Lintner, John. "Distribution of Income of Corporations among Dividends, Retained Earnings, and Taxes." *American Economic Review* 46 (1956): 97–113.

6. Barclay, Michael J., Clifford W. Smith, Jr., and Ross L. Watts. "The Determinants of Corporate Leverage and Dividend Policies." *Journal of Applied Corporate Finance* (Winter 1995): 18.

7. McGee, Suzanne, and Greg Ip. "Stock Buybacks Aren't Always Good Sign for Investors." *Wall Street Journal*, July 7, 1997, C1–2.

8. *Ibid.*

9. Wruck, Eric G., and Karen H. Wruck. "Codependent No More? How Spinoffs Affect Parent and Spinoff Firms' Performance." Draft position paper.

10. Rosenberg, Hilary. "Marriott Corporation's Splitting Headache." *Institutional Investor*, May 1993, p. 42.

3

Amgen Inc.

Amgen Inc. is a leading biotechnology company that develops, manufactures, and markets products based on research in cellular and molecular biology. The company's two current products are Epogen™ and Neupogen™, the genetically engineered versions of natural hormones that stimulate production of blood components. Epogen is a genetically engineered version of human erythropoietin (EPO), a natural hormone that stimulates the production of red blood cells in bone marrow. The drug's primary market is dialysis patients suffering from severe chronic anemia as a result of their failure to produce adequate amounts of EPO. Neupogen is a recombinant version of human granulocyte colony stimulating factor, a protein that stimulates the production of neutrophils, a type of white blood cell that defends the body against bacterial infection. Its principal use is to build neutrophil levels in cancer patients whose natural neutrophils have been destroyed by chemotherapy.

A summary of Amgen's recent financials is contained in table 3.1. The financial summary for each publicly traded case-study in this book includes a calculation of the company's **sustainable growth rate**. That rate is a function of the company's return on sales (net profit/sales), its asset turnover ratio (sales/assets), and the amount of earnings it retains after payment of dividends (1-[dividends/net income]). It is a measure of the company's ability to grow without raising external capital.

Amgen was founded in 1980 by George Rathmann of Abbott Diagnostics with $19 million in seed capital from the parent company, Abbott Laboratories. Recognizing the industry's risks and long product development times, Abbott's management encouraged Amgen to undertake revenue-generating projects with large corporate partners while it was developing its own products for the longer term. This strategy allowed Amgen to show modest profits while other start-up biotechnology companies were concentrating all their efforts on research and development (R&D) and reporting losses. Amgen brought

Table 3.1
Financial Summary: Amgen Inc.

(Dollar Figures in Millions)	1996	1995	1990	1985
Operating Summary				
Sales (Net)	$2,240	$1,940	$381	$7
Operating Profit Margin	42.8%	41.1%	27.7%	−144.0%
Net Profit Margin	30.4%	27.7%	8.9%	−108.5%
Dividend Payout Ratio	0	0	0	0
Sustainable Growth Rate*	24.6%	22.1%	6.6%	−16.0%
Capitalization Summary				
Total Assets	$2,765	$2,432	$514	$48
LT Debt/LT Debt + Equity	2.8%	9.6%	3.2%	17.7%
Total Debt/Total Debt + Equity	7.9%	12.9%	3.4%	17.9%
Market to Book	7.6	9.4	13.9	1.6

*[Net Income/Sales][Sales/Assets][1-(Dividend Payout Rate/Net Income)]

Epogen, its first product, to the market in 1989 and Neupogen, its second product, to the market in 1991. Epogen's first-year sales of $190 million set an industry record. During the period before its first product was launched, one of the company's objectives was to develop a culture of tight cost control and continuous improvement in efficiency.

Capital-Structure Policy

From the beginning, Amgen has been a low-debt company. Long-term debt briefly rose to 25 percent of capitalization just before Epogen was introduced in 1989. At that time, the company issued $50 million in euroconvertible debt that was converted almost immediately because the common stock rose sharply when Epogen was launched. In recent years, long-term debt has risen in dollar terms but has remained between 12 and 14 percent of capitalization.

Amgen manages its balance sheet very conservatively. Cash flow generated from the business is more than enough to cover the company's reinvestment needs, and excess cash is used to buy back stock.

There have been only two questions related to external financing: (1) whether to issue more debt to buy back more stock, a capital-structure question, and (2) whether to pursue possible future acquisitions. Management has an open mind in considering how much debt capacity the company has. An important consideration is maintaining the company's single-A credit rating.

Possible Acquisitions

To keep growing, Amgen considers acquisitions and licenses while continuing its internal new-product research. If the company were to encounter a large acquisition opportunity, management might consider raising new debt or equity. Management could conceivably be willing to let the rating drop for a large, strategic acquisition if it could clearly see that the ratios would improve and the single-A rating would be restored within several years. It would not want the rating to drop to a triple-B for an indefinite period.

Research and Development Spending

Amgen undertakes research and development independently and through both licensing and research agreements and equity investments in partners. In 1996, Amgen spent $528 million on R&D, representing 26 percent of revenues—one of the highest ratios in the industry. The level of the company's R&D expenses is constrained by earnings growth targets and the amount that can be spent efficiently in a given period of time. Management tries to maintain a balance between current returns and long-term investment. So far, management has been able to project sales growth with reasonable accuracy and derive the research and development budget from the sales forecast. Management's preference is to devote what is necessary to R&D and to carefully control the growth of selling, general, and administrative expenses.

Level of Cash

The financial-structure question that management wrestles with the most is how much cash to keep on hand. The company needs a cash reserve for both risks and opportunities. Amgen is subject to business risks common to the industry. The company wants to have enough combined cash and borrowing capacity for a strategic acquisition opportunity if one materializes. On the other hand, it does not want to hold too much cash because investors do not buy Amgen stock to participate in a bond portfolio.

To help determine the appropriate level of cash, Kathryn Falberg, Treasurer, compares it with leading pharmaceutical and biotechnology companies using a ratio of cash-to-market capitalization. She believes that Amgen's risk-and-opportunity profile is in between the smaller biotechnology companies and the larger pharmaceutical companies. Therefore, Amgen's current cash-to-market-capitalization ratio of 1 to 15 is between the 50th and 75th percentile in this combined peer group. Commenting on whether ratios should be based on book value or market value, Falberg says, "We don't think book value is relevant because the value of Amgen is in the intangibles that aren't on the books. We think that the analysts are comfortable looking at market valuations and that they also understand that book values are not the most meaningful measure in our industry."

Asset-Liability Matching

Because of Amgen's low level of debt, Falberg does not spend very much time thinking about the level of fixed- and floating-rate debt. She is more concerned with asset-liability matching. At the end of 1995, the company's $177 million in long-term debt and $70 million in commercial paper borrowings were offset by marketable securities of $984 million. Debt issued for the purpose of buying back stock is under a medium-term note facility at fixed rates. When management has a view about interest rates, it may shorten or lengthen the duration of the bond portfolio or swap some fixed-rate debt into floating rates for a relatively short period. The bond portfolio is conservatively managed with regard to both credit risk and interest-rate risk. Falberg comments, "The fixed income investments are here for risks and opportunities, so we need to keep them liquid. We're not going to put principal at risk."

Timing of Borrowing and Stock Repurchases

Amgen bases stock repurchases and related borrowing partly on its view of market conditions. Recently, management has issued very long-dated debt to buy back more stock because of its combined views that long-term rates are relatively low in their cycle and that Amgen's stock valuation is attractive.

Flexibility

Falberg believes that Amgen has some flexibility to alter its capital structure if it wants to. Management has chosen to be conservative to maintain financial flexibility. Someday, when the company is more mature and has more products, it may want more leverage in its capital structure. But today, management would not want the business to be constrained for lack of liquidity because the company issued too much debt to buy back stock.

Consideration of Targeted Stock

Some investment bankers have suggested that Amgen consider targeted stock similar to what General Motors created when acquiring Electronic Data Systems. Targeted stock is a class of parent company stock that tracks the performance of a specific business group within the company. (See Glossary for more detail.) If such a scheme were implemented, a group of investors that wanted a steady stream of profits could buy stock related to Epogen and Neupogen. Other investors could take the risk of other classes of stock related to product candidates that are still being developed. In theory, the combined market values of the different classes of targeted stock could add up to more than Amgen's current market capitalization.

Falberg has not seen evidence to show that targeted stock would achieve that objective. More important, she believes that targeted stock could create an incentive structure that is alien to the company's culture. Amgen employees would have an incentive to focus on their own pieces of the business rather than working together as part of a company team. In addition, targeted stock would create the administrative burden of separate sets of accounting records and a transfer pricing structure.

Dividends and Stock Repurchases

Amgen has never paid a dividend. Therefore, unlike some of its pharmaceutical peers, it has never set a precedent that would require dividends to be paid in the future. For tax reasons, management believes that stock buy-backs are the most effective way to return excess cash to the shareholders. Another reason the company buys back stock is to off-set the dilution from its stock option plans.

The only reasons Amgen might consider paying dividends in the future would be to broaden its investor base by attracting more yield-oriented investors or to facilitate the use of pooling-of-interest accounting. Having more yield-oriented investors could help stabilize the stock price if Amgen were out of favor with growth-stock investors and unlikely to be back in favor in the near future. The pooling-of-interests issue is more complex. An excess of purchased over issued stock in a rolling 24-month period may be considered "tainted" unless the stock has been purchased in what accounting rules define as a "systematic pattern." If the amount of a company's tainted stock exceeds 10 percent of the value of a merger, pooling-of-interest accounting is not allowed; the merger must be accounted for as a purchase. Some high-technology companies have stopped buying back stock to ensure that they will not have future problems using pooling-of-interest accounting for acquisitions. Amgen's management, however, has made a conscious decision to live with the risk that it would have to "cure" any tainted stock if it ever wanted to do a pooling.

Amgen's stock repurchases have either remained constant or increased over the past few years. Investors tend to think the pattern will continue. This precedent is similar to one established by continuing dividend increases. If management decided to buy back less stock in a given year than it had the year before, it would want to make a particular effort to explain to investors how the company planned to use the extra cash.

Development and Approval of Policies

Every year, Falberg works with the chief financial officer (CFO) to develop a cash-flow budget, discuss it with the chief executive officer (CEO), and present it to the board. The budgeting process triggers all the questions management needs to consider relevant to capital structure: How much cash should be kept? How much stock should be repurchased? Is the number of shares outstanding increasing or decreasing? What would be the impact of issuing debt and buying back more stock?

The effectiveness test of Amgen's capital-structure policies is how well the company can carry out its strategy, how well those policies are received by investors, and how well the stock price performs. Low debt and a substantial cash reserve give management risk-protection and flexibility that it values more than the reduced cost of capital that could come with higher leverage.

Falberg observes, "Investors and analysts tend not to be shy if they think we are doing something wrong. They generally accept our logic and our rationale. They understand the amount of stock we buy back, the amount of cash we have, and our low amount of debt. It all makes sense. It's a matter of appropriate balance."

Instruments and Tactics

Aside from a convertible issue, occasional interest-rate swaps, and stock buy-backs, Amgen has not used many derivatives or other special financial instruments. However, Falberg says, "We always look at things and we don't rule them out for the future." Amgen has used private placements of puts and calls on its own stock, forming costless collars.

Credit Rating

Amgen's management believes the company's current single-A credit rating is appropriate and would like the rating to stay where it is or improve. Falberg explains that the company's balance sheet and ratios are really closer to the requirements for a double-A or even a triple-A, but the agencies are not comfortable raising the rating because the company has only two products. She believes, therefore, that Amgen's ratios could move substantially without jeopardizing its single-A rating. If Amgen were to take on more debt, the analysts would look at the use of the proceeds, not just the balance-sheet and coverage ratios. Falberg believes that Amgen has more debt capacity for a strategic or a cash-positive acquisition than for buying back stock. She also notes that moving up to a double-A rating would reduce the company's borrowing cost by only a few basis points.

Investment and Financing Decisions

Aside from borrowing in order to repurchase stock, there is no connection between Amgen's investment and financing decisions. Management evaluates investment decisions using the weighted average cost of capital as a hurdle rate. When an approved project is implemented, treasury figures out the most cost-effective way to finance it.

For simplicity, treasury uses 15 percent as the standard internal hurdle rate. Its calculations of the weighted average cost of capital range from 12 to 16 percent, depending on assumptions used for the *beta* and the premium of the stock market return over the risk-free rate. Falberg has seen estimates of Amgen's *beta* ranging from 1 to 1.4. The common-stock risk premium varies depending on which period is used for the average. Amgen has used averages from Ibbotson's *Stocks, Bonds, Bills, and Inflation* based on premiums since the 1920s, since World War II, since the 1950s, and in the past 20 years.

Valuation Methods and Performance Measures

Management believes that Amgen's stock price is based primarily on the value of current products and secondarily on the perceived value of future products in the pipeline. The stock price may be influenced by any news that has implications for current or future products. Scientists from Amgen, competitors, universities, and public laboratories are constantly publishing articles and speaking at conferences. There is competition for Amgen's pipeline products. As a result, the market continually picks up bits of information and adjusts its view of Amgen. Falberg believes the market has become more discerning in the past three or four years. A news item such as the success or failure of a critical trial in one company is now less likely to affect stock prices for the whole biotechnology sector.

From time to time, a member of Amgen's treasury staff calculates a discounted-cash-flow valuation of the company using the 15 percent weighted average cost of capital as a discount rate. Falberg believes many securities analysts take some sort of discounted-cash-flow approach to valuation, but that most of them would not forecast as far out as Amgen's internal forecasts. Some analysts try to calculate break-up values, valuing Epogen, Neupogen, and products in the pipeline separately. Some try to make comparisons with other biotechnology companies in order to value the products in Amgen's pipeline. Falberg talks more to sell-side than buy-side analysts. However, she notes that sell-side analysts from major investment banking firms write for institutional as well as retail clients and therefore must keep in mind the interests of long-term as well as short-term investors.

One buy-side analyst values the company using the proprietary **cash-flow-return-on-investment** model (see Glossary), and one firm compares companies using economic value added and market value added as performance measures. The analyst using cash-flow return on investment did internal-rate-of-return and total-shareholder-return calculations with the help of the consulting firm that developed the model.

The corporate performance goals that Amgen communicates internally are sales growth and return on capital employed. The bonus plan is primarily structured around targets for these ratios, and virtually every employee is expected to be familiar with them. Management has considered using economic value added as a performance measure. However, it finds that return on capital employed is simpler to explain, requires fewer accounting adjustments, and does about as good a job in explaining stock-price returns. Falberg emphasizes the importance of sales growth measures as well as return measures. "Without incentives to grow," she notes, "we could have a very efficient, small company."

People Interviewed

Kathryn E. Falberg, Vice President and Treasurer *(Since this case study was written, Ms. Falberg's title has changed to Vice President and Chief Financial Officer.)*

General Electric Company

General Electric Company is the world's largest multibusiness company and has the world's highest market capitalization. In 1996, the company earned $7.3 billion on revenues of $79 billion. General Electric Company can be viewed as two companies in one: General Electric (GE), the industrial company, and GE Capital Services (GE Capital). In 1996, GE Capital contributed $33 billion of the company's $79 billion in revenues. The General Electric 1996 annual report shows both an unconsolidated balance sheet with $60 billion in footings, with GE Capital carried as a $14.3 billion investment, and a consolidated balance sheet with $272 billion in footings. Because this research project is primarily concerned with nonfinancial companies, this case study focuses primarily on GE. A brief section at the end discusses financial structure at GE Capital.

Table 4.1 contains a summary of GE's recent unconsolidated financials, in which GE Capital is carried as an investment on GE's balance sheet.

Although conglomerates have largely fallen from favor, GE, with 12 component businesses, proves the concept can work. In its 1995 annual report, management states it will not follow the current trend of spinning off businesses. Chairman and Chief Executive Officer John F. Welch, Jr., has made management history with programs such as delayering the corporate bureaucracy, encouraging "boundary-less" behavior, and holding workout sessions and driving for six sigma quality levels to bring people at all levels together to solve problems. Between 1992 and 1996, the company's operating margin has increased from 11.5 to 14.8 percent, and working capital turnover has increased from 4.4 times to 6.3 times.

Table 4.1
Financial Summary: General Electric Company (Unconsolidated)

(Dollar Figures in Millions)	1996	1995	1990	1985
Operating Summary				
Sales (Net)	$49,565	$46,181	$44,879	$28,285
Gross Profit Margin	33.4%	32.7%	29.9%	30.1%
Operating Profit Margin	20.5%	20.1%	15.2%	13.9%
Net Profit Margin	14.7%	14.2%	9.6%	8.3%
Dividend Payout Ratio	43.2%	43.3%	39.6%	43.5%
Sustainable Growth Rate*	12.1%	11.8%	9.3%	8.8%
Capitalization Summary				
Total Assets	$59,925	$55,716	$46,364	$26,432
LT Debt/LT Debt + Equity	5.2%	7.1%	15.7%	5.1%
Total Debt/Total Debt + Equity	11.5%	11.8%	23.8%	12.8%
Market to Book	5.2	4.1	2.3	2.4

*[Net Income/Sales][Sales/Assets][1-(Dividend Payout Rate/Net Income)]

Capital-Structure Policy

With consistent growth and strong operating margins, GE recently has been able to generate sufficient cash to make necessary capital expenditures for existing businesses, to maintain a dividend payout above 40 percent of earnings, and to implement a $3 billion-per-year stock buyback program. GE maintains a conservative capital structure with 1996 year-end borrowings under 12 percent of book capital and has no use for option-based instruments such as convertibles and warrants. James R. Bunt, Vice President and Treasurer, has a financial strategy that fits the corporate culture of self-confidence, simplicity, and speed.

Flexibility

Maintaining flexibility is important for GE, and it can do so because of a strong balance sheet, strong operating performance, and strong cash flow. Management tries to keep the balance sheet under control as much as possible throughout the year, although debt-to-capital generally increases several percent above the 12-percent norm because of the natural cyclicality of cash flow during the year. Bunt considers GE's capital structure very much under management's control, with strong consideration given to rating agency ratios. He believes that evidence of the company's control of its capital structure is 60 consecutive quarters of earnings increases and 21 consecutive years of dividend increases.

GE does not pretend to have a formula-driven risk-adjusted capital structure based on some "guesstimate" regarding the market basket of its business risk. The company is about as diversified as it can be, both geographically and in its lines of business. It is impossible to calculate the optimal capital structure for a company like GE because there are so many variables and uncertainties in the calculations. Instead, management has to have a gut feel for how much risk is embedded in its overall activities. Risk involves exposure to geographic groupings as well as products and programs. Management has to have a sense of the possible effect of adverse outcomes on its ability to maintain its desired capital structure. It has to know the company's capability to generate cash flow both now and over the next five years. Then it can base capital-structure decisions on those estimates and the amount of risk the company is willing to tolerate. A company in a low-margin, cyclical business with a 50-percent debt-to-capital ratio would not be rated triple-A even though its earnings growth and stock performance might beat GE's under favorable circumstances. Each company has to decide how much cyclical risk it wants to take, given its investor profile.

During the 1974 recession, GE's ratio of debt to capital reached a high of 39 percent. The company was able to maintain its triple-A credit rating throughout that period, but it embarked on a six-month cash conservation program to reduce the ratio to less than 30 percent. Property, plant, and equipment expenditures were reduced, and collections were accelerated. Bunt observes that GE's corporate management has sufficient control to get everyone in the company focused on such a program and to make dramatic changes quickly. Since the mid-1970s, the most important variance in GE's capital structure has been the increase in debt related to its acquisition of RCA for $6.6 billion in 1986. The company's debt was increased substantially at that time, and since then it has been steadily reduced.

Bunt notes that as debt becomes a smaller component and equity becomes a larger component of the company's capital structure, the weighted average cost of capital increases (with apologies to Miller-Modigliani's seminal work, which assumes away many real-world frictions). On the other hand, he believes the company's record of above-average earnings growth has reduced its cost of capital. He thinks a company such as GE, whose earnings grow at 13 to 15 percent per year, tends to have a lower cost of capital than a company whose earnings grow at only 8 percent per year because a higher earnings-to-growth rate boosts the relative price/earnings (P/E) ratio of its stock.

Internally Generated Capital

For the past five years, all of GE's capital requirements have been generated internally. The only time in recent history that the company raised long-term funds externally was in 1986, when it purchased RCA and financed the acquisition with debt. GE sold off many of the acquired RCA business components and paid down the debt over several years.

Credit Rating

The most important considerations for GE in managing its capital structure are the criteria for a triple-A credit rating. The company would like to maintain that rating unless it decides on its own to give it up. For example, GE could decide to finance a huge acquisition solely with debt. Barring such an event, GE does not intend to lose its triple-A credit rating accidentally or unexpectedly.

Fixed- and Floating-Rate Debt

GE's management does not have a formal policy for fixed- and floating-rate debt. The last time the company raised fixed-rate debt was in 1986 for the RCA acquisition. As that long-term debt has continued to roll off, the company has preferred to use shorter term floating-rate debt and pay it down as much as possible when there is excess cash. Bunt sees no point in keeping any unnecessary debt on the balance sheet, and he notes that with over $30 billion in equity, GE is largely financed with long-term capital.

Tax Considerations

GE's corporate tax position has virtually no effect on its capital-structure policy except for one obvious consideration: It would be hard for GE Capital to be successful without substantial tax-deductible debt.

Capital Structure and Business Segments

GE considers each of its 12 component industrial businesses to have the same capital structure and the same cost of capital for the purposes of hurdle rates and capital budgeting analysis. Bunt believes that trying to figure out the appropriate capital structure and cost of capital for each component business would be excessively complicated. Plant and equipment may be new at one business and fully depreciated at another. One business may be a consistent cash generator showing a relatively small net investment on the books. Another business may have made a recent acquisition or have required more recent capital investment. All these variations have tended to average out in the company's 100-year history.

The capital structures of joint ventures and other affiliates vary considerably, driven by factors such as taxes and partners' objectives. If an affiliate has net operating loss carry-forwards, the parent would want to put in equity. In high-tax countries, affiliates tend to have more debt.

Capital Budgeting Analysis

Hurdle rates and capital budgeting analysis are used mainly for huge investments, such as construction of a billion-dollar plastics plant or development of a new GE aircraft engine. About half of the company's investments are necessary projects such as repairs, replacements, and upgrades of equipment or compliance with environmental and Occupational Safety and Health Administration regulations. Investments in plant and equipment have been relatively flat in recent years because the company is freeing a lot of capacity by improving inventory turns, improving quality, reducing rework, and increasing yields. Bunt says, "We find that we're freeing up all sorts of factory capacity by implementing simple quality process disciplines that we might have been doing all along. Like most American companies, we lagged the Japanese in recognizing the many benefits of such disciplines. But we're now doing a good job at it. Luckily, we and our competitors did not have to

4

go head-to-head against the Japanese, so on a relative basis we're ahead of the people we compete against."

Bunt observes that Monte Carlo simulations, risk adjustment, and present-value analysis look impressive when someone writes an article and compares just five investment alternatives to allocate capital. But he points out that these types of analyses are difficult to do when in one division, such as appliances, there may be as many as 3,000 investment projects annually—rebuilding a machine tool, repaving a driveway, putting a new roof on a plant, building a new plant. What appears to be nice academically is not always practical. Nobody has enough brains or a big enough computer to put parameters around all these projects and rank them. Welch does not rank projects based solely on someone's projection of their internal rates of return; he allocates discretionary resources to those business opportunities that appear, judgmentally, to have the greatest growth and profit potential or are strategically necessary.

Imputed Interest System

Until recently, GE had an imputed interest system to help focus managers on generating cash. An imputed interest charge was based on GE's investment in each business. Some businesses generated more cash over time than the amounts originally invested in them, and as a result they received imputed interest income based on negative amounts invested. To adjust income imbalances, the businesses were recapitalized every three to five years. Bunt believes that the system could have been more realistic if businesses were recapitalized much more frequently, but doing so would have created an administrative and communication nightmare. The imputed interest system is no longer used because new measurements and the emphasis on tying those measurements to the incentive bonus plan better encourage managers to think about working capital turnover and cash generation.

Dividends and Stock Repurchases

GE's dividend payout in 1995 was 43 percent of earnings. The payout has been relatively constant in recent years, increasing along with earnings per share. It was as high as 80 percent in the 1930s, but later it was reduced because of heavy capital requirements in businesses such as aircraft engines and nuclear power. The company decided on a special increase on its dividend in 1992, increasing the payout to 46 percent of earnings, when the share buyback program was temporarily suspended. The dividend increase and the suspension canceled each other out in terms of overall investor expectations and the stock price was essentially unaffected.

GE's dividend policy is determined largely by historical precedent but also by what management perceives to be the interests of its investors. This is not always easy to determine, because different investors have different expectations. Some institutional investors have strict dividend-payout-percentage models. For example, in the third quarter of 1995, GE's stock price had increased nicely since the beginning of the year, but a dividend increase was not planned until the fourth quarter. The dividend-payout ratio therefore fell below one institutional investor's payout requirement at the end of the third quarter, so that investor sold more than a million shares. Although the company explained that the dividend would be raised in the fourth quarter, the institution replied that it would just buy the stock back when the dividend-payout ratio fit its model.

If GE had different capital requirements, its dividend policy might be different. Recently, its cash flow has been strong enough to maintain a steady dividend-payout ratio, to make sufficient capital expenditures to continue growing existing businesses, and to buy back stock. Bunt notes that one large company cut its dividends too late when it ran into trouble and needed the cash. In effect, it had borrowed money to pay the dividend. The stock price of another company rose significantly when a new CEO announced his objective of generating cash and paying down debt, but in the interim he also cut the dividend to shore up the balance sheet and provide resources for growth. Bunt observes that the message a company conveys is just as important as the dividend policy itself. Investors want to know what the company's objectives are and what it plans to do with its cash.

Bunt is also aware that some companies consider no dividends at all to be the most tax-efficient way to reward the investor. It is partly with investor tax considerations in mind that GE has pursued a substantial stock buy-back program. In the first half of the 1980s, while the company was divesting, reinvesting, and restructuring many of its businesses, it returned $850 million in dividends. In the second half of the decade, it paid $1.4 billion in dividends and repurchased $2.6 billion in stock. Between 1990 and 1995, it paid $2.3 billion in dividends and repurchased $5.5 billion in stock. In 1995, the GE Board of Directors approved an additional repurchase of $6 billion in stock through 1997, and in 1996 the program was extended to $13 billion through 1998.

In Bunt's opinion, the company has enhanced its share price by buying back stock rather than leaving cash on the balance sheet in case an acquisition opportunity arises. As a result of the stock repurchased, earnings per share have grown about 2 percent faster than total earnings. GE is currently selling at a multiple above 25, which Bunt notes is about 1.6 to 1.8 times the expected earnings-per-share growth rate. Bunt observes that a company's P/E multiple tends to expand as the market perceives a higher sustainable earnings growth rate. Five years ago, GE's growth rate was above the average for the Standard and Poor's S&P 500. At that time the company's stock sold at a discount to the S&P 500, but now it sells at a premium. GE's performance over the past 10 years has made investors increasingly confident that the company can sustain its above-average growth rate over prolonged periods.

Bunt believes that the company could have made a case to the rating agencies that buying back $6 billion in stock all at once, improving the earnings per share kick, would not be materially different than buying back the same amount over a two-year period. But even he would not want to consider doing this, because it would reduce the company's flexibility should an acquisition opportunity arise or the economy sink significantly.

Development and Approval of Policies

General Electric Company's capital-structure and dividend policies are developed by informal consensus among top management and approved by the Board of Directors. Bunt observes that the company's performance seems to justify its practices. Recently, GE's stock has outperformed the S&P 500 and the Dow-Jones Industrial Average, and the company has been able to maintain its triple-A credit rating. Bunt says, "The proof is in the results." However, asking whether or not GE's capital-structure and dividend policy is absolutely optimal seems to him like asking how many angels can dance on the head of a pin.

Instruments and Tactics

Short-term debt has been useful to GE in recent years because of its flexibility; it can be raised or lowered depending on cash needs. The company has been able to let long-term debt roll off and not replace it.

Leases

GE considers leases to be part of debt for the purpose of capital-structure policy. The use of economic value added as a performance evaluation tool is reflected in the company's practices with respect to leasing real estate. In the 1960s, management thought it was more economical to own land and buildings because the corporation's incremental cost of debt capital was lower than the implicit financing cost of a lease. During the 1980s, Welch and other top management realized that the economic value added to the shareholder arising from owning warehouses and office buildings is simply a money-over-money return that provides adequate returns only to highly leveraged balance sheets. Thus GE now leases much of its real estate because the underlying lessor can operate at much higher leverage than an industrial company. Moreover, given the constant changes in its business environment caused by global competition and technological advances, GE does not want to give up the flexibility of leasing. In a similar vein, Bunt notes shareholders do not obtain a direct return from investments in receivables and inventories. Thus there is a powerful incentive to be as efficient as possible in managing these assets.

Derivatives and Securitization

GE's use of derivatives and other tactics like asset securitization has been relatively minor and for specific risk-management purposes. A couple of long-term debt issues had swaps associated with them. The company has securitized a few leases and uses non-recourse bank financing for certain receivables, particularly those involving long terms in foreign countries. Bunt sees no useful purpose in trying to incorporate optionality into GE's capital structure through instruments such as convertibles, hybrids, warrants, puts, and calls. He says, "You basically have to take a position that you can predict you're going to come out ahead or not come out ahead, but who knows? The one thing for certain is that the banker is in there taking a fee."

Communication with the Markets

GE's dividend and financing decisions have been steady and predictable, in keeping with investor expectations. If earnings increase 15 percent, the company does not want to raise dividends only 10 percent just to save $100 million when it has ample borrowing capacity. Neither does it want to raise the dividend by 20 percent, restricting the stock buy-back program and creating a possibly false expectation that earnings are about to increase by 20 percent. As discussed earlier, Bunt considers the company's credit rating to be where it should be and would not like to see it change unless management consciously decides to change its strategy.

Stock Splits

General Electric announced a 2-for-1 stock split in April 1996. The last four of the company's 2-for-1 stock splits had occurred when its stock price had risen above $100. Bringing the price back to the $50 range makes the stock affordable for smaller retail investors and therefore helps the company continually expand the market for its shares. Also, because GE's stock has risen back to $100 after each split, the split delivers a positive signal to the market.

Most Important Ratios

Among the ratios used by investors, analysts, and rating agencies, Bunt considers free cash flow and the operating margin to be most important. With the increasing globalization of companies such as GE and the variations of accounting conventions across financial markets, it is sometimes easier for analysts and investors to focus on cash than reported net income. Although net income continues to be important, operating margins and cash flow are the most effective measures of GE's efficiency compared with worldwide competitors such as ABB, Hitachi, and Siemens.

In Bunt's view, the operating margin is critical—a fundamental measure of the value added that a company receives from what it is doing. The operating margin also provides a useful measure of a company's ability to survive a downturn in the economy. Imagine a recession in which a company's revenues are off by 10 percent, driving down margins by 5 percent. For a company with a 15-percent margin, income would decline by one-third, but for a company with a 5-percent margin, profits might be wiped out altogether.

Ratios Used by Rating Agencies

The rating agencies consider coverage ratios just as important as debt-to-capital ratios. Book values are used for the debt-to-capital ratios. Recently, GE's debt-to-capital ratio has ranged from 10 to 14 percent. Bunt acknowledges that debt would be a far lower percentage of capital if market values were used, especially given the recent rise in GE's stock price.

Some ratios used differ somewhat among the rating agencies. For example, Moody's has a defined ratio of retained cash flow to debt. S&P has a similar ratio, but dividend and lease payments are not subtracted from cash flow, and debt includes the capitalized value of leases. Although the ratios are different, the resulting trends and relative rankings among companies are similar.

Industry averages can be difficult to use for comparisons because some of the numbers companies publish are not the same as the ones the rating agencies use for their decisions. For example, Moody's does not count working capital changes in its retained-cash-flow measure. GE does not publish changes in progress collections (progress payments received on contracts) separately, and Moody's does not publish numbers that a company has not already published. Therefore, fluctuations in GE's progress collections, which may be as much as $500 million, are not included in the ratio Moody's publishes. In looking at other companies' ratios, Bunt finds some better and some worse than GE's. He assumes that other cases of undisclosed figures account for some of the differences and that knowledge of the additional undisclosed data made available to the rating agencies would reveal a closer convergence.

Investor Mix

GE's common shares are split about evenly between institutional and retail investors, and the company makes no particular attempt to appeal to one type of investor more than the other. The CEO, CFO, and other key managers, along with the investor-relations function, spend substantial amounts of time visiting institutional investors and holding meetings to help analysts get to know the company. Because of the importance of retail investors, the company works closely with sell-side securities analysts who focus primarily on earnings and cash flow prospects.

Bunt does not see a conflict between meeting the expectations of investors with a short-term focus and building value over the long term. In his opinion, companies that say earnings are down because they are investing for the long term generally lack credibility. When a company invests in a big project, competitors learn about it right away. The longer the project, the greater the uncertainty over how well it will be executed and how well marketing and other assumptions will pan out. A company that earns increasing amounts each quarter has the opportunity to invest more for the long term. GE, with a steady run of increasing earnings over a 20-year period, could hardly be accused of short-term management.

Bunt believes that GE has succeeded in changing its image in the investor community. Even as recently as 10 years ago, GE was viewed as a "GNP company" (one that would grow at about the same rate as the gross national product). Today, the company is more successful in portraying itself as a solid, triple-A-rated, conservatively managed company, but also an aggressively managed growth company that is going to continue generating cash for the shareholders. If the company decides to make a big acquisition in the future, investors should be confident that it will be well thought out and that there will be sufficient depth of management to execute it well.

Other Issues

Investment and Financing Decisions

GE's investment decisions are essentially independent of the method of financing. Bunt says, "Either it's a good investment or it isn't." And if the investment cannot be financed from free cash flow, the company has sufficient borrowing capacity. For the RCA acquisition, GE had a choice between issuing stock or assuming debt. GE knew that cash flow from the operations it was buying and the other business components it was selling would be enough to pay down the debt. The rating agencies agreed. The acquisition was executed just as management thought it would be.

Valuation Methods

Bunt believes the most appropriate way to value GE is with a P/E multiple, using companies with comparable prospects as a benchmark. In determining that multiple, investors should consider GE's growth opportunities, infrastructure, products, and depth of management. Bunt thinks GE's multiple should be above that for the S&P 500. In his 30 years with GE, he has seen only a couple studies of GE's stock price based on future cash flows discounted at the company's weighted average cost of capital. He does not think analysts should try to pick apart each of GE's businesses and figure out why transportation had a good year or why results for some other division were down. He thinks it is more important to consider the company's integrated diversity, its growth and profitability initiatives, and its track record in delivering steady, above-average growth and cash flow. It should be no more complicated to analyze GE than single-product companies like Coca-Cola or one of the pharmaceuticals.

GE Capital

GE Capital's balance sheet reflects $227 billion in assets, vs. $60 billion for GE. GE Capital has a triple-A credit rating based partly on a "make-good" agreement, under which GE will ensure that GE Capital has sufficient cash flow for a 1.3 times-charges-earned ratio. Currently, GE Capital's times-charges-earned ratio is above 1.6. Bunt believes it is possible that GE Capital standing alone would merit a triple-A rating.

In the late 1980s, GE Capital diversified into service-type businesses like insurance and active management of leased equipment that are less volatile than pure credit businesses. Currently, GE Capital's business is about one-third financing, one-third insurance, and one-third leasing. In its leasing business, GE Capital acts as the operating lessor for assets such as airplanes, rail cars, containers, and automobile fleets. As a result of this diversification, GE Capital had relatively less exposure to troubled business segments, such as real estate and leveraged buyouts (LBOs), in the early 1990s than some other financial institutions. Moreover, GE Capital's geographic exposures have also become increasingly diversified since the early 1990s. This diversity of less volatile and more predictable sources of earnings is why Bunt believes that GE Capital could be a stand-alone triple-A.

GE Capital's objective is to maintain an 8-to-1 leverage ratio and grow. Management considers this to be a conservative ratio compared with banks and considering its diverse lines of business. The sources of capital are retained earnings and debt. Recently, GE Capital has been retaining 65 percent of earnings. Going forward, it plans to retain 60 percent and pay the remaining 40 percent in dividends—roughly in line with what GE is doing.

GE Capital match-funds its assets and liabilities, carefully managing the maturities. It runs a relatively modest gap (the amount of long-term assets funded with short-term liabilities) that fluctuates around $10 billion. In recent years the gap has been as high as $15 billion and as low as $6 billion. GE Capital is an extensive user of derivatives, but only to replace significant currency and interest-rate risks with the reduced risks of financial-institution counterparties. William Carey, Manager, Financial Planning and Analysis, says that by philosophy, GE Capital believes it has expertise in taking credit risk but prefers to hedge currency and interest-rate risk. The institution never has had a trading mentality. Each of its 27 businesses is considered to have the leverage of the total institution. Before 1982, different businesses had different leverage ratios. Managing this way was discontinued for two reasons. First, it was difficult to analyze the performance of different businesses across interest-rate cycles. Second, the leverage ratios of individual businesses based on peer comparison would not support 8-to-1 for the company as a whole when added up. This result is, in effect, no different than stock portfolio analysis, wherein investment in 15 stocks involves much less risk than investment in a single stock. Today, some of GE Capital's businesses generate higher equity returns than their peers because they benefit from GE Capital's higher leverage ratio. The rating agencies allow GE Capital a couple of times additional leverage because of the reduced risk from the diversity of its 27 businesses.

People Interviewed

James R. Bunt, Vice President and Treasurer

Rhonda L. Seegal, Deputy Treasurer

William Carey, Manager, Financial Planning and Analysis Group, GE Capital Corporation

5

Georgia-Pacific Corporation

Georgia-Pacific Corporation is one of the world's largest forest products companies. It is the leading manufacturer and distributor of building products and one of the leading pulp and paper manufacturers in the United States. In 1996, building products, including wood panels, lumber, chemicals, and gypsum products, accounted for 57 percent of its sales. Pulp and paper products, including containerboard and packaging, communication papers (also called uncoated free sheet), tissue, and market pulp, accounted for the remaining 43 percent. The company owns more than 6 million acres of timberland. It has 9 million tons of pulp, paper, and paperboard manufacturing capacity, representing approximately 8 percent of annual capacity in the United States.

A summary of Georgia-Pacific's recent financials is contained in table 5.1. The increase in debt in 1990 is related to the company's purchase of Great Northern Nekoosa Corporation.

The forest products industry is cyclical—pulp and paper even more so than building products. Georgia-Pacific's net income reached a record $1 billion on sales of $14.3 billion in 1995 and then declined to $156 million on sales of $13 billion in 1996. Year-over-year operating profits in pulp and paper declined 76 percent, primarily as a result of industry overcapacity and substantially lower prices for most of the segment's products.

The effect of economic cycles is amplified by the industry's tendency to overbuild plant capacity when demand is strong. When one company analyzes market demand and considers building a plant to manufacture an engineered lumber product such as particleboard, oriented-strand board, or medium-density fiberboard, it usually does not know how many other companies are considering similar investments. If only one company builds a new particleboard plant, the investment may be successful. If three companies build particleboard plants at the same time, all of them may lose money.

Table 5.1
Financial Summary: Georgia-Pacific Corporation

(Dollar Figures in Millions)	1996	1995	1990	1985
Operating Summary				
Sales (Net)	$13,024	$14,292	$12,665	$6,716
Gross Profit Margin	24.2%	30.1%	23.5%	17.3%
Operating Profit Margin	5.6%	14.7%	10.1%	6.3%
Net Profit Margin	1.2%	7.1%	2.9%	2.8%
Dividend Payout Ratio	113.6%	16.9%	38.1%	43.2%
Sustainable Growth Rate*	1.2%	8.3%	3.0%	3.8%
Capitalization Summary				
Total Assets	$12,818	$12,335	$12,060	$4,866
LT Debt/LT Debt + Equity	55.4%	57.2%	63.7%	35.3%
Total Debt/Total Debt + Equity	61.3%	59.8%	69.1%	37.8%
Market to Book	1.9	1.8	1.1	1.3

*[Net Income/Sales][Sales/Assets][1-(Dividend Payout Rate/Net Income)]

Georgia-Pacific benefits by being on both sides of the forest products industry, because building product cycles usually do not coincide with pulp and paper cycles. The building products business has become less cyclical in recent years as housing starts have become less sensitive to interest rates. Over the long term, the forest products industry grows at 2 to 3 percent per year, along with the national economy. In such a cyclical industry with limited growth opportunities, it is difficult to build shareholder value by making large capital investments to expand capacity. Georgia-Pacific's management has a stated policy of limiting capital expenditures to environmental projects and a limited number of growth projects. In this way, the company will have significant free cash flow it can use to provide investors with returns in the form of dividends or stock repurchases.

Capital-Structure Policy

At the end of 1996, Georgia-Pacific had $5.9 billion in debt outstanding, including $350 million in proceeds from the sale of accounts receivable. Long-term debt was 39 percent of capitalization based on current market values and 55 percent of capitalization based on book values. About 80 percent of the company's debt was long term, with an average maturity of approximately 18 years.

Cost of Capital

Georgia-Pacific's policy is to use debt to optimize the weighted average cost of capital. At the end of 1996, the company's weighted average cost of capital was 10 percent. Its weighted average, after-tax cost of debt was 7.76 percent. Management stated in the 1995 annual report, "Although reducing debt significantly would somewhat reduce the marginal cost of debt, significant debt reduction would likely increase our weighted average cost of capital by raising the proportion of higher-cost equity."

Capital Structure of Business Segments

Both sides of Georgia-Pacific's business are considered to have the same capital structure and cost of capital. However, John F. McGovern, Executive Vice President and Chief Financial Officer, believes the building products side probably can support more debt than the pulp and paper side because it has more stable cash flows.

Role of Treasury Function

The mission of the treasury function at Georgia-Pacific is to maintain a solid liability structure and support the operating side of the business, not to make money independently. Developing good projects that return more than the cost of capital is the first priority; finding the appropriate financing follows. McGovern says, "You cannot make bad projects look good with financing."

McGovern and Treasurer Danny W. Huff see themselves as the people responsible for getting capital. They are on the front line, dealing with the investors. Once the capital is acquired, they have to make sure that it is used properly. Operating managers sometimes have the attitude that the business and the money are theirs. McGovern says the capital does not belong to the company, and the company is not going to retain it if it cannot create value for the shareholders. He has to articulate to shareholders how the company is going to deliver returns. It is management's job to give the shareholders either more cash in their hands or a security with more value.

Credit Rating

Georgia-Pacific's long-term debt is rated Baa2 by Moody's and BBB– by S&P. To preserve its access to capital, the company's policy is to maintain an investment-grade credit rating. This puts an upper limit on debt, which in turn puts an upper limit on capital expenditures unless the company is willing to issue more equity. The company generates enough cash from operations, however, to cover normal capital expenditures in most years. Consequently, there has been a long-established understanding that the company is not capital-constrained and that it will always be able to finance "good" projects. McGovern has seen a danger in that philosophy. Operating managers can propose too many projects for top management to review with appropriate thoroughness. To focus attention on the need for value-creating projects, management has recently adopted a policy to limit capital expenditures, in effect managing the level of capital expenditures to meet the needs of the right-hand side of the balance sheet.

Debt Increase for Acquisition

In 1990, Georgia-Pacific used debt to finance a $5.4-billion takeover of Great Northern Nekoosa Corporation, bringing total debt from 40 to 57 percent of capitalization. The financing for the Great Northern Nekoosa acquisition was in three parts: $1 billion in accounts-receivable securitization, $600 million in credit-sensitive notes, and a $4-billion merger facility with 25 banks.

McGovern believes that packaging receivables is a particularly efficient way to lower the cost of debt when a large amount of financing is needed for an acquisition. No matter where a company's credit rating is, it usually gets an excellent rating on the receivables. Georgia-Pacific does not use accounts-receivable financing today because it is more expensive than commercial paper.

Credit-sensitive notes are securities with an adjustable coupon that is based on the issuer's credit rating. In the event of a ratings upgrade, the coupon on the security is reduced. A ratings downgrade, by contrast, leads to an increase in the coupon. Credit-sensitive notes were developed as a measure to protect investors against event risk—the risk that a major structural change, such as an LBO or a leveraged recapitalization, will cause a ratings downgrade and a consequent loss for bondholders. An investment banker involved with the transaction pointed out that Georgia-Pacific's credit-sensitive notes were issued to finance a strategic acquisition and therefore were more marketable and justified a tighter spread than credit-sensitive notes issued by a typical event-risk candidate. The notes were evenly divided between a 7-year and a 12-year tranche.

The credit-sensitive notes were split-rated, one part below investment grade and the other part above, while Georgia-Pacific's other existing debt remained above investment grade. The investment bankers made the case that the market would not react adversely to a split rating. Pricing on the credit-sensitive notes was significantly more attractive than banks had offered in earlier negotiations for the acquisition financing. This evidence of market access and a reaffirmation of Moody's investment-grade credit rating on the existing debt helped McGovern and Huff negotiate improved terms on the acquisition financing with a syndicate led by one of its long-term relationship banks.

The debt load and the costs of integrating the acquired company placed Georgia-Pacific under significant stress during a subsequent cyclical downturn in the paper industry. High demand for paper in 1989 and 1990 had attracted large amounts of new plant investment, which depressed margins in 1992 and 1993. Despite reporting negative net income, Georgia-Pacific reduced its debt by more than $2 billion during this period by deferring capital expenditures, selling nonstrategic assets, and not increasing its dividend. Management has stated that any similar acquisition in the future will be financed with a combination of debt and equity.

Throughout the difficult three-year period, Georgia-Pacific was able to maintain its investment-grade credit rating with Moody's. Mc-Govern and Huff helped by making a detailed presentation to Moody's analysts at the time the Great Northern acquisition was being financed. They convinced the analysts Georgia-Pacific was capable of managing the additional debt. Subsequently, they kept Moody's up to date on operating results and explained the reasons for variances from projected cash flows. Although earnings were less than forecast for a couple of years after the acquisition, Moody's analysts were satisfied that the character of the credit was not affected.

Economic Value Added

Traditionally, operating managers have believed they earn higher salaries when they manage more assets and more people. To broaden its operating managers' perspective, Georgia-Pacific recently adopted economic value added as a performance measure. The primary benefit of using this measure has been to raise operating managers' awareness of the need to implement projects that return more than the company's cost of capital. The finance function has helped operating managers understand how much capital is employed in each of the company's businesses. Now that part of managers' compensation depends on the performance of the company's stock, they are learning to think more about building shareholder value.

Management expects the economic-value-added metric to encourage continuous process improvements, cost reductions, and divestiture of underperforming assets. Management also tries to make the capital budgeting approval process as rigorous as possible, scrutinizing assumptions about product sales, product price, raw material cost, plant technology, and competitiveness more strictly than ever. Management is not embarrassed to defer a decision when it has doubts or needs more information about a large, complicated project. McGovern compares this approach to the approval process of a bank's senior loan committee, in which a group of experts with many years of experience tries to anticipate everything that possibly could go wrong. Management applies equal rigor to a post-audit program that reviews major investments while projects are under way and after they are completed. These reviews compare the actual timing and amount of expenditures, prices, costs, and other critical success factors with the assumptions that were made when the investments were proposed. McGovern believes that putting an upper limit on capital expenditures helps to ensure that only the best projects are approved.

Fixed- and Floating-Rate Debt

As of early 1997, Georgia-Pacific had $4.5 billion in fixed-rate debt and $1 billion in floating-rate debt. McGovern explains that traditionally the company has borrowed mostly with fixed-rate public debt for the longest possible maturities, protecting itself with call provisions if the funds are not needed. A call provision allows the issuer to buy bonds back from investors at a present price during a specified time period. McGovern believes that the value of call options to Georgia-Pacific is higher than reflected in the option pricing models. The company has taken advantage of the option to call its debt many times. In McGovern's opinion, Georgia-Pacific's current capital structure of mostly fixed-rate debt at reasonable rates allows more capacity for additional borrowing than would a similar capital structure with a higher portion of floating-rate debt. He considers very long-term debt to be a strong form of capital. He believes Georgia-Pacific would have had more difficulty in borrowing to finance the Great Northern acquisition in 1990 if there had been more floating-rate debt on the books.

Tax Considerations

Georgia-Pacific takes advantage of tax-free municipal financing for its plants whenever possible. However, the availability of such financing does not affect the company's decision on whether or not to do a project or its choice of plant sites. McGovern says, "We have to go where the trees are." He considers tax-free municipal financing to be more of a way to save taxes than to reduce the cost of capital. A tax specialist at Georgia-Pacific periodically considers opportunities for structured financing including sales and leasebacks, crossborder leases, and tax arbitrage transactions.

Reinvestment vs. Payout

In 1994 and 1995, Georgia-Pacific reinvested $2.2 billion in its business, partly in projects that had been deferred over the previous three years. The company expects to restrict capital expenditures to about $800 million in 1997 and $700 million in 1998. In the 1995 annual report, management stated, "The paper and forest products industry has traditionally provided shareholders a small portion of their returns through dividend payments. For the most part, however, the industry has endeavored to increase equity values by reinvesting all of its operating cash flow in expansion projects and acquisitions." Considering the industry's cyclicality and limited long-term growth opportunities, McGovern believes a company like Georgia-Pacific should lean toward limiting capital expenditures and providing a cash return to its stockholders through dividends and stock repurchases. He favors Georgia-Pacific's established dividend-payout record because it represents a commitment to pay at least some cash to investors. Georgia-Pacific's board strongly supports a policy of gradually rising dividends. The company's investor relations function believes a portion of the company's shareholders consider dividends important and that cutting them would cause an adverse market reaction. Furthermore, the company would like its stock to be considered a qualified investment by as many institutions as possible, including those whose rules specify that common stock must pay dividends. Nonetheless, McGovern favors returning more cash to investors in the form of stock repurchases because doing so provides flexibility for the company and more favorable tax treatment for investors.

When McGovern presented the company's most recent stock-repurchase program to the finance committee and the board for approval, two alternative approaches were considered. One was the traditional approach of announcing a program to buy back a certain number of shares over a specified period of time, such as one year. The other was to announce the program in more general terms, giving the company the opportunity to repurchase stock more opportunistically based on the amount of its cash surplus and the price of the stock. McGovern prefers the latter approach. Although he considers the program to be more effective if stock is repurchased at favorable prices, he believes that the purpose of the program is to return cash to investors, not to take a view on the stock price. Therefore he does not stop buying back stock when the price goes up.

Development and Approval of Policies

Georgia-Pacific has rather general written policies on capital structure and dividends. When McGovern has specific proposals, such as the stock repurchase program, he first discusses them with the board's finance committee. Then those policies are presented to the full board with the finance committee's support.

Instruments and Tactics

McGovern believes in financing at current market rates when funds are needed rather than prefunding when rates look favorable. He has little interest in exotic instruments. When the company needed funds in the early 1980s, it did an offshore private placement of debt with warrants and hedged it with one of the first currency swaps. McGovern considered the financing expensive. Several years later, he bought back the warrants at a high price because they gave investors the right to lend the company money at 15 percent. Today, Georgia-Pacific focuses on the domestic longer term market. McGovern recognizes that occasionally there may still be opportunities to borrow at favorable rates in overseas markets and swap the debt back into dollars, but he notes that neither the debt instruments nor the currency swaps tend to have the very long terms the company prefers.

McGovern does not want to mix borrowing with bets on where the company stock price is going. Therefore, Georgia-Pacific has never issued debt linked in any way to the price of its stock. McGovern describes convertibles as expensive and as "debt when you need equity and equity when you need debt."

Targeted Stock

In September 1997, Georgia-Pacific announced plans to create a separate class of common stock to allow shareholders to benefit from its profitable timber business. Timber represents a small fraction of sales but a relatively higher percentage of profits. The company will issue a dividend of one share of the newly created timber stock for each share of Georgia-Pacific stock. Management believes the transaction will be tax-free for both the company and its shareholders. A.D. "Pete" Correll, Georgia-Pacific's CEO, said that a spin-off was considered but it would not have been as tax-efficient and would have taken control of timber operations away from the company.

Because earnings from the company's pulp, paper, and building-products businesses are highly cyclical, management believes Georgia-Pacific's stock trades at lower multiples of earnings and cash flow than companies with more predictable earnings. The two classes of common stock will allow each group to either retain cash flow for reinvestment in its business or return the cash directly to investors.

Communication with the Markets

Some investors comment on the relatively large amount of debt Georgia-Pacific carries compared with its industry peers. McGovern believes Georgia-Pacific compares favorably with other forest-products companies, especially when market as well as book debt-equity ratios are used. When the company reviews projected debt-service coverage with the rating agencies, it does worst-case scenarios for both building products and pulp and paper. McGovern and Huff use history to demonstrate that the two sides of the business almost never reach the lowest points of their cycles at the same time. Even under a combined worst-case scenario for 1993, they showed that the company could pay its interest and taxes, maintain its dividend, and still have a $400-million cash flow for capital expenditures.

Distribution of Stock Ownership

Institutions hold between 80 and 85 percent of Georgia-Pacific's stock. McGovern notes Georgia-Pacific does not have many long-term investors because earnings are cyclical. It has mostly momentum investors who make their money on volatility. The company's average daily turnover is 400,000 shares on a base of 90 million.

Investment and Financing Decisions

Except for tax-exempt municipal plant financing, there is generally no connection between Georgia-Pacific's investments and the way they are financed.

Corporate Valuation

McGovern sees some portfolio managers using discounted cash flows to value Georgia-Pacific's stock, but he finds most sell-side securities analysts are more interested in how the price of the stock will move from day to day.

Endnote

1. de Lisser, Eleena, "Georgia-Pacific Plans New Class of Stock Tied to Its Profitable Timber Business," *Wall Street Journal*, September 18, 1997, p. C27.

People Interviewed

John F. McGovern, Executive Vice President and CFO

The Home Depot, Inc.

Founded in 1978, Atlanta-based The Home Depot, Inc. is the world's largest home improvement retailer and ranks among the 10 largest retailers in the United States. As of May 1997, the company had 540 full-service, warehouse-style stores, including 514 in the United States and 26 in Canada. It will start to open stores in South America in the near future. Home Depot employs approximately 112,000 associates, as it calls employees. A summary of The Home Depot's recent financials is contained in table 6.1.

The average Home Depot has approximately 105,000 square feet of indoor selling space and an additional 20,000 to 28,000 square feet for

Table 6.1
Financial Summary: The Home Depot, Inc.

(Dollar Figures in Millions)	1996	1995	1990	1985
Operating Summary				
Sales (Net)	$19,535	$15,470	$3,815	$701
Gross Profit Margin	29.0%	28.9%	28.8%	26.6%
Operating Profit Margin	7.9%	7.6%	7.0%	2.7%
Net Profit Margin	4.8%	4.7%	4.3%	1.2%
Dividend Payout Ratio	11.6%	12.2%	7.9%	0
Sustainable Growth Rate*	10.0%	10.0%	9.9%	2.2%
Capitalization Summary				
Total Assets	$9,342	$7,354	$1,639	$380
LT Debt/LT Debt + Equity	17.3%	12.6%	43.7%	69.2%
Total Debt/Total Debt + Equity	17.3%	12.6%	43.8%	70.2%
Market to Book	4.0	4.4	7.5	3.5

*[Net Income/Sales][Sales/Assets][1-(Dividend Payout Rate/Net Income)]

an outdoor garden center. The stores stock 40,000 to 50,000 different kinds of building materials, home improvement supplies, and lawn and garden products. They offer installation services for many products.

The company has been innovative in combining the economies of scale of warehouse-format stores with a high level of customer service. The corporate culture values entrepreneurial innovation, decentralized management and decision making, and a high level of employee commitment and enthusiasm. In 1997, the company was named America's most admired specialty retailer by *Fortune* magazine for the fourth year in a row. Chief Administrative Officer Ronald M. Brill says, "Our competitors can change their prices and copy our selection, but they haven't been able to duplicate our service levels. Whatever it takes to make the customer happy, we will do." From the beginning, Home Depot has assembled a team of experienced associates to act as the nucleus for the staff of each new store, hiring, training, and inculcating new associates with the company's philosophies.

Home Depot's current P/E ratio of 28 is a function of its consistent growth, which has recently been about 25 percent per year. To continue growing, the company is broadening its product lines and starting to expand internationally. It recently purchased a mail-order company that sells supplies to apartment owners and started selling carpeting in its stores.

Capital-Structure Policy

Except for some short periods, Home Depot has maintained a policy of low leverage. The company has financed its growth with a combination of straight equity, convertible debentures, municipal bonds, capitalized leases, and commercial paper. At the end of fiscal year 1995, long-term debt of $1,247 million was 20.9 percent of book equity. With the help of consistently high P/E ratios, the company has been able to issue new equity periodically to repay its debt and to force rapid conversion of convertible debt.

In the early 1980s, Home Depot was more highly leveraged. Management did not hear many critical comments because earnings were growing rapidly. Then, in 1984, the company made a large acquisition. In 13 months it grew from 20 to 50 stores. Lenders and investors started to voice concerns about the balance sheet when they saw a slight dip in earnings. After all 50 stores were open, earnings began to grow again and leverage was reduced. The company issued new equity and raised cash with a sale and leaseback of six stores. Since 1984, the company has had a bank revolving credit, but has not used it very much. It has been opportunistic in raising equity and convertible debt, sometimes keeping a cash reserve for future capital expenditures for a year or two.

In early 1997, Home Depot completed its third convertible-debenture offering, issuing a $1.1-billion, five-year debenture with a $3^{1}/_{4}$ percent coupon and a 22-percent conversion premium. Brill believes no company has ever done a more successful convertible offering.

Home Depot's book equity was almost $6 billion at the beginning of 1997. During the next two years, conversion of the recent convertible debenture offering plus earnings remaining after dividends will bring book equity to about $8 billion. Brill does not anticipate the need for another equity offering in the foreseeable future. However, the company will continue to borrow to support the acquisition of new real estate.

From the time Home Depot went public in 1981, equity financing has given it an advantage over its competitors. The company has been able to be more aggressive because it does not have to worry about how a possible rise in interest rates might affect its income statement.

Brill is glad Home Depot has never had to borrow from an insurance company. He thinks insurance companies' restrictive covenants can prevent a company from running its own business. Management's position has always been that Home Depot is a great company that will succeed and be sought after by banks and vendors. Those that make unreasonable demands will have to do business with someone else.

Until now, management has focused primarily on return on sales and earning-per-share growth. The company does not use economic value added as a performance measure, but Brill has seen how other companies employ it, calculating capital charges for assets employed at the weighted average cost of capital. He has been gradually familiarizing the company's management with these concepts.

Financing International Expansion

Brill expects Home Depot to use more leverage for opening new stores overseas than it has in the United States. Beyond the company's initial equity investment, sourcing and financing will be local to the extent possible to minimize currency exposure. Currently, 85 percent of the merchandise in Home Depot's Canadian stores is locally sourced, partly from U.S. suppliers that have established Canadian distribution centers at Home Depot's request.

Commercial Paper Classified Long Term

The nature of Home Depot's business puts pressure on its current ratio. The company carries a merchandise inventory of $2.7 billion in its stores, which it supports with accounts payable and commercial paper borrowings. In the past, a portion of the company's commercial paper borrowings have been classified as long-term debt because they have been backed up by a revolving credit agreement rather than just a line of credit. Commercial paper is cheaper, given the current yield curve, and offers more flexibility than fixed-rate public debt. Home Depot's current ratio at the end of 1995 was 1.9. Had outstanding commercial paper been classified short term, the current ratio would have been 1.3. Home Depot has its own credit card but does not carry consumer receivables on its balance sheet; those receivables are owned by a major commercial finance company.

Fixed- and Floating-Rate Debt

Most of Home Depot's borrowing is through commercial paper at floating rates. The company is always aware of the opportunity to use interest-rate swaps to fix the rates. However, it is usually reluctant to use swaps because of the possibility it will refinance its debt with proceeds from an equity offering. In the mid-1980s, shortly after interest-rate swaps were introduced, Home Depot entered into an interest-rate swap to fix the rates on its floating-rate revolver. Then management decided to do an equity offering because the company's stock price was unexpectedly high. This left Brill with an interest-rate swap that was not matched with underlying debt. Because interest rates moved against him, he held the swap for several years until rates swung back and eliminated the loss on the swap. The company has not done an interest-rate swap since then.

Timing of Equity and Debt Issues

Home Depot relies on its principal investment banking firm for advice on timing. Management has generally tried to issue convertible debentures when the company's P/E ratio has been high, interest rates have been low, and there has not been too much similar paper in the market.

Real Estate Ownership

Home Depot owned 73 percent of its stores in early 1997 and will own about 90 percent of the new stores it opens during the year. Having control over its real estate helps the company run its business. Home Depot saves money by owning real estate, because very few landlords can match its credit rating and cost of capital. It also gains flexibility in opening and closing stores. For example, when it decides to close a leased store, the company must find another tenant acceptable to the landlord. It can change store hours only with the landlord's permission. If Home Depot wants to expand a store, the landlord sometimes refuses to reimburse it for the cost of the expansion but still benefits from the property enhancement. Nonetheless, Brill would like the company to scale back over time to owning 80 to 85 percent of its new stores, thereby reducing both the level of capital expenditures required for expansion and the need for external financing. He expects that a relatively high percentage of new stores outside the United States will be leased. At its current rate of growth, Home Depot's capital expenditures, including real estate acquisition, are about $2 billion per year, compared with about $1.5 billion in cash generated from operations.

Leases

The company leases some retail locations, office space, warehouse and distribution space, equipment, and vehicles. It has mostly operating leases but some capital leases as well. Two operating lease agreements signed in 1995 provide the company with purchase options at the higher of cost or fair-market value but also require the company to guarantee the residual value of the leases. The residual value is calculated as the present value of future lease payments; the expense of the residual-value guarantee is recorded as additional rent expense over the lease terms.

Phantom Lease Program

Some real estate is kept off the balance sheet with a phantom lease program. A trust owns the real estate, borrows in the commercial paper market with the benefit of the Home Depot credit rating, and leases the stores to Home Depot. The lease payments repay the commercial paper, which is backed up by a $300-million line of credit. Because the investment bankers own a small percentage of the trust and the banks are not fully secured, the leases are off Home Depot's balance sheet. The primary expense that Home Depot incurs in setting up the trust is fees to the investment bankers.

Real Estate Securitization

Home Depot has considered securitizing its real estate but found it easier to follow a well-established routine of convertible-debenture issues that has been consistently successful and quick to implement. A new offering can be completed in about a week and a half. The Securities and Exchange Commission (SEC) usually approves a new issue a day or so after the company files its S3 form. Investment bankers and officers of the company visit several cities for a "road show" with institutional investors, and the deal is closed.

Shelf Registration

Home Depot has considered a shelf registration but has never done one. Investment bankers have persuaded the company not to do a shelf registration, claiming that it creates an overhang, raising the rating agencies' concern that new debt will be issued. However, Brill believes that the investment bankers' primary concern is the company's ability to shop a new offering among different investment-banking firms for the best rates once the registration is done.

Tax Considerations

Taxes are not a consideration in Home Depot's choice of equity and debt instruments, but they are a consideration in its policy of owning most of its real estate. Depreciation on real estate helps reduce Home

Depot's tax liability. For book reporting purposes, some of the company's real estate is owned by a trust and leased back, but for tax purposes, the company owns that real estate and deducts its depreciation expense.

Stock Splits

Home Depot has done six 4-for-3 and five 3-for-2 stock splits which, compounded, are equal to a 60-for-1 split. The reason for a split is to allow more associates to own 100 shares. Brill does not always think a split is a good idea. Currently, pre-tax earnings of $8 million are equal to a penny per share. After the next 3-for-2 split, the company will have to earn $12 million for each penny per share. The higher the amount, the more difficult it is to produce another penny of earnings when there is a danger of not meeting Wall Street's expectations. In the past, if the company missed those expectations by a penny, it lost $1 billion in market capitalization.

Dividends and Stock Repurchases

Home Depot's dividend policy is based on intuition rather than a defined percentage of earnings. The company declared its first dividend of a penny a share in 1988 because many mutual-fund and pension-fund investors do not buy stock if it has no dividend yield. Since then, the company has raised its dividends every year and also has chosen to keep the dividend constant on a per-share basis with each stock split, thereby continuing to increase the dividend payout as a percentage of earnings. In 1995, the dividend payout ratio was 12 percent. As the company continues to do stock splits, Brill would like to guard against letting the dividend payout ratio get too high, because Home Depot is still a growth company that needs cash. He notes that as long as the company continues to own real estate, it will have to be a borrower. He can tolerate borrowing to pay dividends, but over the long term he would like to minimize the amount of equity sold to pay dividends, including the equity that originates as convertible debentures.

Stock Repurchases

Home Depot has no plans to repurchase stock in the foreseeable future. Someday, however, if the company starts to run out of attractive new store locations and slows its real estate acquisitions, it will start generating a large amount of excess cash. At that time, Brill expects that Home Depot will start buying back its own stock. He has noticed several other large companies whose stock repurchase programs have been successful in raising their share prices. Also, Brill believes that as long as Home Depot is paying enough dividends to qualify as an investment-caliber stock for institutional investors, it should return cash to investors through stock repurchases so their returns will be taxed at a lower rate.

Development and
Approval of Policies

Home Depot's financial structure and its external financing decisions are reviewed by the board's audit and the executive committees. Because the company has a large amount of short-term investments representing proceeds from its recent convertible issue, Brill provides detailed information on the short-term investment portfolio in the board's briefing book. A pie chart shows the amounts of the portfolio invested in government securities, commercial paper, corporate bonds, municipal bonds, and tax-advantaged securities, such as adjustable-rate preferred stock of other corporations. A list of every investment in the portfolio, broken down by category, shows the nominal and effective yield for each investment. The board has approved criteria for short-term investments. They must be fixed-rate bonds with double-A or higher credit ratings. There are no derivative instruments in the portfolio. Maturities are usually not more than one and a half years, and most securities are held to maturity. Occasionally Brill approves single-A investments. He seeks board approval for other instruments that do not meet these guidelines.

One particularly appealing investment instrument has been adjustable-rate preferred stock of other corporations, which allows Home Depot to take advantage of the 85-percent dividend exclusion. Because the dividend is reset every quarter based on current interest rates, principal is not subject to interest-rate risk.

Communication with the Markets

When the earnings rate begins to slow, buy-side analysts tend to ask questions about capital structure, as mentioned above, and about economic value added. They question the company's real estate ownership policy, because additional real estate assets on the balance sheet increase the capital charge in the economic-value-added calculation (see Glossary). Management explains that the benefits of real estate ownership outweigh their effect on the economic-value-added calculation.

Credit Rating

Two years ago, Home Depot's outstanding convertible debenture issue was upgraded to single-A. Because a company's subordinated debentures are usually rated one grade lower than its straight debt, this is equivalent to a double-A rating for the company. Home Depot is currently one of two retailers with a double-A credit rating; the other is Wal-Mart. Aside from credit considerations related to the retailing business, Brill believes that companies with Home Depot's growth rate are seldom rated triple-A. Brill recalls formerly getting credit-enhancement standby letters of credit from commercial banks that now have credit ratings lower than Home Depot's. He would not mind allowing Home Depot's rating to slip to a single-A as a result of a conscious management decision to increase leverage and thereby increase return on equity, economic value added, and earnings per share (although not total earnings).

Distribution of Stock Ownership

About 60 percent of Home Depot's stock and virtually all of its convertible debentures are held by institutional investors. Associates own about 11 percent of the company's stock. There was a time when bond funds would not invest in convertibles, but now they can strip off and sell the conversion features, retaining the straight debt component. Some mutual funds specialize in convertibles.

Employee Compensation

All of the company's officers, corporate managers, store managers, and assistant store managers are compensated partly through a cash bonus plan based on return on assets. For a given fiscal year, a store manager has a plan to achieve both a return-on-assets and a sales target. If the sales target is met but the return-on-assets target is not, the store manager does not receive a bonus. If the store reaches 95 percent of the planned return on assets, the manager is in the bonus pool. A manager who beats the planned return on assets by 15 percent receives a bonus equal to 40 percent of base salary. Once the store meets the return-on-assets target, the manager gets an additional bonus based on achieving certain sales levels.

Going forward, Brill believes that return-on-asset targets are most practical for store managers. However, he would like to see senior management compensation based on a performance measure, such as economic value added, that relates more closely to the creation of shareholder value.

Home Depot also has an employee stock ownership plan (ESOP) and a 401(k) plan. An ESOP is an employee benefit plan consisting of a tax-exempt trust established by the company. The trust must invest primarily in the company's stock, and it is permitted to borrow in order to acquire the stock.

Twice a year, Home Depot associates may buy stock at 85 percent of market value through payroll withholding. At the end of the year, they receive the stock at the lower of the current price or the price in effect when they bought it. All the stock sold to associates is newly issued. Under the 401(k) plan, associates' contributions are matched with Home Depot stock.

Home Depot's ESOP began in the early 1980s as a leveraged ESOP. In a leveraged ESOP, the funds used to purchase the company's stock are borrowed, by either the company or the ESOP trust. To establish its ESOP, Home Depot bought $100 million of its own stock on the open market. At that time, the company recognized the expense of stock sold to employees at cost, and lenders to the ESOP received a tax break on interest income. Now, lenders do not receive a tax break, and the Financial Accounting Standards Board (FASB) has changed the rules to require that the cost of the stock be recognized based on market value rather than cost. Brill observes that if the management of a company is not confident that its stock price will rise, it may be reluctant to leverage its ESOP.

Valuation Methods

When Home Depot's earnings were growing at 25 percent per year, analysts appeared to be concerned primarily with P/E ratios. A couple of years ago, when earnings growth began to slow down, buy-side analysts started bringing up economic value added and discounted-cash-flow valuation. Some of the analysts who measure the company's economic value added disagree with the company's policy of owning real estate. Those analysts have reacted favorably when Home Depot established a trust to own and lease back some of its stores.

People Interviewed

Ronald M. Brill, Executive Vice President and Chief Administrative Officer

Marriott International, Inc., and Host Marriott Corporation

Marriott International, Inc., and Host Marriott Corporation are successors to the Marriott Corporation, which traced its origin to a root-beer stand in Washington, D.C., opened by the late J. Willard Marriott in 1927; the Hot Shoppes restaurant chain; and a motel in Arlington, Virginia, opened in 1957. Today, Marriott International operates in two business segments: lodging and contract services. The lodging business consists of managing full-service, limited-service, and extended-stay hotels and vacation time-share facilities. Brand names include Marriott, Ritz-Carlton, Courtyard, TownePlace Suites, Fairfield Inn, and Residence Inn. The contract business includes senior living communities, food service, food distribution, custodial and housekeeping services, plant operation and maintenance, laundry, and other services. Marriott International owns only a small percentage of the properties it manages. Host Marriott is in the business of lodging ownership. It earns money from hotel and senior living community operating cash flow and capital appreciation in hotel real estate. Most of the hotels and all of the senior living communities that Host Marriott owns are managed by Marriott International.

Summaries of recent financials for Host Marriott and Marriott International are contained in table 7.1 and 7.2.

In 1993, Marriott International was spun off in a special dividend to shareholders, and Marriott Corporation was renamed Host Marriott. The purpose of the break-up was to create two companies with different asset structures and business strategies that would appeal to different investor objectives: Marriott International with steady service revenues, and Host Marriott with ownership positions in hotel real estate. The capital structures and dividend policies of these two entities reflect the differences in their asset structures, revenue sources, and business objectives.

Table 7.1
Financial Summary: Marriott International

(Dollar Figures in Millions)	1996	1995
Operating Summary		
Sales (Net)	$10,172	$8,961
Operating Profit Margin	6.2%	5.4%
Net Profit Margin	3.0%	2.8%
Dividend Payout Ratio	13.1%	14.1%
Sustainable Growth Rate*	6.0%	6.1%
Capitalization Summary		
Total Assets	$5,075	$4,018
LT Debt/LT Debt + Equity	44.5%	43.3%
Total Debt/Total Debt + Equity	44.5%	43.8%
Market to Book	5.5	4.6

*[Net Income/Sales][Sales/Assets][1-(Dividend Payout Rate/Net Income)]

Marriott Corporation grew by building hotels, selling them to investors, and taking back contracts to manage them. The company's growth strategy was very successful in the 1980s, when it developed and sold up to $1 billion in hotel properties each year. The number of hotels the company managed rose from 75 in 1980 to 539 in 1989.

At the end of the decade, Marriott encountered difficulty attracting investors for its hotel properties and arranging purchase financing. Congress had changed the rules on real estate tax shelters in the Tax Reform Act of 1986, reducing their appeal to high-income investors. There was an oversupply of hotels as well as other commercial real estate, compounded by the recession following the Gulf War. Because more hotels than expected were carried on the balance sheet, Marriott Corporation's debt reached 71 percent of book capitalization. Given the nature of the assets, the level of debt was not a major problem. However, a large part of this real estate portfolio was financed with commercial paper. The company had been able to treat the properties it developed as short-term assets because they were constantly rolled over and sold to investors. When the assets could no longer be sold, Marriott

Table 7.2
Financial Summary: Host Marriott

(Dollar Figures in Millions)	1996	1995
Operating Summary		
Revenues (Net)	$717	$474
Hotel Operating Profit Margin	35.7%	40.7%
Dividend Payout Ratio	0	0
Capitalization Summary		
Total Assets	$5,152	$3,557
LT Debt/LT Debt + Equity	70.1%	76.3%
Total Debt/Total Debt + Equity	70.1%	76.3%
Market to Book	2.8	2.8

had more difficulty funding them with commercial paper, and a liquidity problem resulted. At the same time, property values dropped, and recession-related declines in occupancy hurt operating performance.

The purpose of the spin-off, announced in October 1992, was to allow the companies to focus on separate objectives. It also allowed the company's real estate assets to be funded with appropriately long-term debt. Under the terms of the spin-off, Host Marriott was to hold substantially all of the company's real estate assets, worth about $4 billion, and $2.5 billion of the company's $3.1 billion in debt. Marriott International was to make a $600-million line of credit available to Host Marriott.

Initial reaction from some debt investors was negative. Moody's lowered the rating on $1.4 billion of Marriott Corporation's senior debt from Baa3 to Ba2, and the value of the debt fell in the market. The company settled a resulting investors' lawsuit largely by increasing the coupon and extending the maturity of the debt. Some land and related debt was also shifted from Host Marriott to Marriott International. Although the bonds remained slightly below investment grade, a level that Marriott's management considered to be appropriate, the stock market reaction was very positive. The price of the combined entities rose from $17$1/_2$ just before the October 1992 announcement to $33$3/_8$ just after the split in October 1993. The value of Host Marriott's stock was supported by renewed interest in real estate investment trusts (REITs) and other types of real estate investments.

Marriott International Corporation

Marriott International Corporation, headquartered in Washington, D.C., is one of the largest hospitality companies in the world, with more than 250,000 employees and 4,700 operating units in the United States and 29 other countries. For fiscal year 1996, Marriott International reported income of $306 million on sales of $10.2 billion. The company has grown substantially in recent years. In 1995, it paid cash to acquire 49 percent of The Ritz-Carlton Hotel Company LLC, manager of 31 luxury hotels, with the expectation of acquiring the remaining portion over the next several years at a price based on the cash flow of the Ritz-Carlton business. In 1996, it acquired the Forum Group, Inc., owner and operator of about 40 senior housing facilities, for a combination of cash and debt assumption. In early 1997, it agreed to acquire the Hong Kong-based Renaissance Hotel Group, operator and franchiser of 150 hotels in 38 countries under the brand names Renaissance, New World, and Ramada International. This acquisition more than doubled the company's international presence. By year-end 1997, Marriott International's worldwide lodging system is expected to reach approximately 300,000 hotel rooms. By the year 2000, the company expects to be operating twice as many hotels as it did in 1996.

Margins

Marriott International's operating and cash flow margins have increased substantially in the past three years, as shown in table 7.3.

Marriott International's 1996 annual report shows that about one-third of lodging profits comes from base management fees, one-third from profit participations, and one-third from franchise fees, the sale of vacation club time-share intervals, and land rent. While contract services produce lower operating margins than does lodging, it helps diversify Marriott International's revenue sources in the event of a cyclical downturn.

Table 7.3
Marriott International Corporation's Margins (%)

	1996	1995	1994
Operating Margin—Lodging	7.7	6.8	6.1
Operating Margin—Contract Services	4.1	3.6	3.2
Operating Margin—Total	6.2	5.5	4.9
Net Income/Sales	3.0	2.8	2.4
EBITDA*/Sales	7.3	6.6	5.8

*EBITDA=earnings before interest, tax, depreciation, and amortization.

Capital-Structure Policy

Since the spin-off, Marriott International's debt has been between 40 and 50 percent of capitalization. Marriott International's policy is to determine its debt capacity based on the amount and variability of its cash flows. Its debt level is managed so that coverage and balance sheet ratios stay well within the guidelines for a solid, investment-grade credit rating. In its 1996 annual report, the company notes that cash flow, defined as earnings before interest, income tax, depreciation, and amortization (EBITDA) was 7.9 times gross interest cost, significantly exceeding requirements defined by the company's loan agreements.

Marriott International's capital expenditures are used primarily to build new facilities to be sold to investors. Also, as part of its growth strategy, the company provides financing to Host Marriott and other qualified owners to build or acquire lodging and senior living properties to be operated or franchised by Marriott International. It is the company's policy to finance properties on an interim basis with the expectation of selling most of them to investors under long-term management or lease agreements. While Marriott International has the capacity to hold these properties, it opportunistically finances its management and franchise business by selling the properties while retaining the management or franchise rights. The company may participate with the property owners either as a lender or equity investor, but it prefers not to hold the majority of the per-room investment.

Capital expenditures, financing for real estate owners, and acquisitions are funded by a combination of operating cash flow and additions to debt within internal leverage guidelines. In the past three years, cash generated from operations has been more than twice the level of capital expenditures, leaving the company substantial cash flow and borrowing capacity for expansion. The company has no plans to issue new equity in the foreseeable future.

Marriott International's financial objectives include diversifying its financing sources and optimizing the mix and maturity of its long-term debt. In 1995, Marriott International took advantage of favorable market conditions to increase fixed-rate debt to 95 percent of the portfolio and lengthen the average maturity. Three series of senior notes totaling $450 million were issued, with maturities ranging from 10 to 14 years at an effective borrowing rate of 7.5 percent. At the end of 1996, the company's long-term debt had an average rate of 7.3 percent and an average maturity of eight years.

Dividend Policy

In its three years as a separate company, Marriott International has paid dividends of between 10 and 20 percent of earnings, with a stated policy of reinvesting the major portion of earnings in the business. The company periodically repurchases its common stock to replace shares issued under various ESOPs. The timing of its repurchases is based on market conditions. During 1994 and 1995, Marriott International's Board of Directors authorized the purchase of an aggregate 14.5 million shares of the company's common stock. At the end of 1996, the company had purchased 10.5 million shares, and 128.6 million shares remained outstanding.

Development and Approval of Policies

Marriott International's capital-structure and dividend policies are developed by the finance function as an integral part of the company's growth strategy. They are reviewed with the board as part of the annual budgeting process. The effectiveness of these policies is measured by the company's stock price and continuing ability to finance its growth.

Instruments and Tactics

Zero-Coupon Convertible Bonds

In March 1996, Marriott International issued $540 million in zero-coupon convertible bonds due in 2011. Gross proceeds from the issuance were $288 million. Zero-coupon convertible bonds are callable by the issuer and puttable by the investor. The issuer pays a lower rate on zero-coupon convertibles than on regular bonds in exchange for the conversion feature. Imputed interest is tax-deductible each year, even though the issuer does not pay it until maturity. Each $1,000 bond is convertible at any time, at the option of the holder, into 8.76 shares of the company's common stock. The zero-coupon convertibles were issued at a discount representing a yield to maturity of 4.25 percent. At the option of the holder, the company may be required to purchase each bond for $603.71 on March 25, 1999, or $810.36 on March 25, 2006. In such an event, the company may elect to purchase the bonds for cash, common stock, or any combination thereof. The zero-coupon convertibles are redeemable by the company at any time on or after March 25, 1999, for cash equal to the issue price plus accrued original issue discount. The bonds are subordinated to the company's $1.1-billion senior indebtedness.

Michael A. Stein, Executive Vice President and Chief Financial Officer of Marriott International, notes that his company's predecessor, Marriott Corporation, had a successful experience with an issue of zero-coupon convertibles in 1991. Stein and his staff look for opportunities to issue zero-coupon convertibles when rates appear low and conversion premiums high. They like zero-coupon convertibles because they have a low coupon and are less costly than straight equity. Because these bonds are convertible into a fixed number of shares, the conversion price grows at the interest rate. The imputed, or PIK (payment-in-kind), interest is deductible in each period, even though the actual payment of interest is through redemption of the zero-coupon bond at face value. Stein believes financial officers of other companies might find zero-coupon convertibles attractive if they know equity will be needed eventually but would like to take advantage of lower-than-equity financing cost until the time of conversion.

Stein notes that bankers occasionally propose derivatives that allow Marriott International to take a view on its own stock. Stein believes that the company's stock repurchase program gives it an opportunity to benefit when the price is favorable. He is not interested in going beyond that and using derivatives to benefit from the volatility of the company's stock. He says, "Markets can do things we don't understand. There are too many factors other than our company's specific circumstances that drive the stock price."

Commercial Paper

In July 1996, Marriott International entered into a five-year, $1-billion revolving credit facility to back up its commercial paper borrowings. The facility provides for one-year renewal periods after 2001 unless notice of nonrenewal is given. Borrowings under the facility will generally bear interest at a rate based on the company's credit rating. Because of the maturity date of this facility, Marriott International's commercial paper borrowings are classified as long-term debt.

Shelf Registration

In 1996, Marriott International filed a shelf registration with the SEC which, together with an earlier filing, permits the company to issue up to $550 million of straight debt securities. Shelf registration helps issue debt quickly when market conditions are right. Stein likes the SEC's proposed idea of a company, or universal, registration covering all debt and equity instruments in principle because disclosure requirements are the same for all securities. However, he would not like to use this type of registration before the practice becomes widespread because the first filing of a company registration, rather than the usual shelf registration for debt securities, could be taken as a signal to the market that the company plans to issue equity.

Investor Mix

The investor mix for Marriott International's stock is: 50-percent institutional, 30-percent retail, and 20-percent Marriott family. Stein notes that retail investors may add stability to a company's stock price, but they are also more costly for the investor relations function to service.

Related Issues

Investment and Financing Decisions

Marriott International's investment and financing decisions are essentially independent of each other. Funds spent to develop new hotel properties are part of corporate capital expenditures supported by corporate cash flow and borrowing. Marriott International views long-term financing as the sale of these properties to investors such as REITs or individuals. Depending on who the investors are, that financing may or may not be leveraged.

The company sets hurdle rates based on the risk of the project. The vast majority of these projects, whether bricks and mortar, loans, or equity investments, are in new revenue-generating units. It is not difficult to do a return-on-investment analysis. The company sets hurdle rates for each of its businesses (e.g., full-service hotel operation, economy hotel operation, management services, senior living services, distribution services) based on the prototypical business activity. For individual projects, the finance staff risk-adjusts each cash flow to determine whether there is sufficient return to justify going forward.

Valuation Methods

Marriott International's finance staff periodically values the company based on both projected cash flows discounted at the weighted average cost of capital and the P/E ratios and EBITDA multiples used by most securities analysts.

Host Marriott

Host Marriott is one of the largest owners of lodging properties in the world. As of the end of 1996, the company owned 84 lodging properties, all but three of which were operated under Marriott or Ritz-Carlton brand names. In addition, it held minority interests in 25 unconsolidated lodging partnerships with approximately $3 billion in assets. These partnerships own 251 lodging properties operated by Marriott International, 31 of which are full-service hotels. Consistent with its strategy of focusing on the upscale full-service hotel market, Host Marriott spun off the Host Marriott Operating Group at the end of 1995. This business segment is the leading operator of restaurant and retail outlets at airports, toll roads, stadiums, and other tourist attractions. As a special dividend, investors received one share of a new company, Host Marriott Services Corporation, for each five shares of Host Marriott they owned.

Host Marriott's business strategy focuses on opportunistic acquisitions of full-service urban, convention, and resort hotels, primarily in the United States. Robert E. Parsons, Jr., Executive Vice President and Chief Financial Officer, observes that revenue per available room (REVPAR) in the upscale full-service segment has declined only twice in the past 20 years, and that was only briefly, during the recession following the Gulf War. Supply, on the other hand, has varied, and supply is what drives hotel economics. Management believes that the upscale full-service segment of the market offers numerous opportunities to acquire assets at attractive multiples of cash flow and at substantial discounts to replacement value. Many desirable hotel properties are held by inadvertent owners such as banks, insurance companies, and other financial institutions that are looking for the best opportunities to sell. Host Marriott has acquired several properties from these inadvertent owners at significantly less than replacement cost. Management also believes that there are numerous opportunities to improve underperforming hotels through replacement of existing managers and conversion to a Marriott or Ritz-Carlton brand. Conversion is intended to increase occupancy and room rates through Marriott International's worldwide marketing and reservation systems and customer recognition of the Marriott brand names.

Host Marriott works with Marriott International to increase cash flow at each property and maximize profitability throughout its portfolio. It does so by evaluating marginal restaurant operations, exiting low-rate airline room contracts in strengthening markets, reducing property overhead by sharing management positions with other hotels the company manages in the vicinity, and selectively investing where favorable incremental returns are expected.

According to Donald D. Olinger, Senior Vice President and Corporate Controller, the lodging industry as a whole, and the full-service segment in particular, has benefited in the past several years from a shift in the supply-demand relationship, with supply relatively flat and demand strengthening. This is a favorable contrast to the 1980s, a period of significant overbuilding. Upscale full-service room supply increased at approximately 5 percent annually between 1988 and 1990. This increase caused an oversupply of rooms in the industry, especially during the 1990–91 recession.

Since 1991, new hotel construction, excluding casino-related construction, has been modest, largely offset by the number of rooms taken out of service each year. Due to an increase in travel and an improvement in the economy, hotel occupancy has grown steadily over the past several years, and room rates have improved. The company believes that room demand for upscale full-service properties will continue to grow at approximately the rate of inflation. Increased room demand should result in increased hotel occupancy and room rates. According to Smith Travel Research, upscale full-service occupancy for Host Marriott and its competitive set grew in 1996 to 72.4 percent while room-rate growth continued to exceed inflation. While room demand has been rising, new hotel supply growth has been minimal. Smith Travel Research data show that upscale full-service room supply increased at an average rate of only 1 percent annually from 1990 through 1996 for comparable full-scale services. The increase in room demand and minimal growth in new hotel supply has also led to increased room rates. As a result, REVPAR has increased from $67 in 1993 to $93 in 1996. Given the relatively long lead time to develop urban, convention, and resort hotels, as well as the lack of project financing, Host Marriott's management believes the growth in room supply in this segment will be limited for an extended period of time.

Management Agreements with Marriott International

Marriott International has contracts to manage most of Host Marriott's hotels for an initial term of 15 to 20 years, with an option to extend most of those agreements for 16 to 30 years. In addition to on-site management, Marriott International provides certain "chain" services such as a national reservation system, computerized payroll and accounting, and training and promotion. The agreements generally require Host Marriott to pay base management fees of 1.5 to 4 percent of sales and incentive management fees of 15 to 20 percent of the property's operating profits.

Under the terms of its management agreements with Marriott International, Host Marriott is generally required to set aside approximately 5 percent of gross hotel sales to cover maintenance and capital improvements. Guest rooms and common areas are normally refurbished every five or six years. The company spent $54 million on capital improvements in 1994, $56 million in 1995, and $87 million in 1996. Going forward, the company anticipates spending $120 million annually on the renovation and refurbishment of existing properties.

Host Marriott's revenues consist of the house profit from its hotel properties and senior living communities, equity earnings of affiliates, and gains and losses on the sale of properties. A large portion of the company's hotel operating costs and expenses are fixed. Therefore, the company derives substantial operating leverage from increases in revenue. Currently, when revenue increases by $1, EBITDA increases by $1.30 to $1.50. This operating leverage is somewhat offset by an incentive fee structure that allows the manager, in most cases Marriott International, to share in the growth of profits. Base management fees are calculated as a percentage of sales, and variable lease payments and incentive management fees are tied to operating performance above certain established levels.

Capital-Structure Policy

Host Marriott's capital structure is designed to be consistent with its asset base, according to Robert E. Parsons, Jr., Executive Vice President and Chief Financial Officer. Management believes that the most prudent way to finance real estate, a long-life asset, is with equity and long-term, fixed-rate debt. The company is funding its growth with approximately 50-percent debt and 50-percent equity. Management looks at individual markets and tries to fund capital projects opportunistically. However, in making capital-structure decisions, it is concerned primarily with cash-flow coverage of interest expense (defined as EBITDA less maintenance capital expenditures less cash taxes divided by cash interest expense), which has increased from 1.3 to 1.4 times during the past two years. Other important ratios are EBITDA coverage of interest expense and cash-flow coverage of interest expense plus principal payments. Management also looks at debt to total capital, debt-to-market capitalization, and debt to assets, but it gives those ratios less weight than the coverage ratios.

At the end of 1996, Host Marriott had long-term debt of $2.6 billion, representing 70 percent of total market capitalization. Fifty-eight percent of total long-term debt was nonrecourse, in the form of mortgages on individual properties. Management continually reviews all aspects of capital structure, including the maturity schedule and the amount of fixed- and floating-rate debt. It decided to fix a large component of the company's debt over the past 18 months because it believed that rates were at an opportune level. Now, 95 percent of Host Marriott's debt is at fixed rates.

In 1995, the company financed $392 million in acquisitions and $160 million in capital expenditures with $142 million cash from operations, $325 million from asset sales, $191 million from a net increase in debt, and $13 million from the sale of common stock. In 1996, it financed $702 million in acquisitions and $159 million in capital expenditures, with $201 million cash from operations, $338 million from asset sales, $324 million from a net increase in debt, and $454 million from the sale of common stock.

Dividends and Stock Repurchases

Since the spin-off, Host Marriott has neither paid a dividend nor repurchased stock. Management assumes that stockholders are looking for a pure play in real estate, not dividend income. It sees significant investment opportunities and believes it can serve shareholders better by reinvesting capital than by paying out dividends. In 1996, the company invested $1.5 billion in full-service, four- and five-star lodging properties in the United States; in the first half of 1997, it invested $1 billion. Also, Host Marriott was prohibited from paying a dividend while amounts were due under its line of credit from Marriott International. The line of credit has since been eliminated.

Credit Rating

Host Marriott's senior debt is rated Ba3, and its preferred securities are rated B1 by Moody's. Parsons believes that such ratings, just a notch below investment grade, are appropriate for a company focused on real estate. The strengths cited in Moody's analysis are the current favorable supply/demand conditions in the upscale full-service and luxury hotel segments, the potential profit from appreciation of full-service hotel assets, the high brand awareness and quality image of the Marriott and Ritz-Carlton brands, and the strong relationship with Marriott International, including credit support. The risks cited are a highly leveraged balance sheet with off-balance-sheet liabilities, including operating lease commitments and contingent liabilities related to certain leases of divested properties; owned hotels' sensitivity to economic cycles; and the high capital requirements for the acquisition, conversion, development, and refurbishment of full-service hotels.

Instruments and Tactics

In 1991, Host Marriott's predecessor, Marriott Corporation, raised $195 million in an issue of 8.25-percent cumulative convertible preferred stock. During 1995, all of Host Marriott's outstanding preferred stock was converted into common stock or defeased.

In late 1996, Host Marriott raised $533 million, net of issuance costs, of 6.75-percent mandatorily redeemable convertible quarterly income preferred securities (QUIPs). Each $50 QUIP is convertible into 2.2 shares of Host Marriott common stock, which sold for $17⅜ in early May 1997. Parsons believes the after-tax cost was attractive compared with other opportunities in the marketplace. In general, he considers convertible securities to be a cost-effective way of issuing an instrument with certain attributes of debt and certain attributes of equity. Natural-ly, management has to consider the conversion price, the likelihood of stock-price appreciation, and at what levels it would be willing to issue equity.

Valuation Methods

Host Marriott's bottom-line objective is to generate growth in cash flow per share for investors. Parsons believes the most appropriate way to value Host Marriott is based on multiples of EBITDA, cash flow per share, and funds from operations (FFO) per share. FFO, a frequently used measure for REITs and other real estate investment and operating companies, is defined as net income from operating activities before the impact of depreciation and amortization of assets that are unique to real estate. (Assets such as computers, vehicles, and capitalized financ-ing expenses are not considered unique to real estate.)

Host Marriott uses discounted cash flow (DCF) analysis for valuing individual hotel properties, but Parsons does not believe that adding up all of those individual DCF valuations is, without looking at a number of other factors, the most effective way to determine whether the stock market is undervaluing or overvaluing the company as a whole. The company uses four internal-rate-of-return calculations to analyze indi-vidual properties: before taxes, after taxes, with normal leverage, and unleveraged. Management has target ratios for each of the four calcula-tions. The challenge of using DCF analysis for the company as a whole, in Parsons's opinion, is that a number of different fundamental assump-tions can have a substantial effect on the end result. Therefore, such an analysis tends to produce a rather broad range of stock prices—too broad for determining if the market is mispricing the stock by $5 to $7 and deciding whether or not to buy back stock.

Marriott International–Host Marriott Relationship

Marriott International and Host Marriott have agreements that provide for Marriott International to manage lodging properties owned or leased by Host Marriott and for Marriott International to guarantee Host Marriott's performance in connection with certain loans and other obligations. Marriott International has the right to purchase up to 20 percent of the voting stock of Host Marriott if certain events occur that involve a change of control. Management of properties owned by Host Marriott accounted for about 17 percent of Marriott International's sales and 15 percent of its profits.

Comparison of Capital-Structure and Dividend Policies

Although the 1996 year-end balance sheets for Marriott International and Host Marriott reflected about $5 billion in assets each, their composition differs substantially.

Marriott International's balance sheet shows $1.8 billion in property and equipment but also substantial current assets, investments in affiliates, and intangibles. The value of Marriott International is based on future contract revenues. Marriott International is a service company that generates revenue primarily from hotel management fees and contract services. Its business strategy is to increase cash flow by expanding the number of hotel properties it manages and improving operating margins. The purpose of its construction, ownership, and financing activities is to build its service business. Host Marriott is more asset intensive, with $3.8 billion in property and equipment. Host Marriott is a real estate ownership company that derives its revenues from hotel operating profits after the payment of management fees and gains and losses on the sales of properties. Its recent strategy has centered around acquiring full-service hotel properties below replacement cost. Both Marriott International and Host Marriott benefit from high occupancy and operating margins, but Host Marriott as a property owner has higher operating leverage than Marriott International as a service provider. For example, while a decline in hotel occupancy could flatten incentive (profit-related) management fees but not base management fees to the service provider, it could cause an actual loss to the owner.

Marriott International maintains long-term debt of about 50 percent of capitalization to minimize its weighted average cost of capital while protecting its investment-grade credit rating. Host Marriott has a higher level of debt representing about 70 percent of capitalization, reflecting its core business of real estate ownership; a large portion of that debt is mortgages secured by hotel properties.

Marriott International pays a modest dividend and reinvests most of its earnings in the growth of the business. Host Marriott pays no dividend because it is a growth company, and management believes investors are better served by the reinvestment of capital in the business.

People Interviewed

Marriott International

Michael A. Stein, Executive Vice President and Chief Financial Officer

Billie Ida Williamson, Senior Vice President Finance and Corporate Controller

Host Marriott

Robert E. Parsons, Jr., Executive Vice President and Chief Financial Officer

Donald D. Olinger, Senior Vice President and Corporate Controller

Monsanto Company

Shortly before the interviews for this case study were conducted, Monsanto announced plans to spin off its specialty chemicals business. The spin-off was completed on September 1, 1997. The new chemical company is called Solutia Inc. Since the spin-off, Monsanto has adopted a policy of lower dividends consistent with other growth companies.

Monsanto is a $9-billion company, long established in chemicals, that has been diversifying since the mid-1980s into pharmaceuticals and agricultural biotechnology. It has recently decided to split into two companies. One company will comprise Monsanto's chemical businesses, including nylon and acrylic fibers, Saflex™ plastic interlayer for windshields (now trademarked under Solutia, the recently spun-off chemical division of Monsanto), and a large number of specialty chemical products serving the vehicle, aviation, chemicals, packaging, construction, home furnishings, and capital equipment markets. The other will comprise the faster growing life sciences business lines, including agricultural products, food ingredients, and pharmaceuticals. A summary of Monsanto's recent financials is contained in table 8.1.

Although there are some interesting questions to be resolved related to the financial structures of the two new companies, the primary reason for the spin-off is strategic. In recent years, cash flow and divestitures from the chemical businesses have been generating funds needed to develop the life sciences businesses. Proposals for acquisitions and other investments on the chemical side, while financially viable, have been turned down in favor of higher-yielding investments in life sciences. Continuing to operate this way would starve the chemical businesses of the capital they need. Monsanto prefers to divest these stable, established businesses while they are still profitable and hold a number-one or number-two position in their markets.

Table 8.1
Financial Summary: Monsanto Company

(Dollar Figures in Millions)	1996	1995	1990	1985
Operating Summary				
Sales (Net)	$9,262	$8,962	$8,995	$6,747
Gross Profit Margin	47.0%	48.1%	45.5%	35.3%
Operating Profit Margin	6.0%	12.7%	10.1%	5.2%
Net Profit Margin	4.2%	8.2%	6.1%	−1.5%
Dividend Payout Ratio	0	41.0%	44.3%	NA
Sustainable Growth Rate*	3.4%	7.0%	5.9%	−1.1%
Capitalization Summary				
Total Assets	$11,191	$10,611	$9,236	$8,877
LT Debt/LT Debt + Equity	30.4%	30.9%	28.8%	38.0%
Total Debt/Total Debt + Equity	38.0%	35.3%	35.3%	45.0%
Market to Book	6.2	3.8	1.5	1.1

* [Net Income/Sales][Sales/Assets][1-(Dividend Payout Rate/Net Income)]

Capital-Structure Policy

Monsanto's financial policies and capital structure have been relatively stable over the past decade. The capital structure is based on what management considers suitable to the company's needs rather than on the riskiness of the business, industry norms, or market conditions. The company has had sufficient cash flow for internal capital expenditures, dividends, and a stock repurchase program. As a result, management has had wide latitude in defining capital structure. Although the company generally prefers to use internally generated capital to finance its growth, some large acquisitions on the life sciences side have required and will probably continue to require the issuance of additional debt.

Maintaining Credit Rating and Flexibility

The keystone of Monsanto's capital-structure policy has been to maintain a single-A credit rating with a comfortable margin to ensure flexibility. The company tends to stay above the rating agencies' median cash-flow-coverage ratios for a single-A rating, but the debt-to-capital ratio gets out of alignment from time to time. Debt tends to rise after an acquisition or a restructuring, and then it is managed back to its previous level. Juanita H. Hinshaw, Vice President and Treasurer, has told the agencies publicly that Monsanto intends to maintain a 35- to 40-percent ratio of debt to total capitalization. She prefers to keep it closer to 40 percent.

Good communication helps both Monsanto and the rating agencies avoid unpleasant surprises. The company calls the agency analysts the day acquisitions are announced, so they will be as knowledgeable as possible when talking to their rating committees. It has stated its policy of suspending share repurchases and repairing the balance sheet after acquisitions and then followed through on its promises. Recently, one of the agencies discussed the possibility of an upgrade, but Hinshaw reminded them of the company's growth strategy and said that more acquisitions were likely. Monsanto would prefer to maintain its rating than to be upgraded and then downgraded.

Capital-Structure Policy after Spin-Off

Because they will have different risk profiles and capital-structure policies, the two new companies are likely to have different ratings after the spin-off. Management expects the chemical company to have a triple-B rating because such a rating will allow the company to assume more debt and create greater shareholder value than a single-A rating would.

The life sciences company is expected to have a single-A rating, as Monsanto has now. Deciding on the appropriate capital structure and credit rating has been more of a challenge for the life sciences business than for the chemical business. On one hand, the life sciences business will have heavy capital requirements to make acquisitions and round out its biotechnology capabilities and therefore could use additional debt. On the other hand, growth companies tend to have low debt so as not to compound business risk with financial risk. Management believes the life sciences business has more business risk than the chemical business and more need for an equity cushion to provide the flexibility for growth.

To further solidify its operating cash flow, Monsanto would like to continue acquiring pharmaceutical businesses with strong cash flows that fit well with existing product lines. A recent example was the acquisition of the women's health-care business developed by Syntex and later sold to Roche Holding AG. The analysts supported this acquisition as soon as they saw that it would contribute to earnings per share from the first day. But some future acquisitions may not be accretive quite so soon.

As an industry leader in biotechnology, Monsanto will continue to see opportunities for strategic investments with longer term benefits, and it will probably not have much timing flexibility when those opportunities arise. Depending on how much additional debt is required to develop the business, management will have to decide whether it is willing to let the credit rating drop a notch.

Monsanto considered whether to split its existing long-term debt between the two companies when the spin-off occurs, but decided to leave all of its existing long-term debt on the books of the life sciences company. The chemical company will be able to determine its own long-term debt needs after starting with commercial paper funding. The disadvantage of splitting the debt would have been the expensive and time-consuming process of getting bondholders' consent. Although an argument could have been made for leaving the debt on the chemical side of the business because of its predictable cash flows, the market is more enthusiastic about life sciences. Also, that side of the business includes established cash generators such as NutraSweet® and Roundup® herbicide.

Fixed- and Floating-Rate Debt

Although Monsanto does not have a firm policy on fixed- and floating-rate debt, floating-rate debt tends to range from 30 to 50 percent of total debt, reflecting seasonal credit terms offered to agricultural customers. A large part of floating-rate debt is in the form of commercial paper. Depending on her view of the rates, Hinshaw may swap some of that debt into fixed rates. In 1995, a portion of Monsanto's short-term commercial paper, which was rolled over every 30 or 45 days, was classified long term because it was used to finance the Kelco acquisition and because the company intended to replace it with longer term financing.

Timing of Debt Issues

Most of Monsanto's debt issuance is opportunistic. Hinshaw says, "We've had the luxury to be able to look at the market and decide the right time to go in." There are occasional exceptions, when additional debt is needed for a large acquisition regardless of the markets. When Monsanto acquired G.D. Searle & Co. in 1985 for $2.7 billion, it temporarily increased its risk profile. Long-term debt rose from 18 percent of capitalization at the end of 1984 to 45 percent of capitalization at the end of 1985, and then dropped to 35 percent of capitalization at the end of 1986. Since then, the company has had a policy of "repairing its balance sheet" after major acquisitions. The company did a 20-year debt issue immediately after acquiring Kelco, a maker of food ingredients, from Merck for $1.1 billion in February 1995. Fortunately, market conditions were favorable, and the additional debt could be absorbed within the agency guidelines for a single-A rating.

One method of repairing the balance sheet that Hinshaw has considered but not used is the sale of receivables. The use of economic value added as a performance measure might encourage Monsanto line managers to become interested in the sale of receivables, but Hinshaw finds this to be a high-cost method of financing in comparison with commercial paper. The cost would seem reasonable only if the company were beginning to run out of debt capacity under its single-A credit rating and wanted some additional flexibility, perhaps for another temporary debt increase to finance a major acquisition.

Hinshaw watches the markets and talks to a variety of bankers, traders, and other experts on a regular basis. She then makes her own decisions on the timing of intermediate and longer term fixed-rate debt issues based on investments the company has budgeted for the remainder of the year and a probability estimate of funds that actually will be spent.

In December 1995, the company considered issuing 100-year debt with pricing that looked quite favorable. It decided not to go ahead when the U.S. Department of the Treasury made a proposal, as part of the Clinton administration's 1997 budget package, that interest for bonds with maturities greater than 40 years no longer be deductible for tax purposes. Having to make this decision was disappointing for Hinshaw, because the timing of the issue appeared just right, and the bonds would have seemed like inexpensive equity. As of early 1997, the Clinton administration has once again proposed the tax deduction be eliminated, but there is congressional opposition to that proposal. Other companies have issued 100-year bonds recently, but the rates are considerably higher than when Monsanto considered them in 1995.

Tax Issues

For Monsanto's treasury function, the most important tax issues relate to minimizing the tax impact of repatriating dividends from overseas subsidiaries. Tax issues do not affect the company's choice of financing instruments except to the extent that industrial revenue bonds can be used for plant financing. Industrial revenue bonds comprise about 20 percent of Monsanto's long-term debt.

Dividends and Stock Repurchases

Monsanto has increased its dividends every year for 25 years. Historically, management has wanted Monsanto to be considered a great company, and it has observed that great companies pay ever-increasing dividends. Monsanto has had the funds to maintain a payout ratio of approximately 40 to 50 percent of earnings over the years and has wanted to be sure its dividend increases kept ahead of inflation. The company has tried to be consistent with the chemical industry. Since the G.D. Searle acquisition in 1985, it has tried also to be somewhat consistent with the pharmaceutical industry, whose leading companies have higher dividend payouts than most chemical companies.

Hinshaw also points out that a consistent dividend payout makes the stock attractive to yield investors, which tends to set a floor for the company's stock price. This is helpful for a company that is in both the chemical and pharmaceutical industries. The stock price can be hit if there is a problem in either industry.

After the spin-off, the chemical company is likely to maintain a dividend-payout ratio consistent with that of its industry. Determining the dividend policy for the life sciences company is more difficult, because growth companies tend to pay lower dividends and an industry of comparable companies with established dividend patterns does not yet exist. The life sciences company will probably have a lower dividend payout ratio than Monsanto has had recently.

Stock Repurchase Program

Monsanto's stock repurchase program began modestly in 1984. The volume of purchases increased after the crash in 1987 when the company's stock seemed underpriced. Since then, stock repurchases have been opportunistic. The company has had excess cash after capital expenditures and research and development, which Hinshaw has used to buy back shares and adjust the capital structure to the desired level. At a minimum, the company tends to buy back enough shares to offset the exercise of employee stock options.

Development and Approval of Policies

Monsanto has written fairly broad capital-structure and dividend policies. In addition, Hinshaw prepares a comprehensive book each year to facilitate the rating agencies' review of the company. The book is reviewed with the board's finance committee before or after meetings with the rating agencies. For Monsanto, evaluating the effectiveness of capital-structure and dividend policies has been an informal process because those policies have worked well. That is in large part because cash flow has remained strong enough for capital expenditures, dividends, and a stock repurchase program that can be controlled.

Efficient Frontier

Once every year, an investment banking firm prepares an efficient-frontier analysis for Monsanto. (The efficient frontier is the point at which taking on more debt starts to increase rather than decrease a company's cost of capital.) The analysis takes into consideration whether Monsanto should have more fixed-rate or floating-rate debt, longer or shorter maturities, or more foreign-currency borrowings. The purpose of the analysis is to develop an optimal mix of debt, given the company's objective of optimizing the cost of debt capital in light of its risk profile. After the most recent analysis, Monsanto was told that the composition of its debt portfolio was close to optimal. Hinshaw comments that the company has been fortunate in being able to adjust its debt portfolio on an opportunistic basis.

Instruments and Tactics

Monsanto is an active but conservative user of derivatives. Its overall policy is simple and straightforward: "Monsanto will prudently utilize derivative financial instruments to manage interest-rate and currency exposures and costs arising from the operation of its business. Monsanto will not create additional exposures, nor will it initiate or trade such instruments for financial profit." The policies were given a particularly thorough review in 1994, when Robert Hoffman joined Monsanto as its new CFO. He and the board were alerted after some other companies incurred large losses related to derivatives. Hinshaw was able to show Hoffman and the board's audit committee how gains and losses on each derivative transaction were offset by corresponding losses and gains on underlying positions. She and her staff are willing to look at new derivative products offered by bankers, no matter how complex they are, but generally do only transactions customized to fit the company's needs. The company regularly does interest-rate swaps, currency swaps, and swaptions. Monsanto has had relatively little recent need for interest-rate swaps because it took advantage of call provisions to restructure a large part of its debt portfolio in a low-interest-rate market three years ago. Sometimes the company finds favorable rates for borrowing overseas and swaps the debt back into dollars. At other times it uses foreign-currency debt to balance asset exposures in the same currencies.

Several years ago, Monsanto used derivatives to reduce the cost of tax-advantaged financing for expanding its NutraSweet plant in Augusta, Georgia. The lowest long-term fixed rate available for that type of financing was 9 percent. Instead, the company issued a series of one-month and one-year industrial revenue bonds and overlaid those instruments with floating-to-fixed swaps to achieve an overall 8.5-percent fixed rate.

In 1994, Monsanto had yen debt maturing but did not need additional yen financing until 1996. It used a forward-start contract to lock in favorable yen rates for a $100-million debt issue. (A forward-start contract is a contract whose effective life does not start until an agreed future date or until a specific event occurs. All terms of the contract normally are set at the trade date.) The contract was basically a put on a fixed-rate debt instrument; there were no associated swap features. The fundamental reason for the contract was to lock in the cash flows on the debt. However, as it turned out, the dollar strengthened against the yen as Hinshaw had forecasted, and Monsanto also gained $12 million on the $100-million issue.

Monsanto has used call provisions with its bonds when the price seemed reasonable and has used debt warrants under special circumstances. It has considered put bonds but has not found the right market conditions to use them. Hinshaw comments, "They come and go the same way preferred stock does." Put bonds have an embedded feature that permits the holder to sell the bonds back to the issuer or to a third party at par or close to par if interest rates rise or the quality of the issuer's credit declines.

The pricing for preferred stock looked good a couple of years ago, but long-term funds were not needed at that time. Monsanto was one of the first companies approached by investment bankers to float zero-coupon convertible bonds, which are callable by the issuer and puttable by the investor. The issuer pays a lower rate on zero-coupon convertible bonds than on regular bonds in exchange for the conversion feature. Imputed interest is tax-deductible each year even though the issuer does not pay it until maturity. (See Glossary for more detail.) Monsanto was confident its stock price would rise. Consequently, if it issued zero-coupon convertibles, conversion would be highly probable and possibly at an unfavorable price for the company. Therefore, Hinshaw did not consider zero-coupon convertibles suitable to Monsanto's needs.

Another product offered to Monsanto has been equity put warrants, which would provide premium income but also commit the company at least contingently to buy a certain number of shares during a specified period for a defined price. Monsanto has resisted, because even a commitment period as short as 30 days would restrict its flexibility to stop the stock buy-back program when there were seasonal cash needs, when operating cash flow was less than projected, and when the company was repairing its balance sheet after making an acquisition.

Satisfaction with Credit Rating

Hinshaw believes a single-A rating has been optimal for Monsanto and that either a higher or lower rating would have restricted its flexibility. A double-A rating would have required higher coverage ratios but would not have reduced the company's cost of borrowing substantially. If the company had decided to assume more debt to buy back more stock, thereby letting its rating slip to triple-B, it would have lost some of its flexibility to finance acquisitions with debt. Although some proponents of the economic-value-added performance measure recommend increasing leverage in this way, Hinshaw believes such a strategy is inappropriate for a growth company. Monsanto has been willing to pay the price for flexibility of restricting its borrowing to maintain a single-A credit rating.

Communication with the Markets

Sell-side analysts communicate their concerns to Monsanto through telephone calls to the investor-relations function and the treasurer. The analysts focus on strategic business issues and their effects on cash flow and earnings. They are interested in the stock buy-back program but do not pay much attention to capital structure. Hinshaw believes this is because the capital structure has stayed so constant. She observes that what sell-side analysts write indicates they are still interested in earnings per share, even though they profess to have a growing interest in cash flow over the longer term.

On any day Monsanto announces a major event, such as a planned acquisition, the investor-relations function arranges a conference call with securities analysts early in the morning. Hinshaw invites the rating-agency analysts to participate. She generally explains the financial issues after investor relations has discussed the strategic issues.

Discussions with Rating Agencies

The core of Hinshaw's discussions with the rating agencies is a confidential, two-year financial projection. She explains assumptions for sales growth, profit margins, tax rates, and capital expenditures in the context of the company's business strategy. The ratios most important to the rating agencies are the cash flow provided by operations compared with total debt obligations, interest coverage, and debt to capital. The agencies pay particular attention to the cash-flow statement but do not share every ratio they calculate with rated companies. Debt to capital, based on book values, is not as important as the coverage ratios.

Investor Mix

Institutional investors hold 65 to 70 percent of Monsanto's stock. Management would prefer to have a slightly higher representation of retail investors because they tend to stay with a stock longer, but it has not taken any specific steps to bring in more retail investors.

Stock Split

In 1996, Monsanto implemented a 5-for-1 stock split in contrast to its 2-for-1 splits in 1984 and 1990. Management was confident the stock price would continue to rise and also wanted to make the price of the stock more compatible with employee incentive plans. A lower price makes a psychological difference to Monsanto's business managers. Raising the price of a $30 stock through operating performance appears to be easier than raising the price of a $150 stock. Hinshaw believes the market has interpreted the stock split as evidence that management expects the stock price to continue to rise. However, she also believes that companies that do such transactions deliberately to send signals to the market often encounter problems.

Investment and Financing Decisions

There is generally no connection between Monsanto's individual investment and financing decisions. However, the right-hand side of the balance sheet sometimes determines the total level of capital expenditures and acquisitions. In periods following some of its larger acquisitions in recent years, Monsanto tends to hold back on additional investments until it can repair the balance sheet. As a result, some less strategic acquisitions and investments on the chemical side, which might have been approved in other circumstances, have been curtailed.

People Interviewed

Juanita H. Hinshaw, Vice President and Treasurer

Gregory E. Griffin, Director, EVA Stewardship

9

Oracle Corporation

Oracle Corporation develops, markets, installs, and supports computer software products used for database management, network communications, applications development, and end-user applications. Database management systems are used to support the data access and data management requirements of transaction processing and decision-support systems. Oracle's principal product is a relational database management system that allows multiple users to access data for multiple applications while protecting the data against user and program errors and computer and network failures. The system runs on a broad range of massively parallel, clustered, mainframe, minicomputer, workstation, and personal computer systems using an industry-standard SQL language.[1] A variety of applications development products sold as add-ons to the system increase programmer productivity and allow nonprogrammers to design and maintain some applications. Oracle also offers a family of end-user applications, including general ledger, purchasing, payables, assets, receivables, and revenue accounting programs. The company offers consulting, education, and systems integration services to help customers use its products. A summary of Oracle's recent financials is contained in table 9.1.

The demand for database management software to help organizations manage massive amounts of data stored in their computer systems has grown rapidly in recent years. Over the past 10 years, Oracle's sales and profits have both grown at a compounded rate of more than 50 percent per year. In fiscal year 1996, Oracle earned $603 million on revenues of $4.2 billion.

9

Table 9.1
Financial Summary: Oracle Corporation

(Dollar Figures in Millions)	1996	1995	1990	1985
Operating Summary				
Sales (Net)	$4,223	$2,967	$970	$23
Gross Profit Margin	78.1%	77.1%	87.1%	15.9%
Operating Profit Margin	22.6%	21.9%	19.5%	11.8%
Net Profit Margin	14.3%	14.9%	12.1%	6.5%
Dividend Payout Ratio	0	0	0	0
Sustainable Growth Rate*	18.0%	18.2%	14.9%	9.7%
Capitalization Summary				
Total Assets	$3,357	$2,425	$787	$15
LT Debt/LT Debt + Equity	0.05%	6.1%	18.7%	15.9%
Total Debt/Total Debt + Equity	0.3%	6.8%	25.3%	22.1%
Market to Book	11.6	12.4	7.7	NA

*[Net Income/Sales][Sales/Assets][1-(Dividend Payout Rate/Net Income)]

Capital-Structure Policy

Oracle has generally had a policy of low leverage. A summary of financials over the past 10 years shows that debt rose briefly to 18 percent of capitalization in 1990 and again in 1992. There were several reasons for these peaks. First, the ratios are distorted by rapid growth; Oracle's book equity in 1992 was only one-third of what it is today. Vice President and Corporate Treasurer Bruce M. Lange thinks that debt or cash as a percentage of revenue are more meaningful indicators. Second, at that time Oracle offered many of its customers terms as generous as 365 days. Third, even though software is one of the few industries that can throw off cash at high growth rates and Oracle has had limited capital expenditure requirements, any company growing as fast as 100 percent per year needs working capital. Finally, the company's success created a cavalier approach toward spending that management had to recognize and rein in.

In late 1996, Oracle filed a $350-million shelf registration, anticipating the issuance of public debt, and issued the debt in February 1997. The proceeds were used primarily for stock repurchases.

Capital Structure of Business Units

Currently, one capital-structure policy applies to the whole company. Although there are no immediate plans to change that policy, Lange can conceive that future parts of the business might justify higher leverage than the parent company has. For example, today Oracle leases software to customers and assigns the leases to financial institutions. It could consider setting up its own leasing subsidiary in the future. Other businesses, such as customer service and support, with predictable income streams might also be candidates for higher leverage someday. An example is the relational database business that Oracle recently bought from Digital Equipment Corporation.

Stock Repurchases

In recent years, Oracle has been buying back slightly less than the amount of stock required to offset the dilution from stock options granted to employees. The company's overhang (the number of shares on which there are options as a percentage of shares outstanding) is currently between 6 and 6.5 percent. This does not appear to be a huge problem when compared to another large software company's 20-percent overhang, but Lange wants to make sure that it does not become a problem in the future. A couple of years ago, it was relatively easy to buy back enough shares to keep dilution under 1 percent per year. It has been more difficult in the past year or so because Oracle's stock has been stronger, and consequently dilution has been creeping up to 2 percent per year. "To attract the right sort of people," says Lange, "we have to issue the options, but as a practical matter we don't want to use up all of our cash to buy back stock." To reduce dilution, Oracle is likely to put a small amount of debt on the balance sheet. Also, Lange notes that the company will generate more than $200 million in cash from stock issued for employee stock option programs. He thinks it is reasonable to use those proceeds for related stock repurchases as well.

9

Cash Reserves

Although Oracle's management has discussed the effect that debt could have on its cost of capital, the primary reason it plans to borrow is to support the company's substantial cash reserve and thereby preserve its flexibility. In the early 1990s, Oracle did not grow as fast as it might have because its balance sheet was not as strong as it is today. A strong balance sheet allows the company to take advantage of opportunities such as acquiring other companies or real estate. As a caveat, Lange notes management has been cautious about acquiring other software companies, because integrating their products into Oracle's product suite can require almost as much management time and effort as building similar products from scratch.

Lange notes that many of Oracle's competitors also have large amounts of cash on their balance sheets. A rather extreme example is one that recently did a $1-billion financing with $8 billion cash on its balance sheet. Lange would not want to go that far. Oracle has spent about half the cash it has generated in the past three or four years on discretionary items such as stock repurchases, real estate, and cash acquisitions, and the other half on increasing reserves. Going forward, the company's management is comfortable maintaining that balance.

Real Estate Ownership

Lange, in his capacity as treasurer, is responsible for Oracle's real estate facilities because they represent the major capital expense of the company. Because Oracle has been growing recently at 30 to 40 percent per year and added 8,000 new employees last year alone, planning ahead for leased space is a tough job. Sometimes, when real estate prices in a given metropolitan region appear to be cheap, Oracle buys land and starts to create a campus, building new office space at a rate that fits the company's needs. The company has taken this approach with core locations employing more than 1,000 people, such as its Redwood Shores, California, headquarters and its sites in the United Kingdom and Washington, D.C. Even for facilities not quite that large, Lange takes an opportunistic approach. Wherever the company needs a substantial amount of space, it usually has to arrange to construct a suitable building, and the landlord usually wants a 10-year lease. Signing a 10-year lease is not much different from owning the building. So Lange asks, "If we're paying for the building, why shouldn't we be left with the upside?" He adds, "You don't have to be a real estate guru to see that real estate goes in cycles. If a company needs space and has the capital, why should it not take advantage of being at the low point in the cycle?" When the market has been sinking for five or six years, there has been no recent construction, and the region's economy is growing, investing in real estate often appears to be a good decision. Lange believes that spotting real estate cycles is easier than predicting interest rate movements.

Fixed- and Floating-Rate Debt

Because Oracle has so little debt, it has never had to develop a policy for fixed- and floating-rate debt. If Oracle borrows in the near future, it can expect a high credit rating and may find the best opportunities in the public bond markets at fixed rates. However, Lange may then decide to swap some of that debt into floating rates to match the company's floating-rate investments.

Tax Issues

For a company as internationally based as Oracle, tax issues in many ways drive treasury issues. Setting up the right corporate structure in each country where cash is generated and planning how to remit it back to the United States has greater dollar implications than earning an extra five basis points on the company's investment portfolio. If cross-border cash management is not done properly, the company may accumulate large cash balances that are not needed for reinvestment in the business overseas but cannot be repatriated without a large tax penalty. For example, if an Oracle subsidiary in a given country does a local public offering and keeps the funds in that country, it will probably not incur any taxes. But if it sells secondary shares and brings the cash back to the United States, it may have to pay substantial taxes. Although generally Oracle would prefer to keep cash in countries with low tax rates, some countries have more favorable regulations than others for paying dividends from local subsidiaries to a parent in the United States. Every quarter, treasury reviews with the company's tax counsel which overseas subsidiaries should and should not be paying current dividends.

Dividends and Stock Repurchases

Oracle has never paid a dividend; instead, it has a regular stock repurchase program. The company's first priority for using excess cash has been to build up a substantial reserve, but it does not want to keep as high a cash reserve as some of its peers. This leaves the option of dividends or stock repurchases. Oracle's management prefers stock repurchases to dividends for two reasons. The first is flexibility. Although dividends are theoretically discretionary items, companies tend to maintain steady or increasing payouts that are difficult to reverse when cash is needed. Second, Lange believes that stock repurchases are a more tax-efficient way to return cash to investors.

Development and Approval of Policies

As part of the annual budget process, Lange reviews with the board expected dilution from employee stock options, cash forecasts, and how much cash he feels comfortable spending to repurchase stock. He also reviews these issues and their expected effect on the balance sheet with the board's finance committee on a quarterly basis. In calculating potential dilution, Lange assumes that all options granted will be exercised eventually and that all the proceeds from options exercised will be used to buy back stock.

Instruments and Tactics

In 1994 and 1995, Oracle sold put warrants and used some of the proceeds to buy call options on its common stock. This combination is sometimes called a costless collar. Most of these transactions were done at a time when Oracle's stock price had taken a fairly big hit, and management did not believe it would drop any further. Writing put warrants that would probably not be exercised was a good source of cash. If the puts had become exercisable, the company would have had the opportunity to settle up for net cash or buy back its stock. To the extent that premium income from the puts was used to buy calls, the company had an opportunity to repurchase its stock at a favorable price if the market price rose. Though Lange considered this an effective strategy a couple of years ago, he thinks it would be less effective today. Lange notes that a costless collar is analogous to borrowing money to own the stock, and that there are cheaper sources of funds than investment banking firms, especially when transaction costs are factored in. He explains that a costless collar has both a forward-contract and an option component. The prices of put warrants and call options differ because of the bid-offer spread, the volatility of the stock, and the time remaining until the expiration date. As those prices move closer together, the costless collar becomes less an option and more purely a forward, and the cost of the transaction is the interest carry on the stock position.

Oracle's treasury staff recently spent substantial time and legal fees investigating convertible debt securities, synthetic convertibles, and performance equity redemption cumulative stock (PERCS). PERCS is a form of mandatorily convertible preferred stock with a cap on the investor's upside opportunity. The treasury staff concluded that neither PERCS nor convertible debt securities, both bundled transactions where the debt has implicit options, is as efficient as a synthetic convertible. A synthetic convertible entails issuing debt and selling call warrants on the issuer's common stock, both at standard rates, either together or at different times. A synthetic convertible also has tax advantages. With a bundled transaction, the investor accepts a lower coupon in exchange for the warrant component. The lower coupon reduces the tax shield. If the warrants are sold separately, the premium income is not taxed, and the coupon on the straight debt provides a larger tax cover. Oracle did a synthetic convertible offering recently, issuing $350 million debt in February and selling warrants a month later.

Communication with the Markets

Securities analysts tend not to be very concerned with balance sheets in the software industry. The main balance-sheet issue for a software company is the small amount of assets that can be used as a borrowing base. Oracle's market capitalization is $36 billion, but the capitalized software development costs on its balance sheet are only $99 million. Under FASB Statement 2, almost all R&D expenses must be recognized when incurred. The only exception is development expenses for software products that will be sold. FASB Statement 86 permits those expenses to be capitalized after the company has ascertained that development of the product is technically feasible. Because Oracle currently borrows so little, the small amount of assets it can use as a borrowing base is not a problem. However, the small borrowing base did present a temporary obstacle when the company securitized some of its receivables in the early 1990s.

Distribution of Stock Ownership

Although 70 percent of Oracle's stock is held by institutions and only about 30 percent by individuals, the company still has a broad base of about 200,000 shareholders. Management is reasonably happy with the distribution. It sometimes has difficulty distinguishing between retail and institutional shareholders because many individuals hold shares indirectly through mutual funds.

Valuation Methods

Lange and his staff have done discounted-cash-flow valuations of Oracle, but the valuations they see in sell-side securities analysts' reports are based mainly on P/E ratios. In one recent report, an analyst set a target of twice the current growth rate for several well-known companies, meaning that the P/E ratios should be twice the companies' growth rates. Lange has difficulty seeing how the mathematics of such valuations work. The problem with discounted-cash-flow valuations for a company like Oracle is the future growth rate is difficult to project. Extrapolating Oracle's recent growth rate 10 or 15 years into the future produces revenues, earnings, and valuations that are too high to believe, but the management of a fast-growing company is sometimes reluctant to forecast a slowing growth rate.

Investment and Financing Decisions

In Oracle's core business of developing software, there is no direct connection between investment decisions and how projects are financed. However, as mentioned earlier, the company's decision to borrow is linked to its stock purchase program. It would also be conceivable for the company to compare the cost of borrowing to buy real estate with the cost of a 10-year lease.

Banking Relationships

Lange finds commercial banks and investment banking firms to be the best sources of new financing ideas. Of particular interest are firms that can discuss structuring transactions throughout the world. The other reason Lange likes to keep in touch with a variety of financial institutions is to help them understand Oracle and the software business so they will be receptive to future credit requests. He says, "Software can be a difficult industry for people to understand unless they have been involved for some time. It's not easy to get up to speed in a week or two."

A software company such as Oracle has substantial financial flexibility because 65 percent of its operating costs are employee expenses; it has very low capital expenditure requirements and almost no inventory. The most important planning issue is matching revenue growth and expense growth. In Lange's opinion, it is almost inevitable Oracle's growth will slow some day and the company will find it has hired too many people. Management is aware of this danger and is tracking revenue and expense growth carefully to ensure that a little margin compression does not turn into a major drop in earnings. Bankers also need to understand that modest margin compression does not mean the end of the company. That type of understanding comes from getting to know the business over time.

Endnote

1. SQL, pronounced "sequel," is a simple, English-like command language in which users define, retrieve, manipulate, and control data stored in a relational database management system (DBMS). IBM published the specifications for SQL in 1976. Oracle was founded in 1977 to develop a relational DBMS using IBM's SQL specifications.

People Interviewed

Bruce M. Lange, Vice President and Corporate Treasurer

Paychex, Inc.

Paychex, Inc., provides comprehensive payroll processing and human resource services to small and medium-sized clients. Payroll includes check processing, payroll tax preparation and filing, direct deposit, W-2s, and check signing. The human resource services include a professional employee organization (PEO), employee handbooks, 401(k) plan recordkeeping, and Section 125 plans. A PEO acts as a co-employer of a client's employees, relieving the business owner of responsibilities such as employment regulatory compliance, workers' compensation, health care, and 401(k) administration.

A summary of Paychex's recent financials is contained in table 10.1.

Table 10.1
Financial Summary: Paychex, Inc.

(Dollar Figures in Millions)	1996	1995	1990	1985
Operating Summary				
Sales (Net)	$325	$267	$120	$41
Gross Profit Margin	70.2%	70.6%	62.5%	63.1%
Operating Profit Margin	20.7%	19.1%	10.1%	11.2%
Net Profit Margin	16.0%	14.6%	7.2%	7.3%
Dividend Payout Ratio	28.7%	25.2%	22.8%	0
Sustainable Growth Rate*	17.6%	16.5%	13.5%	9.5%
Capitalization Summary				
Total Assets	$220	$168	$62	$21
LT Debt/LT Debt + Equity	0	0.4%	3.3%	16.2%
Total Debt/Total Debt + Equity	0	0.5%	4.5%	17.6%
Market to Book	15.8	9.4	4.4	5.3

*[Net Income/Sales][Sales/Assets][1-(Dividend Payout Rate/Net Income)]

B. Thomas Golisano founded the company in 1971 after recognizing that smaller businesses were an untapped segment of the payroll services market. He continues as its chairman and chief executive officer.

Through 75 branch centers and 23 sales offices, the company serves over 260,000 clients with an average of 14 employees, within a normal range of 1 to 200 employees. This represents 4.5-percent client penetration of a national market of 5.3 million businesses. The average penetration in the company's top 10 offices is 5.1 percent. Approximately 15 percent of businesses in the United States use outside payroll services; 5 percent use an in-house computer; 80 percent process their payrolls manually.

Paychex is one of three large players in the payroll outsourcing market. The other two are Automatic Data Processing, with 360,000 clients ranging from small to large, and Ceridian, with 40,000 clients, focused primarily on the large end of the market. Paychex has historically avoided the large end, where complex accounting requirements and customizing are more prevalent.

In the fiscal year ending May 31, 1997, Paychex earned $75 million on service revenues of $400 million. The company's total shareholder return has averaged more than 30 percent over the last ten years. Its NASDAQ-traded stock, part of the S&P MidCap 400, has traded over the past year at 40 to 50 times earnings.

The Paychex growth strategy is reflected in the formula Tom Golisano uses to manage and drive the business. The annual goal is to achieve a net 11-percent client gain, which should generate a 17- to 19-percent revenue gain, accompanied by profit gains over 25 percent. Recent profit growth has been 35 to 40 percent per year. A net 11-percent client gain requires hard selling. The company loses 22 percent of its existing clients each year and therefore must bring in new clients equal to 33 percent of its customer base to meet its growth objective. Approximately half the client losses relate to bankruptcies. There is some swapping among competitors, and Paychex believes it gains more than it loses.

Capital-Structure Policy

Golisano started Paychex with borrowed funds and expanded the business nationwide through franchises. In the late 1970s, the franchise network was consolidated into the company, and the franchisees became shareholders. Paychex raised funds with debt at that time and with an initial public offering of equity in 1983. The debt was paid down systematically as the company grew. Now Paychex has virtually no debt and does not expect to borrow in the near future. In recent years, cash flow from operations has been more than three times capital expenditures.

Cash and Short-Term Investments

Total balance-sheet assets of $1.2 million include cash and investments of $183 million and Electronic Network Services (ENS) investments of $897 million. The ENS investments relate to Taxpay® and direct deposit services, wherein the company acts as temporary custodian of funds between the time they are debited from client accounts and the time they are paid to the government or employee. The total investment account has recently averaged $1 billion. The funds are invested 50-percent long term and 50-percent short term, mostly in tax-free municipal securities.

Acquisitions for Stock

Despite a large cash balance, Paychex has taken advantage of its high P/E ratio to acquire other companies for stock. It has made two acquisitions over the past year and accounted for each as a pooling of interests. Pooling-of-interest accounting is helpful to Paychex because it does not require the recognition and amortization of goodwill. Pooling-of-interest accounting is also beneficial to sellers of acquired companies because it allows them to receive Paychex stock in a tax-free exchange. The disadvantage of pooling for Paychex is that it does not allow any part of a final purchase price to be based on future performance or contingencies not known as of the transaction date.

Reporting of Earnings and Cash Flow

In the opinion of John Morphy, Vice President and Chief Financial Officer of Paychex, one of the most important considerations in looking at earnings and cash-flow statements is whether earnings are calculated on an accurate and consistent basis. They should represent the actual performance of the entity as well as provide a basis to evaluate future earnings potential. Cash flow is extremely important. At Paychex, cash flow and earnings track very closely.

Tax Considerations

Tax considerations are not a major issue for Paychex when evaluating financing or capital requirements. All of its business is conducted in the United States. The company's primary tax considerations relate to its large tax-free municipal investment portfolio. Paychex has a very risk-averse position in investing both its corporate funds and those provided by its ENS product lines. Because the tax-free investment portfolio is so large, the company's effective tax rate is about 28 percent. The securities are classified as available for sale and, in accordance with accounting regulations, gains and losses are recognized in the income statement only when the securities are sold or a loss is deemed to be permanent.

Flexibility and Safety

Maximizing flexibility and minimizing risk are important considerations in Paychex's capital-structure policy. Maximizing income is not a capital-structure consideration, and control has not been an issue. Timing is an issue to the extent that favorable stock performance has helped the company make recent acquisitions for stock. The company has not had a recent equity offering and has no need for one in the foreseeable future. Paychex's capital structure has not changed since it repaid the debt incurred to start the company and consolidate the franchise operation. One capital structure applies to the entire company, because it is all essentially the same business.

Dividends and Stock Repurchases

Paychex paid its first dividend in 1988. Since then the dividend payout ratio has risen from 14 to 31 percent. Because of the rapid growth in earnings and free cash flow, dividends were increased 50 percent per year between 1992 and 1997. Management believes the level of dividends is appropriate and wants to continue sending positive signals on how it feels about the future.

Stock Repurchases

Paychex does not buy back stock, because at current prices buy-backs would dilute earnings per share and could prevent it from utilizing a pooling-of-interest accounting on acquisitions for as long as three years. In Morphy's opinion, a company repurchases stock primarily because it believes the stock is undervalued and that doing so will benefit the remaining shareholders.

Stock Splits

Paychex has declared seven 3-for-2 stock splits since public trading began in 1983. It believes the ability to do splits more frequently offsets the administrative benefits of doing 2-for-1 splits.

Development and Approval of Policies

The company developed its policy of minimal debt more than a decade ago. There has been no reason in recent years to consider changing it. Dividend policy is discussed at each board meeting. Historically, increases in the dividend have been announced close to the annual shareholders' meeting in October.

Instruments and Tactics

Paychex has virtually no need for short-term debt, has not considered convertibles, puts, or calls, and generally avoids capital leases. The company leases most of its office space, but Morphy recognizes that Paychex may have missed some real estate opportunities related to depressed prices in some areas of the country. Leasing property is usually considered preferable when the benefits of moving or expanding locations for a rapidly growing business are considered. Morphy is approached often for capital leases on data processing equipment but finds that owning the equipment is generally more economical. Paychex does not change software often and can generally use computer equipment for five to 10 years. Recently the company leased some of its printers because the vendor's pricing strongly favored leasing over buying.

Communication with the Markets

Paychex's performance, capital structure, and dividend policies have been simple and consistent. Morphy believes its stock price has benefited from this consistency, as well as from Tom Golisano's strong commitment to create shareholder value for both the short and long terms. Wall Street tends to not ask many questions about the company's capital structure or its large cash balance. The analysts are mainly interested in performance and earnings. They have been impressed with Paychex's high total shareholder return. Morphy says, "We have a well-known reputation for providing outstanding year-over-year earnings performance and are fully committed to do so in the future."

Credit Rating

Paychex has a very high credit rating based on its strong balance sheet. Because it has no public debt, it is not covered by the bond-rating agencies.

Investor Mix

About 55 percent of Paychex's stock is held by institutional investors.

Other Issues

Corporate Valuation

Morphy is not aware of any institutional investors who have valued the company based on estimated future cash flows discounted at the weighted average cost of capital. He believes that cash flow is usually a better basis than earnings for valuing a company. The difference between cash flow and earnings is not very large for Paychex because there are not many non-cash charges or significant balance-sheet issues.

Cost of Capital and Hurdle Rate

Morphy uses the approximately 6-percent pre-tax return on the company's investment portfolio as an informal hurdle rate. He believes Paychex would have a hard time increasing the return rate without taking substantial risk. Therefore, if someone in the company proposes a project with a return higher than 6 percent, he tends to favor it. He finds it hard to believe the company's real cost of equity capital would be as high as 16 to 18 percent, as calculated by the capital asset pricing model (CAPM), and that therefore its weighted average cost of capital (WACC) would be that high.[1] He does not find WACC to be a meaningful figure because it is not a practical hurdle rate, nor does he see any benefit in taking on debt to reduce WACC.

Business Strategy and Operating Performance

Whether or not a project clears the hurdle rate is not the only question, in Morphy's opinion. More important is whether the company can implement the project successfully and whether it helps the company achieve its growth strategy. To be successful, a company needs to be in a market that will reward its investment. Morphy's thinking about capital structure is similar. Of course a company needs to have an appropriate debt-equity ratio and needs to be able to show it can repay its debt. Some businesses can benefit from debt that is cheaper than equity and adjust their capital structures with stock repurchases. But a company's success is determined more by whether it can grow and generate a good return than by its capital structure. Too much attention to financial gimmicks or technical assumptions can divert management from what it should be focusing on—meeting the needs of all its customers.

Pitfalls of High Leverage

Morphy can see why a company generating excess cash might want to repurchase stock. He has a harder time understanding the logic of deliberately leveraging a company through a transaction such as a very large dividend coupled with a leveraged recapitalization. Perhaps it could be justified if a major shareholder or group of them wants to remove cash without selling the company or introducing a new group of shareholders. But if a leveraged recapitalization is required to motivate management, he thinks the principal owner or shareholder would be better served to look for a management team that can successfully grow a business without the burden of self-imposed liquidity pressure.

Endnote

1. Paychex's cost of equity capital is 16.73 percent, calculated by the following CAPM formula: Cost of equity capital = risk-free rate plus (common stock risk premium times beta). This is based on a 5-percent risk-free rate, the current rate for short-term Treasury bills, an 8.5-percent common-stock risk premium based on the 1926–1994 average calculated by Ibbotson and Associates, and Paychex's beta of 1.38.

People Interviewed

John Morphy, Chief Financial Officer

Sheplers, Inc.

S heplers, Inc., a private company headquartered in Wichita, Kansas, owns the world's largest chain of stores devoted completely to western wear and the world's largest western-wear retail catalog business. It has 23 stores serving nine states in the Midwest and Southwest and mails 20 million catalogs every year. The company's core function is summarized in its mission statement: "Sheplers Inc. is a customer-driven company whose mission is to generate reasonable profits by selling a complete assortment of high-quality, and good-value, western-wear merchandise at the retail level through high-quality facilities by providing excellent customer service." Former owner Harry Shepler put it a different way in 1968: "If it ain't western, if it ain't denim, if it ain't a jean or jean-related, it probably doesn't belong at Sheplers."

Company History

The company began in Wichita as the Gibson Harness Company in 1899. Founder J.W. Gibson continued to expand his harness and saddle business until 1946, when he sold it to Shepler. Over the next 20 years, Shepler added boots, jeans, and hats to the merchandise line and built a 10,000-square-foot store. Robert Dry, a local entrepreneur, bought the business in 1968. He built a new 24,000-square-foot store with Spanish-American architecture, high-beamed ceilings, and Southwestern decor, setting the style for future retail locations. Dry also added ladies' and other apparel to make Sheplers a well-rounded western store with goods for the entire family. The Sheplers catalog was initiated in 1970 with a mailing of 80,000. The first branch store, patterned after the parent store, was opened in Oklahoma City in 1973.

Part of a Conglomerate

W.R. Grace & Co., one of the nation's largest conglomerates, bought Sheplers in 1976 as part of a specialty retailing strategy that included the acquisition of chains such as Herman's World of Sporting Goods, Berman's Leather Goods, and Robinson's Jewelers. At the time of purchase, plans were already under way to open new Sheplers stores in Colorado and Texas. Under Grace's ownership, Sheplers continued to expand its store network as well as staffing, information systems, and a 50,000-square-foot warehousing and distribution center in Wichita for the mail-order catalog.

Urban Cowboy, a 1979 movie starring John Travolta, caused a surge in demand for western wear. A boom in sales caused retailers and manufacturers to add capacity. The fad died down several years later, causing a steep decline in western wear sales. Grace's strategy for resuming sales growth was to broaden the merchandise line beyond western wear to leisure wear, including items such as Izod sport shirts and espadrille shoes. This turned out to be a poorly conceived plan that failed to increase sales and blurred the store's identity with its core, western-wear customers.

New Management

After a period of losses in the early 1980s, Grace replaced Sheplers' president with the current CEO, Louis Cohen. It also brought in vice presidents of finance, stores, operations and personnel, merchandising, catalog marketing, and sales promotion who had broad experience in other retail organizations. John Mosley joined the company as chief financial officer and built a strong financial analysis, budgeting, forecasting, and reporting system to conform to Grace's requirements. The management team formed at that time owns and runs the company today.

Return to Core Strategy

After talking to customers and employees and becoming familiar with the business, Cohen decided that Sheplers needed to return to its foundation as a store with the best available selection of western wear. Other merchandise was marked down and sold. Mosley worked with merchandising and purchasing functions to develop realistic sales and cost projections based on continuing demand in the core market for western wear. The projections had to be modified slightly because it was not politically feasible to submit a budget showing a sales decline to the management of a large conglomerate—particularly one headed by Peter Grace. Sheplers' performance stabilized over the next couple of years and was modestly in the black by 1985.

Management's Buy-Out Offer

In December 1985, Grace announced that it planned to sell its retail holdings and retained two investment banking firms to find buyers. By this time the catalog side of the business was stronger than the retail side. Grace was willing to sell them together or separately. Sheplers' management indicated an interest in buying the company but had more difficulty than it expected convincing Grace that its offer was serious and credible. Throughout 1986, management cooperated with Grace by showing the company to other potential buyers while continuing to plan and negotiate its own leveraged buy-out.

In November 1986, Grace agreed to a price with Sheplers' management and set a year-end deadline for closing a sale. However, it did not give the management team an exclusive right to buy the company. There were still two other potential bidders who could have offered a higher price. The need for high leverage, the lack of a firm commitment from Grace, the state of the regional economy, and the tight deadline made the management team's negotiations with potential lenders almost impossible. Banks in the area were suffering from problems in oil, gas, and mining and a related decline in real estate values. They were also concerned about the fading fashion appeal of western wear.

Structure of the Initial Financing

During its search for financing, the management team benefited from a lucky coincidence. In late 1985, the Kansas Public Employees Retirement System (KPERS) decided to carve out a portion of its $4-billion portfolio for venture-capital investments in Kansas companies with proven track records. Sheplers approached the fund and appeared to fit its criteria. Because time pressure precluded Sheplers from arranging other funding prior to the year-end deadline, KPERS agreed to provide mezzanine financing, a bridge loan, and equity financing to supplement the equity provided by the six-member management team and an outside advisor. The deal was closed on December 29, 1986, with a traditional LBO balance sheet and equity ownership evenly split between management and KPERS.

The initial capital structure after the buy-out was as follows:

Bridge loan	$ 5,000,000
Working capital revolver	4,000,000
Mezzanine financing	4,000,000
Preferred stock	1,000,000
Common equity	1,200,000

Transition to Private Ownership

The transition to private ownership in early 1987 went relatively smoothly. Only three people had to be let go; two of them held jobs related to Grace's reporting requirements. The company assumed responsibility for its own taxes, insurance, and legal work. The control side of the finance function remained strong, and because management hoped to buy the company, it had made sure that the company was in good shape. While the company was for sale in 1986, management had adjusted both the level and the type of inventory to projected sales, getting rid of slow-moving stock and paring down expenses.

Since the LBO, Sheplers has been run by the six top members of management, who comprise an executive committee. Before the KPERS loan was repaid, a five-person board of directors consisted of the CEO and four outside members, two elected by the shareholders and two by KPERS. This structure gave the insiders control with three votes. But if the company defaulted on its loan, KPERS had the right to elect a third director, replacing one of the directors elected by the shareholders and thereby gaining a majority vote. In addition to the directors, John Mosley and Mike Anop, the Executive Vice Presidents of Finance and Administration, respectively, attended the meetings. Meetings were held once a month in the beginning, and have been held once a quarter since then.

Long-Term Bank Financing

At the time of the LBO, Sheplers' borrowing capacity was based not only on proven cash flow but also on the $10-million appraised value of its wholly owned stores in Wichita and Oklahoma City. The $5-million bridge loan from KPERS gave the company the time it needed to negotiate a senior loan collateralized by real estate as take-out financing.

To find a lender, Mosley first approached all the commercial banks, savings and loan associations, and insurance companies in Wichita. None of them was interested in lending to an LBO with recent losses. KPERS continued to extend its bridge loan, having little choice but comforted by continuing interest payments. Then it occurred to Mosley that Sheplers had been doing business in Oklahoma City for many years. Banks that were suffering from the oil bust might be interested in a nonenergy loan outside of Oklahoma. Through a Kansas banking commissioner, Mosley obtained contacts in the three largest Oklahoma City banks. Two were interested in talking. One agreed to a $5-million mortgage with a 30-year amortization, and it remains one of Sheplers' banks.

In early 1989, KPERS expressed an interest in liquidating its investment. The original agreement gave KPERS a put, but also gave the shareholders a call when the debt was repaid. An investment banking firm was hired to conduct an arm's-length appraisal of the company. In July, the shareholders exercised their right to pay off the mezzanine debt, to purchase the preferred stock, and to call the common stock owned by KPERS at the appraised value. Just two and a half years after the buy-out, $21 million was returned to KPERS, including $14 million for equity with a cost basis of $600,000. This represented the fund's greatest investment success story to date.

Sheplers' refinancing requirements exceeded the capacity of any bank in the Wichita area; most of them had legal lending limits of about $3 to $10 million. A $20-million, seven-year, senior term loan with no mezzanine financing was provided by a large regional bank that had developed substantial investment banking capabilities and had made several marketing visits to Sheplers following the LBO. The credit analysis was based almost entirely on projected cash flows. The regional bank was not constrained by the need for hard assets as back-up collateral to the degree most local banks were at the time. The company was leveraged more than five to one, but it had a strong management team and a good track record of sales and earnings growth. Covenants in the bank loan agreement included required working capital and ratios of debt to operating cash flow, cash flow to fixed charge, debt to equity, and current ratios.

Capital-Structure Policy

Mosley comments that if a company is doing well, capital structure is under its control, but if it is not doing well, capital structure is under the bank's control. Sheplers has never been a debt-free company and never intends to be. The timing of the company's debt issues has been driven by the chain of events related to the buy-out. It became a highly leveraged company in 1986 and again in 1989 because an LBO was the necessary tool for the management buy-outs. Since then, the company has reduced its leverage by retaining earnings and paying down the term loan. Management has been sufficiently confident in the company's continued strong operating performance and its ability to survive worst-case recession scenarios that it has paid down the term debt on schedule, but not ahead of schedule.

Internally Generated Cash

Internally generated cash is Sheplers' preferred source of funds for expansion. This source allows a comfortable pace of two or three new stores each year. Management does not want to take on additional external financing to expand more rapidly. More debt would increase the company's risk profile. Going public would change the company culture. At least some control would be ceded to outside investors and quarterly performance would be scrutinized by Wall Street analysts.

Cash Balances

When the company was owned by Grace, it held no cash. Holding cash would have hurt its return-on-capital-employed ratio. All cash was controlled at the corporate level, and subsidiaries wrote checks on zero-balance accounts (ZBAs). Mosley still prefers to hold virtually no cash, but instead to draw checks on a ZBA. Borrowings are adjusted every day under a revolving credit facility that he asked a local bank to coordinate with the ZBA. Usage under the revolver tends to rise during the summer and fall as the company is stocking up for the back-to-school and Christmas seasons and then drop again in the spring.

Financial Forecasting

The foundation of Sheplers' capital-structure policy is realistic financial forecasts. The company does both five-year forecasts and monthly forecasts going out 12 months. This allows Mosley to forecast usage under the revolving credit and compliance with the covenants well ahead of time. He has never had problems with debt repayment or covenants, but he has a system to spot potential problems and discuss them with the banks up to a year in advance.

Advantage of Operating Leases

Rather than borrowing to finance additional real estate for new stores, Sheplers prefers to sign operating leases. Sheplers has capital leases for two of its stores and operating leases for all the rest. The two capital leases are included in debt-coverage-ratio calculations, but Mosley comments that in substance the capital leases are no different from the operating leases.

To be conservative, Sheplers limits the term of its operating leases to five years and negotiates early-out clauses whenever possible. These clauses tend not to be unduly expensive because usually landlords are trying to attract Sheplers to their shopping centers. Early-out clauses were helpful in Houston, which Mosley describes as the most western big city in the country. The problem was an overcapacity of western-wear stores, all advertising and discounting heavily and none earning a good profit. After two years, Sheplers decided to leave Houston, exercised its early-out clauses, and moved all of its store fixtures to other locations. Having minimized its operating and financial exposure, the company was able to do an about-face without suffering any financial damage.

Mosley explains that this would have been a more difficult decision for a public company to make. "Even if it's the right decision, and profits are going up, Wall Street is going to clobber you because sales are going down." Unlike companies owned by the public or by conglomerates, Sheplers can make decisions based on the bottom line and not be overly concerned with volatility in the top line.

Fixed- and Floating-Rate Debt

All of Sheplers' bank debt has been at floating rates. In the beginning, the company paid 7 percent above prime on its term loan; now it pays 2 percent above LIBOR (London Interbank Offered Rate) on its revolving credit, term loan, and real estate facilities. When the company had higher leverage, half of its bank debt was covered by an interest-rate collar. Given the decline in interest rates since then, such protection could have seemed like a poor financial decision, but management preferred security of eliminating the risk of higher interest rates.

Employee Stock Ownership

Sheplers believes owning stock is the ultimate motivation for management. Although the company's senior executives made the best decisions they could in Grace's corporate interests before the buy-out, they started to think differently when they were owners. Their decisions were better thought out and more conservative.

The managers who bought the company took out personal bank loans and invested everything they had. They do not believe in stock options because no financial commitment is required of the people who receive them.

The company has offered a small amount of stock to key managers each year. The ownership group has gradually expanded to about 50, most with small holdings. Except for the directors, no outsiders own Sheplers stock, and only the director who acts as the company's management advisor holds a substantial interest.

Managers usually borrow money to buy their stock from local banks that are familiar with the company. None of them has ever been turned down. Upon termination—voluntary or involuntary—the company has a call on a manager's stock. Since the buy-out, all transactions have been at book value. Rather than constantly updating the appraised market value for stock transaction purposes, management prefers to be conservative and provide extra compensation in the form of bonuses.

Bonus Pool

Since the buy-out, a percentage of Sheplers' pre-tax income has been allocated to a bonus pool shared by all salaried employees. The CEO and the two executive vice presidents decide on each employee's bonus every year based on their perception of that person's value to the organization. The top six managers of the company have not received salary increases since the buy-out. A large part of their compensation is in the form of bonuses, which vary with company performance.

Financial Restructuring Alternatives

By 1992, the company was generating excess cash after paying down the bank term loan. With the help of the regional lending bank and several investment banking firms, it considered both a public offering and a leveraged ESOP to help the original six manager/stockholders, who had all of their wealth invested in the company, diversify their personal portfolios. The ESOP would have purchased about 20 percent of Sheplers' stock held by the original shareholders. Going public appeared to be feasible. Estimated valuations from the investment banking firms were considerably higher than management had expected.

These discussions caused the management team to reexamine its own objectives. It came to two conclusions. First, the purpose of a public offering is to raise money for expansion. A company that uses a public offering just to take out money is likely to be penalized. Second, the company would receive a premium over book value for its stock only if projected annual growth were 20 percent or greater. To achieve this growth, Sheplers would have to open five stores per year rather than two or three. Management would have to accept advice from the outside world on how to run the company. In an industry of mostly private companies, it would have to release financial information to the public, including its competitors. Therefore, management decided not to go public at that time.

Another alternative considered at that time was a leveraged recapitalization coupled with a substantial one-time dividend to the shareholders. Even though this would have created a huge negative equity number on the company's balance sheet, the regional lending bank was willing to support it. This alternative was rejected because the shareholders would have had to pay taxes at the ordinary-income rate on the dividends.

Corporate Legal Structure

Before the buy-out, Sheplers, Inc., was a C corporation wholly owned by Grace. Sheplers Catalog was organized as a wholly owned subsidiary of Sheplers, Inc., giving Grace the flexibility to sell the catalog separately if it so desired. When the management team bought the company, it formed a new C corporation, Sheplers Enterprises, Inc., as a holding company to own the two existing C corporations. From a legal standpoint, it was easier to sell shares or incur debt at the holding-company level, leaving assets to guarantee those obligations at the operating-company level. When management bought out KPERS, it formed another new company, Sheplers Western Wear, Inc., to buy the stock in Sheplers Enterprises that had been owned by both management and KPERS. Sheplers Enterprises was merged down into the operating subsidiary, leaving Sheplers Western Wear as the owner of Sheplers, Inc., and Sheplers Catalog.

Conversion to S Corporation

In 1993, management decided to convert from a C corporation to an S corporation, which Sheplers remains today. Earnings for an S corporation are not taxed at the corporate level. Instead, each stockholder is taxed for his or her proportionate share of the earnings, whether or not cash dividends are paid. Subsequent cash dividends are not taxed because they are considered a return of capital. Normally, an S corporation pays shareholders at least enough in dividends to cover their tax liability.

For Sheplers, the purpose of the conversion was to go beyond that level of dividends. Mosley said to his colleagues, "You don't have to sell the company to realize value." The dividends helped the shareholders realize some of their increased equity value in Sheplers with the least possible tax burden. For the first 18 months after the conversion, the company kept its level of equity constant and paid out all of its earnings in dividends. Distributing cash to the shareholders and helping them diversify their personal investment portfolios was a carefully considered alternative to reinvesting the funds in the company for faster growth. The directors and employees were offsetting forces that caused management to seek a balance between bonuses and dividends.

The directors hold stock but are not eligible for bonuses. Conversely, many employees are eligible for bonuses but do not own stock.

Phantom Stock Plan

In order to convert to an S corporation, Sheplers was required by tax law to replace its subsidiaries with limited partnerships and to reduce the number of its shareholders from 50 to 35. A phantom stock plan was created for managers who could not be actual stockholders. Holders of phantom stock received every stockholder's right except for a vote. Dividends were paid. Funds used to purchase the phantom stock (also known as a stock appreciation right) were deducted from a manager's pay and put into a deferred compensation account. When the manager left the company, the amount received from the deferred compensation account was based on the audited book value of the company's stock as of the prior fiscal year-end.

Management Philosophy

Immediately after the buy-out, management discussed and carefully articulated a corporate philosophy. Mosley recalls, "We were conservative by nature and wanted to win the game by hitting singles, not home runs." Part of management's conservative policy was always to beat the budget. A conservative sales forecast was the basis for cost and inventory planning. Mosley says, "If things are going better, it's easy to add more expense and more inventory. It's a lot more difficult to go the other way."

Expansion Program

By 1988, Sheplers was able to resume its expansion program. It experimented with 3,000-square-foot boot and accessory stores in shopping malls but decided to stick mainly with the proven larger store format it established in Wichita. The new stores ranged from 15,000 to 25,000 square feet, depending on the size of suitable space in the market. During the next several years, the company opened additional units in Arizona, Kansas, Nevada, Tennessee, Texas, Utah, and other locations with well-established demand for western wear.

Strategic Planning

Since the buy-out, the management team has held an annual, off-site strategic planning meeting. The dean of Wichita State University's business school acts as a facilitator. For two days, members of the executive committee discuss the company's long-term direction, addressing issues such as how many stores it should open, whether the current capital structure is still suitable, and whether the owners would ever want to cash out through a public offering or sale to another company. Each executive also shares his personal goals—how much longer he wants to work at the company, when he might want to sell his stock back to the company. This helps the company and its management owners ensure that corporate and personal goals are aligned. After discussing these issues in depth, management can return and concentrate on running the business.

Development and Approval of Policies

Financial policies are generally developed by Mosley, coordinating closely with Cohen and Anop. In developing these policies, Mosley also works closely with the regional bank, the company's Big Six accounting firm, and its law firm in Kansas City.

Communication with Shareholders

Management holds a shareholders' meeting every year to provide an in-depth review of results for the prior year, the budget for the coming year, and the five-year plan. The shareholders, who are also the key people who run the company, are also briefed whenever major events such as the KPERS buy-out occur.

External Communication

Sheplers does not share financial information with rating agencies. It provides financial information to parties with a need to know, such as vendors, banks, and landlords. Every page has a confidentiality stamp that forbids the party to show the information to another party. For example, if a landlord needs to provide Sheplers' financial information to the institution that has mortgaged the shopping center, it notifies Sheplers, and Sheplers sends the financial information directly to the institution.

Ratios and Analytic Tools

The most important financial measures for Sheplers are pre-tax profit, operating profit, direct store profit, gross profit, and inventory turnover. The company also calculates gross margin return on investment to measure the return on its inventory investment for merchandise classifications such as jeans, shirts, and boots. Mosley comments that the retail business is measured mostly by profit and loss because the primary asset is inventory.

Valuation Methods

On the two occasions when investment banking firms were hired to value Sheplers, their primary method was to use comparable companies' multiples of price to earnings and price to earnings before interest, income taxes, depreciation, and amortization. Mosley is not aware of any valuations using projected free cash flow discounted at the weighted average cost of capital.

Reasons for Success

Mosley believes that the most important factors in Sheplers' success have been the management team's prior experience, the team's ability to work well together, its conservative philosophy, the fresh perspective of the outside board of directors, the favorable price of the buy-out, and the support of the regional lending bank. The board acts as a check to keep management from being self-serving. Management's conservative approach has helped the company weather economic cycles. The management team was able to avoid the pitfall of many other LBOs: paying too much and making unrealistic assumptions about assets that could be sold or spun off. The bank was confident enough to base its loan on projected cash flows. Since then, as the loan has been paid down, the bank has been willing to finance several acquisitions management has considered based strictly on Sheplers credit, with no consideration of the targets' cash flows.

For the time being, the management team is comfortable retaining ownership and continuing to expand the company at a moderate pace. No one feels that now is the right time to consider a sale, a partial sale, a public offering, or a leveraged recapitalization, but any of these alternatives could be considered in the future.

People Interviewed

John T. Mosley, Executive Vice President and CFO

SymmetriCom, Inc.

SymmetriCom, Inc., formerly Silicon General, Inc., began as an electronics company in 1956. It now conducts business through two separate operating units: Telecom Solutions, a division that generates about 60 percent of revenues, and Linfinity Microelectronics, a subsidiary that generates 40 percent of revenues. The company's current sales level is $150 million. A summary of SymmetriCom's recent financials is contained in table 12.1.

Telecom Solutions was started in 1986 to take advantage of the competition introduced to the North American telecommunications market by the break-up of AT&T. Its primary manufacturing facility is located in Puerto Rico. Telecom Solutions is a leading worldwide supplier of advanced network synchronization systems for the telecommunications industry. A synchronization system provides a regulating pulse that enables various data streams to merge without losing message packets or allowing electronic collisions that degrade or slow transmission. The division's Navstar Systems, Ltd., unit, based in England, designs and manufactures equipment that calculates precise geographic locations based on satellite global positioning technology.

Linfinity Microelectronics, Inc., formerly the Silicon General Semiconductor Group, designs and manufactures linear and mixed-signal integrated circuits as well as modules used in power supply, data communications, and signal-conditioning applications for commercial, industrial, defense, and space markets.

Capital-Structure Policy

The only debt on SymmetriCom's balance sheet is a mortgage on a semiconductor plant. The company has several operating leases that are not capitalized. Total debt as a percentage of capitalization has declined from 33 to 7.5 percent in the past eight years. Therefore, debt-equity and coverage ratios are not a material issue.

Table 12.1
Financial Summary: SymmetriCom, Inc.

(Dollar Figures in Millions)	1996	1995	1990	1985
Operating Summary				
Sales (Net)	$106	$103	$58	$46
Gross Profit Margin	43.6%	45.6%	33.6%	41.9%
Operating Profit Margin	7.8%	10.5%	4.0%	18.4%
Net Profit Margin	7.1%	10.0%	2.0%	20.8%
Dividend Payout Ratio	0	0	0	0
Sustainable Growth Rate	8.0%	12.1%	2.8%	12.8%
Capitalization Summary				
Total Assets	$94	$85	$41	$75
LT Debt/LT Debt + Equity	7.5%	8.8%	16.3%	19.8%
Total Debt/Total Debt + Equity	7.5%	8.8%	18.6%	33.2%
Market to Book	3.0	5.5	1.5	2.0

Cash Reserve

More important than debt as a percentage of capitalization is the level of cash and short-term investments, currently about one-third of book assets. J. Scott Kamsler, Senior Vice President and Chief Financial Officer, says, "A substantial amount of cash gives us peace of mind, the opportunity to finance our growth internally, and the ability to repurchase stock when the price is low. It helps us weather significant changes in business that typically have impacted high-technology industries. In the longer term, it gives us the ability to acquire companies for either cash or stock, although we don't have a specific acquisition strategy."

Investment Decisions and Capital Requirements

The nature of investment decisions and capital requirements in the two businesses is quite different. On the telecommunications side, reinvestment to grow is more through R&D than plant and equipment, and therefore new external capital is not required often. In developing its

R&D budget, Telecom Solutions' management must decide how much to restrict current earnings for future growth and how to allocate funds among projects based on their risk/reward profiles to create a balanced portfolio. Higher risk/higher return projects must be balanced against lower risk/lower return projects. Resources must be spread to avoid "betting the company" on any one project. Kamsler can remember learning in business school about the advantages of net-present-value analysis and the weaknesses of payback analysis for investment decision making. For a large investment in plant and equipment, net-present-value analysis would be necessary. However, for a company such as SymmetriCom, trying to grow within two fast-changing industries, payback is a particularly helpful measure as risk increases with lengthened time to market. Therefore, it is easier to justify higher risk projects with shorter paybacks. The faster the payback for a project, the faster the impact on sales, the sooner the return of cash to invest in new projects, and the lower the risk of technological obsolescence.

The semiconductor business requires more capital assets than the telecom business. "Make-or-buy" decisions must be made. A relatively small player such as Linfinity can make a substantial investment in its own wafer fabrication plant, known in the business as a "fab," or it can subcontract wafer fabrication to a manufacturer with excess plant capacity, known in the business as a "foundry." If revenues from semiconductor products are sufficiently high, the company can earn higher margins by having its own fab. Even in these circumstances, some smaller companies prefer to subcontract wafer fabrication, accepting lower margins but also minimizing the risk associated with a large plant investment.

Challenges in the Semiconductor Business

During the past several years, Linfinity has confronted two challenges: the need to develop new products and the cyclical nature of the industry. Until recently, Linfinity survived by selling analog semiconductor products, many of which were developed more than 10 years ago. Sales were flat primarily because the company chose to use most of the cash generated by its semiconductor unit to fund the start-up of its telecom business rather than investing significant amounts in new semiconductor product development. In 1992, the company began to reinvest in its semiconductor business as its telecom unit was able to fund itself. Linfinity hired a new chief operating officer, set up a new marketing department, and raised R&D expenditures from 3 to 15 percent of revenues. Sales of new products began to pick up in early 1996, just in time to lessen the impact on the company of the cyclical downturn in the semiconductor industry. The 1996 downturn, like many previous ones, was particularly severe because of a ripple effect. When personal-computer orders are strong, plant capacity tends to become tight. Original equipment manufacturers (OEMs) often attempt to protect themselves by placing simultaneous orders for components with several suppliers. When more plant capacity becomes available, delivery times usually shorten, and OEMs cancel their excess orders, causing a disproportionate drop-off in suppliers' sales.

Linfinity's management is currently evaluating whether or not it should expand its fab facilities, and if it does, how it will finance them. The business is currently running at a sales rate of about $50 million per year. The expansion could cost $20 million to $40 million or more. This is a relatively small amount by industry standards but a huge capital expenditure for a company of Linfinity's size. Kamsler explains that the plant can be expanded in steps, but that the first step is very large. "We would have to go up several flights of stairs all at once." The expansion would have to be financed either with new equity, which would dilute the stake of existing shareholders, or with debt, which would raise the level of fixed costs and put the company at risk in case of another industry slowdown. Although the company could possibly generate higher margins by manufacturing all of its wafers—assuming a sufficient level of sales—there are other successful semiconductor companies that subcontract to foundries. Also, in today's market there are foundries with excess capacity looking for business. Because Linfinity has begun just recently to introduce successful new products and to start growing again, management is inclined to be conservative and postpone a major plant expansion for as long as possible.

Possible Spin-Off

Telecom Solutions and Linfinity Microelectronics are run as two entirely separate companies under one corporate umbrella. There are no transactions or other business relationships between them. Being in two separate businesses hampers SymmetriCom's access to the capital markets. Semiconductor companies and telecommunications equipment companies are usually followed by separate securities analysts in large investment banking and brokerage firms. Because SymmetriCom is small and requires two analysts, most large investment advisors prefer not to allocate the resources to follow it. Most of the company's coverage is from analysts in smaller regional firms who cover a broad range of high-technology companies or special situations. Consequently, management believes the two businesses ultimately could have higher market values as separate companies, each with a separate, focused business strategy to convey to the capital markets. Kamsler says, "We think the sum of the parts would be greater than the whole." SymmetriCom has considered selling Linfinity but does not need the cash. An investment banker has been hired to help management consider all possible alternatives, such as a partial or full divestiture, a spin-off, or even keeping the company and building it through acquisitions.

When Linfinity's new chief operating officer was hired, Linfinity was incorporated as a separate subsidiary and allocated a portion of the corporation's cash, other assets, and liabilities. The business was valued as a separate concern but without the benefit of tax-loss carry-forwards, which were retained at the corporate level. A stock compensation plan was developed to link Linfinity's management to the future performance and valuation of the business. When the subsidiary can demonstrate a good financial track record and market conditions are favorable, it will probably be spun off.

Currently, Telecom Solutions has substantial cash balances and modest capital requirements, while Linfinity has less cash and significant capital requirements. Even if Linfinity decides not to build a new fab, its existing fab needs capital for new equipment. However, because management wants to keep the two businesses separate, any corporate funding for new investment in the semiconductor business will be through arm's-length transactions at market rates.

Tax Considerations

Under current tax law, the tax shield from stock options exercised is an important source of equity capital for a company with a rising stock price such as SymmetriCom. Kamsler illustrates this with a simple example. An employee is granted an option to purchase stock at $30 when the company's stock price is $30. During the year following the option grant, the stock price rises to $40 and the employee decides to exercise the option. The employee pays the company $30 and gains $10. Under Accounting Principles Board (APB) Opinion 25, the company accrues no compensation expense because there is no difference between the option price and the market price at the date of grant. However, the difference between the option price and the market price on the exercise date is treated as a tax-deductible compensation expense for the corporation and compensation on the employee's W-2 if the option is a nonqualified option; or in the case of an incentive option, if the option is disposed of within one year of the exercise date.[1] Because of tax benefits related to a plant in Puerto Rico, and other tax benefits such as California production and R&D equipment tax credits, SymmetriCom's effective tax rate has been in the 20-percent range in recent years.

Dividends and Stock Repurchases

Kamsler believes that investors normally do not expect a growing high-technology company to pay a dividend, and SymmetriCom has never paid one. He cites Intel as an exception because it is generating such a large amount of cash. But SymmetriCom continues to have strategic reasons to maintain a substantial cash balance. Someday, if such a surplus is not needed, Kamsler believes that buying back stock to increase the return on equity would be a more effective use of cash than paying dividends—particularly if the stock price falls, making repurchase more of a bargain. Recently, SymmetriCom started a stock repurchase program to offset the dilution created by shares issued under its stock option plans.

Development of Policies

Because SymmetriCom is a relatively small company, financial policies can be developed informally among Kamsler, the CEO, and the division heads. There is a mutual understanding of why the company does not pay dividends and how divisional performance results are affected by capital expenditures and increases in inventory and receivables. Division heads are measured primarily by their P&Ls. Inventory and receivables increase interest expense, and capital expenditures increase both depreciation and interest expense.

Kamsler attends all board meetings. Each operation proposes a capital expenditure program as part of the planning process each year. In unusual circumstances, important capital expenditures outside the plan can be approved by the board in a conference call.

Management develops a strategic plan before preparing the annual budget each year. The CEO and Kamsler have monthly financial reviews with the division heads and also work with them on a day-to-day basis. For example, they might question whether the expectation of large orders justifies increased inventory or whether credit terms are needed to increase international sales. Kamsler is aware of the implicit interest cost of inventory and receivables but is more concerned about the danger of having to write them off.

Financial Instruments

SymmetriCom's only reason for using derivatives has been to hedge accounts receivable in foreign currencies. Most of its current overseas customers are willing to pay dollars, but Kamsler foresees the need in the future to bill in foreign currencies to stay competitive. He cites a large high-technology equipment manufacturer that has a competitive advantage because it has natural hedges that help it quote prices several years forward in currencies throughout the world.

Distribution of Stock Ownership

Institutional ownership of SymmetriCom's stock was 40 percent in the late 1980s, but has since declined to 20 percent. At one point, a venture capital and investment banking firm specializing in high-technology companies owned 10 percent of the company. In the early 1990s, SymmetriCom's stock was selling for $1 or $2 a share. When it rose, many institutions that had bought the stock at lower prices cashed out of their positions. Many of the shares sold by the institutions were purchased by retail investors. Kamsler observes that retail shareholders tend to stay with a stock and ride the ups and downs. SymmetriCom has had to contend with momentum players who buy in when the stock starts going up and then dump their positions whenever there is any sign of weakness. On the other hand, Kamsler believes that if more of the company's stock is held by institutional investors with a long-term perspective, volatility in the stock price could be reduced without significantly impacting liquidity.

Corporate Valuation

SymmetriCom's management periodically compares the semiconductor and telecommunications businesses with their peers based on ratios of their market prices to earnings, sales, invested capital, book assets, net assets, earnings before interest and taxes (EBIT), and EBITDA; compound annual growth rates (CAGRs), and performance ratios such as return on sales and return on assets. Kamsler states that some analysts value a company based on a rule of thumb that equates the CAGR with the P/E ratio. He notes that SymmetriCom has a capitalized lease for its new office, but that many companies avoid capitalized assets whenever possible because of their effect on operating ratios. When Linfinity was organized as a separate subsidiary, the two principal methods the appraiser used to value the business were based on discounted future cash flow and the comparison of Linfinity with its peers based on various market-multiple ratios.

Endnote

1. Accounting for stock options is covered in APB Opinion 25 and FASB Statement 123. In a stock option and purchase plan, an employee is granted the right to purchase a fixed number of shares at a certain price during a specified period. The option or purchase price may be either at or below the stock's current market price. Under APB 25, the cost of compensation to the employer corporation is measured by the excess of the quoted market price of the stock over the option price on the measurement date, which is the first date that the number of shares the

employee is entitled to receive and the option price are known. This is known as the intrinsic value method.

Statement 123, effective for financial statements for fiscal years beginning after December 15, 1995, describes a method of accounting for stock compensation plans that is based on the fair value of employee stock options and similar equity instruments. The fair value of the stock option is estimated using an option pricing model such as Black Scholes. As of the grant date, the following factors are taken into consideration: the exercise price of the option, the expected life of the option, the current price of the underlying stock, the expected volatility of the underlying stock, expected dividends on the stock, and the risk-free interest rate for the expected term of the option. The fair value of the option estimated on the grant date is not subsequently adjusted for changes in the price of the underlying stock or changes in other variables, such as the volatility, dividend, or risk-free interest rate. Compensation cost is recognized over the period during which related employee services are rendered. Because this method was controversial when it was introduced, FASB now encourages but does not require the new method to be used for accruing the compensation expense related to stock options on corporate income statements. If a company continues to use APB 25, it is required to disclose the pro forma net income and earnings per share as if the fair-value-based accounting method described in Statement 123 were used.

There are different tax implications for incentive stock options and nonqualified stock options. An incentive stock option is granted under a plan approved by a company's shareholders within 10 years of plan adoption. The option is neither transferable nor exercisable more than 10 years from the grant date. The option price may not be less than the fair market value of the stock on the grant date. A nonqualified stock option is one that does not meet the requirements for an incentive stock option.

For incentive stock options, there are no tax implications on the grant date for either the corporation or the employee. There are no tax implications on the exercise date for the corporation except for disqualifying dispositions, which is explained below. For the employee, the difference between the amount paid for the stock and its fair market value on the exercise date is recognized as compensation for alternative minimum tax purposes in the year the option is exercised. The compensation is considered an increase in the employee's basis in the stock. The basis is the purchase price for the purpose of calculating the capital gains tax. There are no other tax implications for the employee for regular tax purposes. When the stock is sold, there are no tax implications for the company except in the case of a disqualifying disposition. The employee must recognize the difference between the sales price and the exercise price as a capital gain.

A disqualifying disposition is the sale of stock within two years of grant or within one year of exercise. The excess of the fair market value over the option price on the exercise date or the sale date, whichever is less, is included in the employee's W-2 in the year the stock is sold. The employee's basis in the stock is the amount paid for the stock plus the compensation recognized. The corporation deducts as compensation expense the same amount the employee recognizes as compensation.

For nonqualified stock options, there are no tax implications for the corporation or the employee on the grant date but tax implications for both on the exercise date. The difference between the amount paid for the stock and the fair market value on the exercise date is included in the employee's W-2 in the year the option is exercised. The employee's basis in the stock is the amount paid for the stock plus the compensation recognized. The corporation deducts as compensation expense the same amount the employee recognizes as compensation.

People Interviewed

J. Scott Kamsler, Senior Vice President, Finance and Chief Financial Officer

TELUS Corporation

TELUS Corporation, based in Edmonton, Alberta, is a management holding company whose subsidiaries provide voice, data, and visual telecommunications services, and advertising services. TELUS, formerly the Alberta Government Telephones Commission, is the third largest telecommunications company in Canada. TELUS Communications, TELUS' largest subsidiary, provides voice and data communications services throughout Alberta. TELUS Edmonton Holdings, operating through its largest subsidiary, TELUS Communications (Edmonton), provides voice and data communications in the local Edmonton market. TELUS Mobility is Alberta's leading supplier of wireless, voice, and data communications through cellular, paging, and private radio systems. Canadian Mobility Products provides distribution services for cellular telephones, pagers, and accessories across western Canada. TELUS Advanced Communications markets high-speed data and Internet services to business customers. TELUS Advertising Services publishes 30 White and Yellow Pages™ and special directories in Alberta. TELUS Marketing Services provides call center services. TELUS Multimedia conducts experimental technical and marketing field trials. TELUS also, until recently, held interests in two partnerships: ISM Alberta, the largest Alberta-based information technology services company, and Telecential Communications, which provides cable television and telephone services in the United Kingdom. ISM Alberta was jointly owned with an IBM Canada subsidiary, and Telecential Communications was jointly owned with a subsidiary of KPN, the largest communications company in the Netherlands. A summary of TELUS' recent financials is contained in table 13.1. All currency amounts in the chapter are in Canadian dollars.

TELUS was formed in 1990 when the Alberta Government Telephones Commission was reorganized and privatized. In Canada's largest initial public offering to that date, $896 million was raised from the sale of TELUS common shares. Most of the shares were sold at $12

Table 13.1
Financial Summary: TELUS Corporation

(Dollar Figures in Millions)	1996	1995	1991
Operating Summary			
Sales (Net)	$1,914	$1,664	$1,238
Operating Profit Margin	20.5%	19.7%	21.5%
Net Profit Margin	12.7%	11.5%	14.8%
Dividend Payout Ratio	54.1%	67.6%	66.9%
Sustainable Growth Rate*	5.5%	4.2%	5.6%
Capitalization Summary			
Total Assets	$4,404	$4,572	$3,234
LT Debt/LT Debt + Equity	42.8%	50.3%	42.4%
Total Debt/Total Debt + Equity	46.8%	52.6%	43.9%
Market to Book	1.9	1.5	1.5

*[Net Income/Sales][Sales/Assets][1-(Dividend Payout Rate/Net Income)]

Note: All currency amounts are in Canadian dollars.

per share to individuals in Alberta on an installment basis, with $6 per share payable at the time of purchase and the balance due in a year. In 1991, the provincial government sold its remaining shares for $870 million, also on an installment basis. TELUS entered into the ISM Alberta partnership in 1992 and the Telecential Communications partnership in 1993. It purchased Edmonton Telephones, now TELUS Edmonton Holdings, in 1995.

TELUS' corporate strategy is centered on providing excellent customer service, growing the business, and maintaining strategic focus in its lines of business. To grow the business, the company is conducting trials to develop new multimedia services, pursuing enhanced services, and making investments outside Alberta to develop or leverage core skills. In pursuing excellent customer service, the company strives for continuous improvement in the quality of its processes and unit costs. For example, the company has significantly reduced employment through voluntary separation programs, outsourced terminal equipment sales, and disposed of assets connected with an international consulting and venture capital operation. To maintain strategic focus, the company is concentrating on four lines of business: voice, data, visual, and advertising. In pursuing these lines of business, TELUS, where practical, is organizing its sales effort so that one salesperson represents all TELUS telecommunications products to a given customer. TELUS is striving to have the Canadian federal government and the Canadian Radio-television and Telecommunications Commission eliminate regulated subsidies and handicaps that restrict competition in the telecommunications market.

Capital-Structure Policy

TELUS Corporation has a board-approved capital-structure target of 60-percent equity and 40-percent debt. It is the board's policy to review that target periodically to make sure it is appropriate for TELUS and its business environment. Also, the regulator of the two telephone subsidiaries uses a guideline for equity of 55 percent of capitalization for TELUS Communications.

The target ratio of 60-percent equity and 40-percent debt is influenced by several factors, including credit rating, business risk, and the need for flexibility. TELUS, the parent, has not borrowed in the public markets and does not have a credit rating, but TELUS Communications has a single-A rating issued by the Canadian credit rating agencies.

When TELUS was organized in 1990, it was essentially a regulated telephone utility. Since then, it has built up a substantial group of telecommunications businesses that are not regulated on a rate-of-return basis. During that time, technological and structural changes have increased the level of business risk in the telecommunications industry. As management has perceived greater risk, it has preferred to increase the equity portion of the capital structure. To preserve capital, it has kept the level of dividends flat while earnings have risen. A conservative balance sheet gives the company not only risk protection but also borrowing capacity in the event of strategic acquisition opportunities.

TELUS' strong cash-generating capacity allows it to increase debt temporarily and then return to its longer term debt-equity target. In 1995, the company financed its $467-million acquisition of Edmonton

Telephone with bank debt, moving total debt from 40 to 50 percent of capitalization. By early 1997, debt was reduced to 41 percent of capitalization, and subsequently with the divestiture of ISM Alberta and Telecential Communications, the level of debt was reduced to 35 percent.

Use of Internally Generated Funds

TELUS prefers to use internally generated funds for capital investments because it has strong cash flow driven by significant depreciation on its fixed assets. As long as the nature of its business does not change, the company expects to be able to satisfy all of its current investment needs internally with the possible exception of future acquisitions.

Floating-Rate Debt and Taxes

In 1995, floating-rate debt was restricted to 12.5 percent of assets to limit the company's income volatility. At that time, TELUS was paying no taxes because of a heavy depreciation tax shield resulting from assets that were transferred to its tax books on an undepreciated basis at the time of privatization. Therefore, the company had no tax shield against interest-rate volatility. Treasury expects to review this policy in 1998 and perhaps recommend a higher floating-rate debt limit to the board, because TELUS is becoming taxable, and the company's overall level of profitability is sufficient to cover an increase in interest-rate risk. The purpose of the floating-rate debt limit is to limit the impact of interest-rate movements on net income. The limit is defined as a percentage of total assets rather than total debt because total assets are representative of the size of the business, while total debt can vary.

Timing of Debt Issues

Because of strong cash flow and a good credit rating, TELUS has considerable flexibility in the timing of its debt issues. TELUS Communications issued $200 million of public debt in 1995, primarily to refinance another debt issue that was maturing within a few months. At that time, there was uncertainty over the referendum in Quebec and concern in the market that interest rates might rise. In early 1997, TELUS Communications followed an opposite course. It financed a $200-million maturity with commercial paper, with the expectation of refinancing some of that amount in the long-term market later in the year. Jim Drinkwater, Vice President and Treasurer, says, "We do try to time it, but we don't pretend we can pick the exact day."

Control over Capital Structure

When TELUS was largely a telephone utility, the regulators had a strong influence over its capital structure. They set upper limits on the percentage of equity because less equity and more debt resulted in a lower cost of capital and therefore lower telephone rates for the consumer. As TELUS' unregulated businesses have grown, Drinkwater explains that overall capital structure has come more under management's control. He expects the regulatory influence over capital structure will largely disappear in the next few years.

Subsidiary Capital Structures

While TELUS follows a capital-structure guideline for the corporation as a whole, Theresa Walton, Corporate Financial Analyst in Treasury, explains that management has the flexibility to vary the capital structures of its subsidiaries considerably. Unlike the United States, in Canada each subsidiary within a corporation such as TELUS files an individual tax return. Subsidiaries with higher effective tax rates are sometimes capitalized with higher levels of debt.

The capital structures of the two telephone companies, TELUS Communications and TELUS Communications (Edmonton), are still influenced by regulation. For TELUS Communications, maintaining the single-A credit rating is a consideration. None of the other subsidiaries borrow directly, so their capital structures do not have to conform to bank lending criteria. Before the sale of its interest in Telecential, TELUS and its Dutch partner considered higher leverage for the subsidiary. It was strong enough to support unsecured, high-yield, capital market debt with minimal covenants, but it elected to pledge assets for bank project financing.

Dividend Policy

Telephone companies in Canada have historically been rate-of-return and rate-base regulated. They have grown with the national economy and increased their dividends steadily over time. When TELUS went public in 1990, the government wanted to start with a relatively high dividend payout ratio of 65 to 70 percent of earnings to support the value of the stock and ensure the success of the privatization. Since 1992, the dividend per share has stayed the same in dollar terms while earnings have grown. The corporation has deliberately not articulated a dividend policy. It realizes that lowering the dividend would have a significant, negative, short-term impact on the company's stock price. But now that the nature of the telecommunications business has changed, earnings growth may not be as steady as in the past, and a greater portion of internally generated funds may be needed for reinvestment. Management is concerned a dividend increase would lead investors to expect continual increases that might not be sustainable.

Development and Approval of Policies

Management developed capital-structure policies and recommended them to the board based on industry norms, rating-agency considerations, regulatory considerations, and business risks the company expects to face in the future. The effectiveness of these policies will be evaluated based on several factors: (1) the company's ability to finance its normal operations at reasonably favorable interest rates and to access other forms of debt when it wants to do acquisitions; (2) stock price; and (3) investor feedback, principally through securities analysts. The board reviews the level of the dividend on an ongoing basis.

Distribution of Stock Ownership

TELUS' initial public offering in 1990 was structured to enable individuals in Alberta to buy their telephone company. Since then, the balance of ownership has shifted. It is estimated that institutional investors now hold 60 percent of TELUS' stock and retail investors hold 40 percent. As TELUS becomes less of a regulated telephone utility and more of a diversified telecommunications company, it becomes riskier and more complicated to follow. Institutional investors tend to be more capable of following such a stock than retail investors. TELUS' management is primarily concerned with satisfying institutional investors' information needs. However, it also recognizes that a base of retail investors can dampen stock price fluctuations as long as the company continues to pay dividends. Management is not unhappy with the current investor mix.

Communication with the Markets

Management hears investor opinions through securities analysts, regular institutional shareholder meetings, and telephone calls to the investor relations department. Investors and analysts are aware of the company's capital-structure targets and interested in knowing how capital structure might change in the future, but these issues usually are not their highest concerns. Their questions mainly relate to changes in the technological, regulatory, and competitive environment. They are particularly concerned about the ability of TELUS' management to recognize problems and issues and develop useful ideas to address them. They ask about the level of future dividends and occasionally about the potential dilution from possible future equity offerings. Investors also are interested in the company's dividend reinvestment and share purchase plan. Until mid-1997, TELUS sold treasury stock through this plan and the company's employee share-purchase plan. In all, these programs raised $40 to $50 million in equity per year. This is a relatively modest amount in relation to total equity, but it helped the company return more quickly to its target ratio of 60-percent equity and 40-percent debt after having raised debt to 50 percent of capitalization to acquire Edmonton Telephones.

Although the nature of the discussion does not vary significantly between buy-side institutional investors and sell-side securities analysts, Drinkwater finds the institutional investors tend to take a longer term view. A sell-side analyst may change a buy recommendation to a sell or hold when the company's stock price reaches a target. Institutional investors sometimes have targets too, but they are more willing to reassess whether those targets are still appropriate and whether the company's stock is still a good value.

Credit Rating

Drinkwater considers single-A to be the minimum acceptable credit rating for TELUS Communications, at least over the medium term. He observes the Canadian capital markets on the debt side are not as robust as those in the United States. Even at the triple-B level, there is a noticeable drop-off in the reliability of a company's access to the capital markets.

Although the rating agencies in Canada are starting to look more at cash-flow-based ratios, the interest-coverage ratio still appears to be most important to them. In comparing future debt maturities with underlying cash flow, the agencies usually look at the company's performance over the past five years and whether there are circumstances that may materially change future performance.

Repurchase of Stock

TELUS received about $400 million in cash from the sale of its 50-percent interest in Telecential. Approximately one-half of that cash is expected to be used to buy back 5 percent of its shares under a normal course issuer bid. The remaining 50 percent of the proceeds will then be available for investments or acquisitions.

Instruments and Tactics

Drinkwater describes TELUS' balance sheet as plain vanilla. Floating-rate debt is only a small portion of the total. Treasury has entered into a few interest-rate swaps based on analysis of yield curves and a view of the market. Drinkwater describes this as interest-rate as opposed to capital-structure management. TELUS has not used any other derivatives.

Other Issues

Investment and Financing Decisions

TELUS' decisions on making acquisitions and investments are independent of its decisions on how to finance them. The largest acquisition so far has been Edmonton Telephones. It was financed with unsecured bank debt based on the overall strength of the TELUS balance sheet.

Valuation Methods

Most analysts appear to use P/E and market-to-book ratios in valuing TELUS, but Drinkwater can see a growing number using cash flow as well as earnings measures. When analysts talk to TELUS' management, one of their principal objectives is to identify anomalies and determine a normalized level of earnings to use as a base year in their projections. Then they use their own methods for valuation. They tend not to discuss assumptions such as the weighted average cost of capital or the duration over which cash flows can be projected.

In its efforts to get the best possible return for the shareholder, management cannot ignore the valuation methods the market uses. But it is trying to encourage analysts to look past the accounting and focus more on cash flows. Drinkwater points out that TELUS has higher depreciation rates than its Canadian peers, which management considers appropriate because technological change and competition have been reducing the useful life of telecommunications assets. As a result, the "quality" of TELUS' earnings is unusually strong.

People Interviewed

J.M. Drinkwater, Vice President and Treasurer

Theresa Walton, Corporate Financial Analyst—Treasury

Vermeer Manufacturing Company

Vermeer Manufacturing Company, located in Pella, Iowa, is a privately owned maker of agricultural and industrial equipment. The company was founded in 1947 by Gary Vermeer, who had developed a mechanical wagon hoist to improve productivity on his Iowa farm. Growth has been rapid in recent years. Sales were just $100 million in 1985 and reached $200 million in 1992. Since then, Vermeer has grown to $450 million in sales, with 2,000 employees and more than 1 million square feet of manufacturing and parts facilities—still right next to Gary Vermeer's farm. The company has an international sales subsidiary in Holland. This is an appropriate location given Pella's strong Dutch heritage, reflected in the background of many of its residents, its architecture, and a tulip festival every spring.

The company's business is the design and manufacture of special-purpose, innovative, labor-saving equipment with demonstrable reliability and performance advantages that enhance its customers' productivity. Vermeer manufactures a diverse line of trenchers, directional boring systems, haying equipment, and tree equipment. In addition to the first mechanical wagon hoist, Vermeer's innovations include the first stump cutter, the first tree spade, and the first large, round hay baler. The company's marketing strategy is to sell throughout the world to the infrastructure, environmental, and hay-harvesting markets, where dedicated dealers can add service and support value.

Vermeer Manufacturing Company has approximately 30 shareholders. Most are in the four generations of the founder's family, but a few are in a related family that does not play an active role in the business.

Capital-Structure Policy

Except for some short-term, working-capital financing with bank lines of credit, Vermeer has financed all of its growth with internally generated capital. Throughout the company's 49-year existence, founder Gary Vermeer's policy has been to have no debt. He grew up in the Depression and has experienced both business and agricultural cycles. Business downturns always create problems, but one problem Vermeer has avoided has been a banker knocking on the door asking if the company will be able to service its debt. The second generation of family management, which runs the company now, completely agrees with the no-debt philosophy. The company's leadership position in many of its markets, its lack of debt, and the Vermeers' stated intention of maintaining their family ownership create a sense of security among the employees. They do not worry about a larger company buying Vermeer, leaving production management in place and eliminating everyone else. The owners feel a strong sense of responsibility to the employees. Occasionally during business downturns, Vermeer has had to cut back hours and even employment, but very little of that has been necessary in recent years. In its estate planning, the Vermeer family has tried to ensure that estate tax needs under normal circumstances will not jeopardize the company's policy of remaining debt-free and financing its growth internally.

Off-Balance-Sheet Financing

To support continued growth, Vermeer uses creative off-balance-sheet financing. The company has worked with several large financial institutions to set up inventory financing programs for its industrial equipment. Vermeer provides dealers with some interest subsidy for terms ranging from 90 to 120 days, but it does not borrow money to carry the inventory and does not guarantee dealers' indebtedness. Unlike some industrial equipment manufacturers, Vermeer does not try to ship merchandise into the dealer network as soon as it leaves the factory. It would rather carry inventory than receivables. As soon as a dealer needs to replenish its stock of small equipment, needs to refill its rental fleet, or has a customer order and arranges financing, Vermeer ships the equipment to the dealer—and expects payment in 10 to 15 days.

Because of the seasonal nature of agricultural equipment sales, Vermeer provides contingent support to help its dealers build up inventory from November through May. The hay harvesting season starts in the South in mid-April and runs as late as September in some areas. Most payments for equipment are received between the middle and the end of summer. This is partly because of the seasonality of the business and partly because of a tradition set by the largest players in the agricultural equipment market, Deere and Case. Vermeer has to live by those market-wide rules. As with industrial equipment, the actual financing is extended by a financial institution, not Vermeer. The financial institution has partial recourse to Vermeer, which is capped at a small percentage of the total financing extended to the dealers. In the past, Vermeer has provided similar dealer support through its own credit subsidiary. Vermeer records most of its recourse financing arrangements as off-balance-sheet contingent liabilities. As long as Vermeer provides contingent support, dealers are generally willing to carry debt on their own balance sheets supporting equipment on their showroom floors. Providing contingent support appears to help Vermeer's marketing efforts just as much as providing direct financing to the dealers would.

Allocating Capital among Business Units

Since the late 1980s, Vermeer has been organized by product division. Recently, a cultural shift has occurred in which division managers have been encouraged to manage the balance sheet as well as the P&L. Compensation has become more aligned with the balance sheet, with goals set in terms of net assets as well as profit margins.

Each division is allocated capital on which its pays interest at a uniform rate, such as prime. Division managers are compensated based on achieving a return on net assets above a threshold; until their results reach the thresholds, they get no bonuses, but above the thresholds, bonuses are leveraged in their favor. Minimum risk-adjusted rates of return are based on a consultant's study of a cross-section of agricultural and industrial equipment manufacturers.

The early and mid-1970s were a boom period for the sales of agricultural equipment. This boom helped Vermeer generate the cash to develop its construction equipment lines. The company has always used cash generated from established product lines to develop new ones, but in recent years it has made the process more systematic, establishing an internal bank and requiring each independent business unit to stand on its own. Each division is allowed a defined amount of capital. If the division's net assets are above that amount, it is charged prime on the excess; if net assets are below that amount, the division is credited at a rate that approximates the company's market rate for short-term investments. Division managers are motivated to collect payments from dealers by the end of the month because that is when net assets are measured.

Debt-equity ratios are not relevant to Vermeer, but the founder established some guidelines on the asset side of the balance sheet that the company continues to follow. Each business is managed with targets of receivables 10 percent of sales, inventory 25 percent of sales, and fixed assets 10 percent of sales. These three asset categories add up to 45 percent of sales, representing a two-and-a-half times asset turn. As the company has grown, it has been able to leverage its manufacturing capacity and achieve asset turns considerably above this benchmark. Sales have increased five times since the mid-1980s, but receivables have only doubled and inventory has only tripled.

Management continually tries to improve inventory turns to provide cash for the company's growth. It reduces manufacturing cycle time through shop-floor controls and improved software. A new enterprise resource planning system is in the process of being implemented. The company is establishing closer partnerships with steel companies, tool companies, and other suppliers. It prefers to deal with a couple of suppliers rather than a dozen for a given product, and it orders and bills electronically. All of these policies streamline the process, keep cash flowing, and help the company maintain its policy of no debt.

Although Vermeer does not have a policy on fixed- and floating-rate debt on its own balance sheet, it has in effect a fixed-rate-only policy for the interest subsidies it provides to dealers. Dealer financing programs are generally tied to the prime rate. Vermeer's subsidy to the dealers is not a percentage of total interest but the top three points. If prime is 6 percent and the dealer is paying prime plus 1 percent, Vermeer buys it down to 4 percent. If prime goes to 8 percent and the dealer pays 9 percent, Vermeer still pays only 3 percent, bringing the dealer's cost to 6 percent.

The financial arrangements that come closest to long-term debt are three-year leases on some highly technical equipment, such as computers and printing systems. These are operating leases and therefore not capitalized.

Dividend Policy

Vermeer's dividend policy is driven by a formula that starts with earnings and employee bonuses. There is a profit-sharing plan under which a discretionary percentage of each year's operating profits is allocated for employee bonuses and retirement funds. Vermeer wants employees to know they are at the top of the list in profit-sharing. Management compensation is in the form of salaries and annual bonuses only; there are no stock ownership, phantom-stock, or long-term incentive plans. From the remainder of earnings after employee compensation, a percentage is paid to a charitable foundation devoted primarily to local causes. Then taxes are paid, and dividends for the shareholders are calculated as a defined percentage of what is left after taxes. The formula approach eliminates the need for year-by-year decisions on dividend policy, and it has worked to everyone's satisfaction.

The family and minority shareholders essentially are unified in supporting management's policy of no debt, careful growth, and a small but steady dividend payout. A factor that helps the company achieve this unity is that, currently, only two generations of family shareholders, including the founder, are actively involved in management. The company's financial results and dividend policy are reviewed in an annual shareholders' meeting.

While dividend policy remains consistent, management is willing to explore new ideas. For example, it has considered a dividend policy similar to the management compensation plan, in which minimal dividends would be paid until earnings reached a threshold amount and then a higher amount would be paid. Also, it has considered quarterly payment dividend instead of the current annual payment cycle.

Concerning corporate and investor tax considerations, Steve Van Dusseldorp, Vice President–Finance, says the company would like to see some legislation that makes dividends either nontaxable to the recipient or deductible by the corporation paying them. For several years in the mid-1980s, the company elected S-corporation status and paid out 100 percent of profits to its shareholders in dividends. After a period of rapid sales growth related to the round hay bailer in the late 1970s, the company's sales leveled off, but cash flow remained strong. The company took advantage of that cash flow by distributing extra dividends.

Vermeer's shareholders own an interest-charge domestic international sales corporation (DISC) through which the company channels most of its export sales. Commissions paid by Vermeer to the interest-charge DISC are tax-deductible.

Van Dusseldorp believes that the growth in demand for the company's products is the outside factor that helps it most in maintaining a no-debt policy. Some of that growth has come from market-share gains—designing better products and sometimes being a little more aggressive in pricing than the competition. But the company also benefits from worldwide growth in demand for infrastructure equipment. Trenching equipment is required where anything has to be installed underground, including electric, telecommunications, water, and sewer systems. The company has sold a great deal of equipment in the former Soviet Union and sees China as an important growth market.

Vermeer could decide to limit its growth but wants to take advantage of increasing demand for its equipment. So Van Dusseldorp says, "We have to be financially creative in figuring ways to grow and still maintain a no-debt status." A few years ago, the company started to use short-term financing under its lines of credit. Management found this practice unnerving in the beginning but gradually adjusted. Recently, the founder approved construction of a new plant as long as funds were not raised from operations or from debt. The company sold a $3-million tranche from the credit portfolio to help finance the plant.

Van Dusseldorp admits that on paper this might not have looked like the best financial decision, because the cost of borrowing would have been less than the rate of return in Vermeer's credit subsidiary. But that wasn't the point. The issue was not the bottom line but control. Vermeer wants to have complete control over its balance sheet, rather than yielding part of that control to a bank or the public. However, if the company continues to grow as fast as it has in recent years, it may run out of creative financing options. It may have to start thinking about some broader strategic measures, such as allocating more resources to fast-growing business lines and less to others.

If growth in Vermeer's markets were to slow down and the company wanted to keep growing, it might consider an acquisition. This possibility is sometimes casually discussed when an opportunity comes up, but it has never been pursued seriously. The company has always been able to grow internally, and its no-debt, no-additional-stock policy would limit the size of any target company.

Development and Approval of Policies

Vermeer's capital-structure and dividend policies stem from what the founder considers a simple, logical approach and good stewardship of resources. The effectiveness of these policies can be evaluated by the company's performance over time, and the policies are continually discussed and reevaluated among the shareholders. If there continues to be general agreement, management has no incentive to consider any substantial changes.

Instruments and Tactics

Vermeer's Dutch sales subsidiary, worth several million dollars, is largely self-funded and has more of a normal debt-equity ratio than the parent company. The company also has a subsidiary called Vermeer Credit Corporation. The founder has never been terribly enthusiastic about this operation, but management believes it is a necessary tool to support the dealers' sales efforts. Three-quarters of the credit subsidiary's loans are to customers who have purchased equipment from dealers. Most of the remainder is dealer-floor-plan financing. The parent company has securitized assets by selling off blocks of Vermeer Credit receivables on a couple of occasions, to financial institutions. This was done to reduce the amount of cash tied up in the credit corporation. If Vermeer starts doing more business through its credit subsidiary, it will probably sell off blocks of loans more frequently to minimize the amount of cash invested.

Credit Rating

With no public debt, Vermeer is not rated by the agencies. However, the company is concerned about how banks score its credit internally. At one point Vermeer was assigned a major bank's second highest credit ranking. The only reason it did not receive the highest ranking was its lack of audited financial statements. Vermeer wanted the highest ranking, and now its statements are audited by a Big Six accounting firm. Van Dusseldorp points out this is one of many ways Vermeer must do things like a public company, now that it is approaching a half-billion dollars in sales.

Valuation

Vermeer has bought back stock on several occasions. Also, family members occasionally donate stock to charity as part of their estate or tax planning, and at a certain point the company buys back the stock to provide cash to the charity. For these transactions, the valuation is based on an independent stock valuation done by a recognized investment banking firm. The firm uses several methods, including discounted cash flows and P/E multiples of comparable companies. Vermeer is compared to competitors such as Agco, Alamo Group, Case, Caterpillar, Deere, and Gehl. The ratios used for comparison include book value to operating income and book value to EBIT. A capital-asset pricing model calculation is used, taking into account the risk-free rate, a market risk premium, a small stock risk premium, and a risk premium specific to Vermeer. Because the company has no debt, its weighted average cost of capital is estimated to be 18 percent. The resulting valuation is usually above book before subtracting a percentage to account for the stock's limited marketability and minority holdings.

Van Dusseldorp does not see very much connection between Vermeer's capital structure and dividend policy and its valuation. Dividends are based strictly on book profits. Dividends could conceivably rise at the same time the company value falls.

People Interviewed

Steve Van Dusseldorp, Vice President–Finance

15

The Role of High Debt

The majority of the case-study companies prefer low leverage. The case studies show only two examples of high leverage, Host Marriott and Sheplers. The capital structure of Host Marriott, the real-estate-ownership company specializing in upscale hotels, is designed to be consistent with its asset base. More than half of the company's long-term debt is nonrecourse in the form of mortgages on individual properties. Sheplers, the western-wear retailer, was taken private through an LBO in 1986 by the management team that continues to run the company. Debt remains an important part of the company's financing, but strong operating cash flow has allowed the company to pay it down steadily. Two other case-study companies, Home Depot and Paychex, were started largely with debt but have used strong operating cash flow to become low-leverage companies.

Reasons for Low Debt

Managements of the case-study companies cite several reasons for low debt. John Morphy, CFO of Paychex, sees no reason for assuming debt when the company generates more than enough cash to sustain its growth and its stock trades at a high price-earnings ratio. Low debt allows Amgen and GE the flexibility to assume more leverage someday, if necessary, for a large acquisition. Several case-study companies have investment-grade credit ratings they consider to be optimal trade-offs between lowering their costs of capital and providing flexibility, risk protection, and continuing access to capital markets. Another reason for low debt is that the good economy of the 1990s has allowed companies to build war chests for bad times. Finally, low leverage reduces risk and may make life more comfortable for management potentially at the expense of shareholders, who might prefer higher risks and higher returns. Conflicts between the interests of management and those of shareholders, known as "agency conflicts," are explained in Chapter 1.

Although low leverage is the norm in many industries today, debt is more prevalent in some industries than others. For example, with consistent strong cash flow, companies in the food industry can often justify relatively high levels of debt.

The preponderance of low leverage in the case-study companies was more than the researchers originally intended. Several high-leverage companies were invited to participate in the study but declined. Several other companies that offer particularly good examples of highly leveraged transactions (HLTs) had already been well documented in published articles. Some of these articles are briefly summarized in this chapter.

Reasons for High Debt

Even if low leverage is preferred by the "silent majority," HLTs have played an important role in recent financial history. The purpose of this chapter is to describe the reasons for HLTs, the extent to which they have succeeded and failed in recent years, the reasons for success and failure, and to suggest the permanent place for HLTs. A brief historical background of HLTs is followed by summaries of academic studies covering LBOs and leveraged recapitalizations. The first nine studies summarized assess large groups of HLTs; the concluding six are company case studies. In general, the studies cited show that high leverage is appropriate for certain industries and for certain unusual situations (such as the opportunity for management to buy a company), but often is employed only for a short period of time.

History

High leverage has a long history. Early in this century, U.S. Steel was founded with high leverage. Previous security holders were given various types of senior securities, and new equity was floated to the public. In 1902, three du Pont cousins bought E.I. du Pont de Nemours & Co. from other members of their family with a large amount of debt and a cash outlay of less than $3,000.

Leverage grew in the 1980s for several reasons. Michael Milken, of Drexel Burnham Lambert, developed corporate bonds rated below investment grade, known informally as "high-yield bonds" or "junk bonds," from obscure instruments to important, though controversial, financing tools. The availability of junk-bond financing, in conjunction with insurance companies, thrift institutions, and commercial banks looking for high-yield loans, facilitated the growth of hostile takeovers and LBOs.

Hostile takeovers and LBOs were motivated by fundamental changes in the way the capital markets defined financial objectives. Some companies, despite growing revenues and earnings per share, were recognized to be diminishing shareholder value by investing in projects returning less than their costs of capital. Managements were encouraged to consider growth in shareholder value more important than growth in revenue or earnings per share. Companies failing to manage for value became vulnerable to hostile takeovers, particularly when they had excess cash or debt capacity. Among the targets were conglomerates that had sustained their earnings-per-share growth with acquisitions. Conglomerates fell out of favor, with notable exceptions, such as GE. Investors began to prefer making focused "pure-play" investments, taking responsibility for their own diversification rather than letting the conglomerate's management do it for them. Some subsidiaries of conglomerates could be managed better independently, particularly by managers with an equity stake who knew their businesses. They became candidates for LBOs. High leverage was considered to be a necessary financing tool and a good disciplinary tool as well.

The wave of LBOs that began in the early 1980s was initiated by Prudential Insurance in an effort to compensate for the effect of high inflation on its fixed-income portfolio and hence on its earning power. Working with Henry Kravis and Jerome Kohlberg, who were then still with Bear Stearns, Prudential was an innovator in taking public companies private. Prudential held all the senior securities in a variety of forms, and the investment bankers and management held the equity. In the beginning, the equity was a nominal amount, but the debt securities that Prudential held could be converted into most of the equity at the time the entity was sold or taken public again.

Others copied this practice, notably former Salomon Brothers partner and Treasury Secretary William Simon with Gibson Greetings. Eventually, high-yield senior securities attained their own identity as a securitized alternative to commercial bank debt and a medium by which troubled thrift institutions attempted to raise their earnings and restore their capital.

Institutional investors had several criteria for target companies that would enable them to create value. These companies were generally undervalued with little existing debt and assets that could be redeployed. Other criteria included strong operating cash flow; low technology; minimal requirements for plant and equipment; a minimum of environmental, labor, and litigation problems; and good management. When managers were given a direct stake in the business, they were often motivated to create value where before they had been content with a comfortable status quo. From a theoretical perspective, agency theory justified the positive social and economic benefits of LBOs.

During the 1980s, high leverage was not confined to just a few HLTs. The ratios in table 15.1, based on figures from the U.S. Department of Commerce, show that leverage increased on average for the whole corporate population during the 1980s. Both long-term debt and total debt as a percentage of capitalization increased sharply in the 1980s and then tapered off by the mid-1990s. Total debt declined less than long-term debt in these ratios, reflecting the increased use of commercial paper and other short-term facilities in place of long-term debt.

Table 15.1
U.S. Department of Commerce Average Financial Ratios and Percentages for All Manufacturing Companies

	1970	1975	1980	1985	1990	1995
Long-Term Debt as Percentage of Capitalization	24.8	25.0	25.1	29.3	37.3	34.7
Total Debt as Percentage of Capitalization	30.8	29.5	30.2	34.6	42.7	41.0

Financial Structure of LBOs

A recent study by Dianne M. Roden and Wilbur G. Lewellen addressed the relationship between company characteristics and the financial structure of LBOs.[1] The authors analyzed the composition of financing packages used in a sample of 107 LBO transactions, effected between 1981 and 1990, to test a set of hypotheses developed from prior literature about the determinants of corporate capital-structure decisions. They found evidence that LBO financing decisions are systematically affected by the target firm's growth prospects, the level and variability of its return on assets, its pre-buyout liquidity position, tax considerations, and post-buyout restructuring plans. The financing criteria for LBOs are thus similar to those for less-leveraged companies.

The authors tested nine hypotheses:

1. The larger the target firm, the greater the proportion of debt in the buyout financing package.

2. The more target company assets the buyout group plans to sell, the greater the proportion of debt in the financing package.

3. The higher the target firm's return on assets, the larger the proportion of debt in the financing package.

4. The greater the target firm's growth prospects, the larger the proportion of common equity in the buyout financing package.

5. The greater the variability of earnings for the target firm, the greater the proportion of common equity in the buyout financing package.

6. The higher the level of the target firm's free cash flow in relation to the total price paid, the larger the proportion of debt in the buyout financing package.

7. The likelihood that reduced-cash-flow securities will be issued increases when the proportion of debt in the financing package is relatively high, when a relatively high acquisition premium is paid, and when the target firm has substantial growth opportunities.

8. The likelihood that the financing package will include reduced-cash-flow securities decreases when the target firm has large free cash flows relative to the acquisition price paid.

9. The proportion of bank debt in buyout financing packages decreases over time as the proportion of junior-debt securities increases.

The authors' statistical analysis supported all hypotheses but the first and sixth. While the evidence was not strong enough to prove these two statistically, it did not contradict them.

LBO Structure

The immediate post-buyout structure of the typical LBO resembles an inverted pyramid. At the top are large amounts of senior secured bank loans. In the middle is mezzanine financing consisting of unsecured, subordinated long-term debt known as junk bonds or high-yield bonds. These are sold in public and private offerings to institutional and individual investors. At the bottom are relatively small amounts of preferred and common equity, the bulk of which are provided by the buyout group, including the management of the newly acquired company. The authors found that on average, bank financing provided 62 percent; subordinated debt, 24 percent; preferred stock, 4 percent; and common stock, 7 percent of the funds raised for the sample LBOs. The remainder came from the proceeds of asset sales at the time of the transactions and the target firms' cash and marketable securities.

Increasing Use of Debt Securities

The key secular phenomenon the authors observed was the trend toward heavier reliance on debt securities. Between the first and second halves of the 10-year study period, there was a shift of 20 percentage points away from bank financing toward junk-bond financing. The proportion of bank financing declined from 72 percent to 52 percent, while the proportion of subordinated debt securities increased from 13 percent to 33 percent. Furthermore, in the late 1980s, there was increased use of reduced-cash-flow instruments that lessen the immediate requirements to pay interest after the buyout. These instruments included

zero-coupon bonds, which promise a single payment of principal and interest at maturity; **split-coupon bonds,** which stipulate low cash interest rates during their earlier years and predetermined higher interest rates during their later years; **PIK securities,** which allow the issuer to pay interest in the form of additional securities for a time and then require interest on the augmented amount; and **reset bonds,** which initially pay relatively low interest rates but on a specified later date require the rate to be set to the level that allows the bonds to trade at par in the market.

The authors observed that the companies using reduced-cash-flow securities tended to have higher leverage and a heavier component of junk bonds than did other LBOs in the sample. They also found that a buyout financing package was more likely to include reduced-cash-flow securities when the proportion of debt was relatively high, when substantial growth opportunities were present, and when the company had paid a relatively large acquisition premium. Conversely, the likelihood of reduced-cash-flow securities diminished when the target firm generated large free cash flows in relation to the acquisition price. A company with significant future growth opportunities but little cash flow to fund them would find securities that defer debt-service obligations particularly attractive.

How HLTs Can Improve Operating Performance

LBOs have been criticized as attempts to "rip off" other players, such as bondholders and employees. Another view, however, is that an appropriately structured LBO can benefit all stakeholders by motivating management and creating a better run company. A leading proponent of the notion that LBOs can add value to society is Michael C. Jensen, who sees takeovers, corporate break-ups, divisional spin-offs, and LBOs as signs of an organizational change in the economy.[2] They are a threat to senior managers of many large public corporations, but they resolve a central weakness in those institutions: agency conflicts over the control and use of corporate resources. Jensen believes that new organizational forms, such as LBO associations with active investors, have created new models of general management. They have motivated remarkable gains in operating efficiency, employee productivity, and shareholder value. The conventional 20th-century model of corporate governance, dispersed public ownership, professional managers without substantial equity holdings, and a board of directors dominated by management-appointed outsiders is more suited to companies whose profitable investment opportunities exceed the cash flow they generate internally.

But Jensen does not believe the conventional model is appropriate for companies in slow-growing industries where internally generated funds outstrip investment opportunities or where downsizing may be the most productive long-term strategy. For this type of company to operate efficiently and maximize value, Jensen believes that free cash flow must be distributed to shareholders rather than retained. But he notes that in large public companies, managers have few incentives to distribute funds. For example, cash reserves reduce a company's dependence on the capital markets. Where middle managers are rewarded for increasing the scope of their responsibilities rather than for increasing shareholder value, retaining funds increases the size of the company and justifies the creation of new positions. Large cash reserves thus can lead to waste and inefficiency, imposing agency costs on shareholders. With large cash balances, Jensen observed, managements are tempted to make diversifying acquisitions rather than distribute excess cash to shareholders so they can reinvest.

Jensen believes that taking on debt and paying out the proceeds helps companies limit the waste of free cash flow. This practice represents more of a commitment than regular dividends or stock repurchases, which can be cut back at any time. According to Jensen, debt can be a powerful agent for change. Even overleveraging can be desirable when it makes sense to break up a company, sell off parts of the business, or focus on core operations. It requires managers to slash unsound investment programs, shrink overhead, and dispose of assets that have better use outside the company.

Management methods in LBOs go well beyond the motivating effects of high leverage. In LBO associations, there are three main constituencies: an LBO partnership that sponsors the buyout transaction, company managers who hold substantial equity stakes, and institutional investors. The LBO sponsor tends to have much more hands-on involvement and industry expertise than the typical public-company board of directors.

Compensation systems are more sensitive to performance for LBO managers than for public-company managers. These systems usually have high upper limits or no limits at all, tie bonuses to cash flow and debt retirement, and include equity holdings as a vital part of the reward system.

Jensen asserts that the relationship between debt and insolvency in LBOs is not well understood. He explains that taking on high debt is more feasible than it used to be because derivative-based hedging techniques developed in the 1980s protect companies against unexpected high interest rates. Furthermore, the higher the level of debt, the less costly to shareholders insolvency is likely to be. A company financed mostly with equity can underperform over a long period while its going-concern value sinks toward its liquidation value. When it becomes insolvent, there is little incentive to salvage it. Underperformance causes a company financed mostly with debt to become insolvent sooner, arresting the erosion of its value as a going concern. When a company's going-concern value is substantially above its liquidation value, there is a strong incentive to preserve the remaining value by restructuring creditors' claims.

Performance of Management Buyouts

Jensen was primarily studying the LBO phenomenon, but his concepts also apply to the LBO category known as management buyouts (MBOs). Steven Kaplan notes that MBOs increased in both size and number during the 1980s.[3] In the typical MBO, buyout investors, including some of the company's current managers, pay pre-buyout shareholders a premium, often more than 40 percent above the prevailing market price, to take the company private. Kaplan analyzed operating performance for 48 large MBOs of public companies completed between 1980 and 1986 in the three years following their buyout. He found that operating income for this group, net of industry changes, was essentially unchanged in the first two post-buyout years but was 24 percent higher in the third year.

Kaplan explained that the change in operating income did not measure the effect of post-buyout divestitures. But changes in the ratios of operating income to assets and operating income to sales, which were affected by divestitures and acquisitions, exceeded industry averages by 20 percent in the first three buyout years. The median net cash flow (the difference between operating income and capital expenditures), net of industry changes, in the three post-buyout years was, respectively, 22 percent, 43 percent, and 80 percent larger than in the last pre-buyout year. The buyout companies' increases in net cash flow to assets and net cash flow to sales exceeded industry averages by approximately 50 percent during this period.

Kaplan presented three possible explanations for the operating performance improvements and value increases: wealth transfers from employees, superior information available to management, and improved management incentives. He rejected the wealth-transfer hypothesis, that the owners created value at the employees' expense, because the MBO companies did not reduce headcount much. He also rejected the information-advantage or underpricing hypothesis: that buyout managers had information about potential value increases that public shareholders did not have and could therefore purchase the company for less than public shareholders would accept if they had the same knowledge. Kaplan found significant numbers of managers who decided not to participate in MBOs and sold their shares to buyout groups. They may not have done so had they known that the true values of the buyout companies exceeded their buyout prices. Kaplan supported the reduced-agency-cost or improved-incentive hypothesis—that the debt burden, the equity incentives, and the monitoring associated with the buyout significantly reduced agency costs within the company. These improved incentives led to value-increasing decisions and post-buyout operating improvements.

How Financial Distress Affects Organizational Efficiency

Karen H. Wruck found that financial distress has benefits as well as costs and that financial and ownership structure affects net costs.[4] She explained that financial distress is often accompanied by changes in management, governance, and organizational structure. Financial distress forces decisions to improve the use of resources, which in turn creates value. For example, companies in declining industries often continue to reinvest in plants and equipment even if market analysis and efficiency suggest capacity reduction. Financial distress forces decisions, such as capacity reductions, that are less likely in companies with equity cushions.

Without outside intervention, management often failed to change strategy or was unaware that the company's strategy was the wrong one. This was one of the problems with Revco, discussed later in this chapter. When the value of a company deteriorated because of poor management, or when the value of the company was highest in liquidation but management refused to liquidate, Wruck concurred with Michael Jensen that financial distress could create value.

Performance of Reverse LBOs

Another angle on the effects of leverage is the reverse LBO, an LBO that subsequently goes public again. Robert W. Holthausen and David F. Larcker examined the operating performance of a sample of 90 reverse LBOs for periods extending from one year before to four years after their subsequent initial public offerings (IPOs).[5] The LBOs for the sample companies occurred between 1976 and 1988, the majority between 1983 and 1986. The IPOs took place between 1983 and 1988, the majority in 1986 and 1987.

Many reverse-LBO companies did not stay public for very long. According to Holthausen and Larcker, by the end of 1993, 36 of the 90 companies in the sample had been acquired by other companies, and 8 had been taken private again through LBOs. For those 44 IPOs, the average time to acquisition was 30 months. Thirty-seven companies in the sample were still public at the end of 1993; eight had what the authors defined as a significant event of default, a covenant violation, missed interest or principal payment, or bankruptcy filing. For the total 90-company sample, debt as a percentage of capitalization declined from an average of 83 percent to 56 percent of capitalization, management's share of equity declined from 36 percent to 24 percent, and nonmanagement insiders' share of equity declined from 39 percent to 25 percent.

Holthausen and Larcker found the operating performance of the reverse LBOs in the sample was significantly better than the performance of the median firms in their industries in the year prior to and the year of their IPOs. Performance for these companies also was better than that of their industries for at least four years following their IPOs, although there was some evidence of deterioration during this period.

The authors found declines in operating performance after IPOs correlated with declines in percentage of equity owned by operating management and other insiders, such as LBO sponsors, but they did not find changes in operating performance correlated with post-IPO decreases in leverage. They also found that as the ownership stakes of managers and nonmanager insiders fell, capital expenditures and working capital both tended to increase, even after acknowledging that some IPOs are undertaken for necessary capital expenditures and additions to working capital. These increases might have indicated a slackening of the discipline LBOs had imposed earlier.

Holthausen and Larcker suggested that the changes in performance, correlated with changes in insider ownership, could be interpreted in two ways: (1) Less concentrated ownership led to an inferior incentive structure or (2) managers timed their IPOs to take advantage of information known by insiders but not the market. They noted studies in recent years documenting poor stock-price performance of both IPOs and seasoned equity offerings, presumably at least partly caused by such information asymmetry. But for the reverse-LBO sample, they concluded stock-price performance was sufficiently positive to indicate the IPOs were priced correctly.

The authors observed that there were competing economic predictions on the effects of leverage and managerial equity ownership on a company's financial performance. Leverage could cause managers to reject projects with high-risk and high-net present value in favor of low-risk projects to reduce the likelihood of default. However, the authors believe that this study reinforced Jensen's and Wruck's conclusions that leverage and managerial equity ownership can have a positive influence on performance.

Voluntary vs. Defensive Leveraged Recaps

One way to classify leveraged recapitalizations is to determine whether companies initiated them as defensive measures or undertook them voluntarily. Krishna G. Palepu and Karen H. Wruck showed the consequences of defensive and voluntary leveraged shareholder payouts differ radically.[6] Defensive payouts in their 33-company sample blocked hostile takeovers but were followed by weak profitability, poor stock performance, and reduced capital spending. In contrast, improved profitability, positive stock performance, and unchanged capital spending followed voluntary payouts.

The authors recalled that during the 1980s many publicly traded companies made large distributions of cash, debt securities, or both to shareholders. Some of those companies, such as GE, accomplished this through long-term programs to repurchase shares using internally generated funds. Other companies borrowed and substantially increased their leverage to make cash distributions, through either special dividends or self-tender offers.

The 18 defensive-recapitalization companies in the sample experienced better stock-price performance than the 15 voluntary-recapitalization companies between the announcement and the completed payout but far worse performance after the payout. After the payout, defensive firms experienced large stock-price declines, while voluntary firms experienced substantial stock-price appreciation. Post-payout stock-price performance for defensive payouts was so poor that it eliminated the gains between the announcement and payout completions. Significant differences also favored the voluntary-payout firms in post-payout operating profitability, capital expenditures, and employment.

The voluntary and defensive firms showed no major differences in payout percentages, but they differed in the use of securities in the payout structure. Seven of the nine firms that used securities as part of their payouts were defensive. Also, the defensive payouts were completed more quickly, with a median completion time of 55 days, compared with 83 days for voluntary payouts.

Palepu and Wruck cited several possible reasons the defensive firms increased in value more than the voluntary firms between announcement and completion. The defensive payouts could have been predicated on more optimistic estimates of future profitability than the voluntary payouts. Those companies may have been poorly managed and had a greater opportunity to create value, or they may have had more severe information problems. The defensive payouts may have been financed more aggressively, and perhaps less realistically, than the voluntary payouts. By the end of 1991, seven of the 33 sample firms were in financial distress: Three were in Chapter 11, and four were on the verge of default. All but one of these distressed firms were defensive recapitalizations.

In the authors' view, it is easy to understand why leveraged share-holder payouts appeal to managers under siege, but it is more difficult to understand why companies might undertake them voluntarily. For a takeover target, the payout eliminates the bidder's opportunity to create additional value and forces management to take the same type of action the bidder would. In unthreatened companies, managers might undertake leveraged payouts for two reasons. First, they might recognize they are not maximizing firm value and view the payout as a preemptive measure. Increasing leverage and paying out cash to share-holders forces organizational change to solve free-cash-flow problems, and it also reduces returns available to a potential bidder. Sealed Air Corporation, discussed later in this chapter, is an example of a leveraged payout undertaken for this reason.

Second, a voluntary payout might solve an information problem. If management believes the market is underestimating the firm's true value, it can use the payout to signal more certain future cash flow than the market is predicting. CUC International, also discussed later in this chapter, illustrates a leveraged payout done for this reason.

How HLTs Can Hurt Operating Performance

Despite the many benefits of HLTs, some do not succeed. Tim C. Opler and Sheridan Titman found highly leveraged companies lose substantial market share to their more conservatively financed competitors in industry downturns.[7] In a sample of industries that experienced significant contractions, the authors found that companies in the decile with the most leverage saw their sales drop by 26 percent more than did companies in the decile with the least leverage. The authors believe these findings underscore the significance of indirect financial distress costs.

Their findings support their hypothesis that more highly leveraged firms will have difficulty in an economic downturn, because of the cost of financial distress. But if financial distress had the benefit of forcing more rapid moves toward efficiency, the more highly leveraged firms should have outperformed their peers. Specifically, Opler and Titman found that highly leveraged firms suffer greater market-share losses than their less leveraged competitors during economic recessions. Such losses could be customer driven, reflecting the customers' reluctance to do business with distressed firms; competitor driven, reflecting efforts of financially strong companies to exploit the financial weaknesses of their competitors; or manager driven, indicating that the firms take the initiative to downsize in response to an industry downturn.

Opler and Titman also hypothesized that competitor-driven losses are more likely in concentrated industries with more potential for strategic interaction among competitors, and that customer-driven losses are more likely with companies that have specialized products, as indicated by relatively high R&D expenditures. (In the quadrant model used for this study, these would be secular-growth, intangible-asset companies.) They also hypothesized that small firms may be more financially vulnerable, and thus more subject to customer-driven and competitor-driven sales losses, while large firms may be more subject to manager-driven sales reductions. The authors also found that companies with specialized products, supported by substantial R&D expenditures, are especially vulnerable to financial distress.

The authors reasoned that if sales losses are customer or competitor driven, indicating that financial distress is costly, the more highly leveraged firms should lose value during an industry downturn. However, if the financial discipline of high leverage produces a more efficient competitor, the highly leveraged firms should gain in value relative to the less-leveraged firms in their industries.

The authors found the stock prices of more-leveraged companies are more sensitive to industry downturns. This relationship is partly explained by the leverage effect. But the authors found that operating income, which is not biased by leverage, falls for more highly leveraged companies during industry downturns. They also found that the relationship between leverage and performance tends to be more pronounced for companies with significant R&D expenditures and companies in more concentrated industries. This finding would indicate that customers and competitors at least partially drive losses in sales, rather than cost-cutting managers optimally downsizing in declining industries.

How LBOs Can Lead to Bankruptcy

A major controversy has existed from the early phase of the LBO period in the 1980s about whether a highly leveraged recapitalization tends to propel a company into bankruptcy. Those arguing that this is the case received a boost when the banking authorities issued regulations restricting the HLT loans in an institution's portfolio. David J. Denis and Diane J. Denis attempted to sort out the reasons for the failures that befell nearly a third of the leveraged recapitalizations completed between 1985 and 1988.[8] They found that 31 percent of the companies completing leveraged recapitalizations between 1985 and 1988 encountered financial distress by the end of 1991. Following their recapitalizations, the distressed firms exhibited poor operating performance caused by industry-wide problems, surprisingly low proceeds from asset sales, and negative stock-price reactions to economic and regulatory events associated with the demise of the market for HLTs. The authors attributed the high rate of distress primarily to unexpected macroeconomic and regulatory developments rather than to characteristics previously linked with poorly structured deals.

Two hypotheses could explain why so many of these transactions failed. First, the market for HLTs became overheated in the late 1980s, resulting in overpriced and poorly structured deals that should not have been undertaken.[9] The authors' alternative, though not mutually exclusive, hypothesis is that many of the HLT problems in the late 1980s stemmed from macroeconomic and regulatory developments, such as the recession, the collapse of the junk-bond market, and the credit crunch of 1990.

In the Denises' sample of 29 recapitalizations, the 9 companies that experienced distress had, on average, higher leverage and tighter interest coverage ratios than the other companies. This finding is consistent with both the overheating hypothesis and the hypothesis that the distressed firms expected to take more restructuring steps, such as asset sales after the recapitalizations, but were prevented from doing so by unfavorable events. Because other firms in the same industries experienced similar declines, the authors conclude broader economic factors were largely responsible for the poor performance of the distressed firms.

The authors estimated that five of the nine distressed firms would have been able to meet required debt payments in the year of default had asset sales produced the anticipated proceeds. However, the rate of asset sales for the distressed companies was no greater than for the other companies in the sample. This finding is surprising because tight interest-coverage ratios and poor operating performance should have made asset sales urgent. The authors concluded the distressed companies had difficulty selling assets and received lower-than-expected prices for the assets they did sell because of an unanticipated contraction in the liquidity of the asset markets and because their poor financial condition reduced their bargaining power.

The authors found negative stock-price reactions often met announcements of asset sales. These negative reactions were concentrated among firms in poorly performing industries and among firms with ratios of operating earnings to interest and principal obligations of less than one. While the market could have been reacting negatively to evidence that these companies needed cash, the companies had announced their intentions to sell assets at the time of their recapitalizations. A more plausible interpretation, in the authors' opinion, was that the stock market thought the poor financial condition of the distressed companies would weaken their bargaining power and reduce the prices they received for their assets, regardless of the liquidity of the asset markets.

The Denises' study suggests an unexpected decrease in asset liquidity was an important cause of financial distress for the sample companies. One contributor to this phenomenon was the onset of the recession in 1990, but several other legal and regulatory events also reduced the funding available for corporate control transactions. They included pressure by the Securities and Exchange Commission (SEC) on Drexel to remove Michael Milken from control of junk-bond operations in March 1989; a congressional ban on investment in junk bonds as part of the Financial Institutions Reform and Recovery Act in July 1989; and the inability of Robert Campeau, the Canadian real estate developer and investor, to make a $50-million interest payment in September 1989. Other events included widespread financial distress resulting from the collapse of the proposed UAL (the parent company of United Airlines) buyout in October 1989 because banks were reluctant to provide the financing, Drexel's filing for bankruptcy in February 1990, and an October 1990 congressional proposal to limit money-market-fund investment in low-grade commercial paper. The negative **abnormal returns** in response to these events were more pronounced for the distressed firms than for other firms in the sample.

The authors examined several characteristics previously linked to poorly structured recapitalizations, including junk-bond financing, management cashing out in the transactions, and takeover bids prior to recapitalizations. These factors were no more present with the distressed companies than with the other companies in the sample, leading the authors to conclude that poor deal structure was not the primary explanation for financial distress.

Financial distress was concentrated among the most recent transactions rather than in those done early on. The financial distress encountered by seven of the nine firms encountered occurred in 1990 and 1991. Whereas only one of the recapitalizations completed in 1985 and 1986 encountered financial distress, 8 of the 19 recapitalizations completed in 1987 and 1988 had encountered some form of distress by the end of 1991. In the authors' view, this time pattern suggested either that the later transactions were more likely to be poorly restructured or that the later completion dates allowed these companies less time to accomplish the restructurings they had planned before the onset of macroeconomic and regulatory problems.

Organizational Changes Resulting from an LBO

George P. Baker and Karen H. Wruck prepared a detailed study of the effect on O.M. Scott & Sons Company of its sale to a group of managers and an outside LBO firm.[10] The objective was to determine whether the combination of a heavy debt load and significant management ownership would lead to a more efficient organization. Consistent with agency theory, the authors found the pressure of servicing a heavy debt load and management equity ownership can lead to improved management performance.

Founded in 1870 to sell farm-crop seed, Scott became the largest producer of lawn-care products in the United States. The company was closely held until 1971, when it was purchased by ITT and became part of that conglomerate's consumer products division. In 1986, ITT sold several subsidiaries as part of an effort to focus on fewer, larger lines of business. It sold Scott to a group of managers and Clayton & Dubilier (C&D), a firm specializing in LBOs. Financing for the buyout consisted of common stock (9 percent), subordinated notes and debentures (33 percent), a bank working capital loan (21 percent), and a bank revolving credit (37 percent). C&D believed that equity ownership gave managers an incentive to maximize the value of the company. It required managers to buy stock with their own money. (Sheplers, a case-study company, has a similar policy.) Managers purchased 14 percent of Scott's common stock.

C&D increased managers' salaries but also set higher standards for performance than ITT had set. The increase in compensation also served as remuneration for increased risk bearing. Scott's managers were more valuable to C&D than they had been to ITT, which had created a control system that allowed headquarters to manage a vast number of businesses. A redesigned bonus plan with an emphasis on EBIT and working-capital management covered more managers and had higher ceilings based on corporate, divisional, and individual performance goals. A small, active board of directors was chartered to monitor, advise, and evaluate the CEO. In line with policy, a C&D partner with extensive operating experience served as liaison between the firm and Scott, advising the CEO but not making decisions for him.

Baker and Wruck explained that in some distressed situations there is a conflict between the goals of servicing debt and maximizing shareholder value. Scott's managers had an incentive to avoid even technical default on the loans because of a debt-for-equity provision that could affect their stock holdings.

Scott's managers were able to implement more changes and get more capital spending requests approved than under ITT, which had maintained control through a formal, inflexible reporting structure. As a result, operating performance improved substantially. Marketing, R&D, and capital spending continued to increase. The company reduced working capital and also employment, although only through attrition.

Voluntary Leveraged Recap to
Spur Management Performance

In a case study of Sealed Air Corporation, Karen H. Wruck described how a leveraged recapitalization can solve a free-cash-flow problem and restore a sense of urgency to a management lulled into complacency by corporate success.[11] Sealed Air, founded in 1960, manufactures protective packaging products such as plastic packaging bubbles, padded mailing envelopes, moisture-absorbing pads for supermarket meat packaging, and foam and equipment for custom-fit packaging.

Leveraged Recapitalization

Dermot Dunphy has been President and CEO since 1971. During the first 18 years of his tenure, sales grew from $5 million to $345 million and profits improved from a small operating loss to $25.3 million. But during the mid-1980s, despite continuing increases in earnings per share, Sealed Air's stock-price performance lagged behind that of its competitors and the overall market.

In April 1989, Sealed Air declared a one-time special dividend of $40 per share, representing 90 percent of market capitalization. The cash payout of $330 million was financed with a $137-million senior secured bank loan, $170 million in subordinated bridge notes, and $21 million from internal sources, including dividends from subsidiaries and cash and short-term investments. The subordinated bridge notes were refinanced through a public offering of 10-year senior subordinated notes rated "B" by Standard & Poor's and "B1" by Moody's. Debt rose to 65 percent of market capitalization and 135 percent of total assets, resulting in negative accounting net worth.

Market Response

The market response to Sealed Air's leveraged recapitalization was mildly favorable at the time of the transaction but very favorable over the next several years as a result of constantly improving operating performance. The company's stock price rose 9.8 percent at the time of the announcement and another 5.2 percent by the time the leveraged recapitalization was completed. Over the five-year period following the special dividend, Wruck calculated a 36 percent annualized stock return for Sealed Air, compared with a 6.6 percent annualized return for the S&P 500, 5.3 percent for a sample of 33 leveraged-payout firms, and 17.7 percent for a sample of leveraged-payout firms without the pressure of a takeover offer.

Operating Performance Improvement

Before the leveraged recapitalization, Sealed Air's performance was slightly below average for its industry. In the five years following the leveraged recapitalization, Sealed Air's operating performance improved substantially, while that of the industry remained essentially unchanged. The company's value, measured by the sum of long-term debt and the market value of equity, increased by over 100 percent.

World-Class Manufacturing Initiative

Six months before the special dividend, Sealed Air began a world-class manufacturing initiative. Despite early success and involvement of operators at all levels, enthusiasm for the program dissipated after a few months. Because the company was highly profitable and increased future competition after the expiry of certain patents seemed remote, managers became complacent. The company showed symptoms of a free-cash-flow problem. It began to overinvest, with not all projects earning the cost of capital, and to tolerate manufacturing inefficiencies. Ironically, success caused the company's complacency and its free-cash-flow problem.

Need for a Crisis

Dunphy believed employees needed a crisis to shake them out of their complacency. The reorganization required for integrating newly acquired companies had provided crises for Sealed Air in the past. A new acquisition could have addressed the free-cash-flow problem, but management could not identify any suitable candidates. Another alternative management considered was simply to fire employees who did not change their behavior. Management preferred a leveraged recapitalization, believing it would motivate people to change their behavior voluntarily. The free-cash-flow problem would be solved by distributing cash representing the company's future earning power to its existing shareholders. Management did not consider an LBO because it would result in too much leverage and could put the company in play. It also ruled out the use of exotic securities, such as pay-in-kind bonds, to keep the transaction simple.

Lack of Sponsor

While Sealed Air was negotiating debt financing, lenders voiced reservations about the lack of a sponsor and the large special dividends that officers and directors who were equity owners would receive. Because LBO partnerships such as C&D and Kohlberg, Kravis & Roberts (KKR) had reputations for establishing strong governance and effective internal controls, banks sometimes were more willing to lend when they were involved. Lenders questioned managers' commitment to the future success of the company after they received their dividends. However, these concerns were somewhat allayed by Dunphy's experience sitting on the boards of several successful LBOs.

Performance Measures

After the leveraged recapitalization, Sealed Air implemented a new performance measurement system. Management adopted new company-level and plant-level performance measures and a new management bonus plan. The company-level measures emphasized earnings before interest, income taxes, depreciation, and amortization (EBITDA) and earnings above the cost of capital rather than earnings per share. The plant-level measures reflected management's view of the factors that contributed most directly to shareholder value. They fell into seven categories: service, quality, inventory, training, suggestions, change-over time, and material yield. Under the new management bonus plan, payouts were based on EBITDA, inventory turns, accounts receivable, and working capital. For the first time, balance sheets had to be managed at the divisional level.

Employee Stock Ownership

Management put new emphasis on employee stock ownership, believing it to be an important motivator. Employees were encouraged to hold onto their stock after it was awarded to them. Between 1988 and 1993, employee ownership increased from 8.2 to 18.6 percent of outstanding shares. Dunphy wanted employee ownership to remain under 20 percent to preserve the discipline of serving outside shareholders.

Shareholder Mix

Before the leveraged recapitalization, 109 institutions held approximately 62 percent of Sealed Air's stock. After the transaction, the percentage of institutional ownership remained about the same. However, the actual institutions owning the stock turned over almost completely, even though existing shareholders had the opportunity to participate in the special dividend and preserve their proportional ownership. Some pension funds sold because they were required to hold stock that paid dividends, whereas Sealed Air planned to discontinue its dividend. One money manager sold because he was evaluated strictly on capital gains. In the words of Sealed Air's management, the investor clientele changed from "earnings-per-share" investors to "cash-flow sharpies." The new investors appeared to be smarter, to understand the company better, and to be more actively involved in evaluating its progress.

Improvement in Performance

The combination of high leverage and new performance measures helped revitalize the world-class manufacturing program. High leverage increased the urgency of program objectives, such as reducing working capital and improving cash flow by reducing waste and streamlining manufacturing processes.

The seven-year bank credit agreement required a covenant specifying the maximum capital expenditures each year. Management originally agreed to an unrealistic cap significantly below capital expenditure levels in recent years and had to negotiate several increases in the cap over the following three years. The restrictions were frustrating, but they forced the company to prioritize and to be more selective in its capital expenditures. Management realized that before the leveraged recapitalization, capital allocation procedures had become lax because of excess free cash flow.

According to *The Wall Street Journal's Shareholder Scorecard,* published in February 1997, Sealed Air's average total shareholder return was 49 percent over the previous year, 38 percent per year over the past 3 years, and 35 percent per year over the past 10 years. As of May 1997, Sealed Air's stock sold for 27 times recent earnings.

In summary, Sealed Air created a value-building culture by making two mutually reinforcing changes: (1) an increase in leverage and (2) new, cash-flow-based performance measurement and reward systems. The increase in leverage solved a free-cash-flow problem and added urgency to other value-building measures such as the world-class manufacturing program.

Leveraged Recap to Send Signals to the Market

Empirical studies have shown mixed results on the extent to which capital structure is used to signal the market about a company's prospects. Paul M. Healy and Krishna Palepu showed how a company used a leveraged recapitalization to send positive signals after the market showed concerns about the company's practice of capitalizing marketing expenses.[12] CUC International, founded in 1973, markets membership programs to credit card holders of major financial, retailing, and oil companies. The company's most popular product is Shoppers Advantage™. For an annual fee, users of this service are entitled to call the company's operators on a toll-free line or use online computer access to inquire about or buy brand-name products.

Because only a small fraction of the people reached through direct marketing sign up for the service, membership acquisition costs generally exceed membership fees in the first year. But there are no direct marketing costs for renewing members. Renewals are billed each year automatically by credit card companies; members must elect to cancel the service. The average annual renewal rate for Shoppers Advantage between 1971 and 1988 was 71 percent, making the program very profitable. Recognizing the importance of high sign-up and renewal rates, the company did substantial market research on customers most likely to subscribe and carefully analyzed responses to marketing campaigns and renewal rates.

In 1988 and 1989, based on its experience with Shoppers Advantage, the company added other membership products. During this period, the number of members, revenues, and operating cash flows increased substantially, but marketing expenses increased even faster. On the basis of its experience with previous marketing efforts, however, management had calculated its investment in marketing to have a positive net present value. With the approval of both the auditors and the SEC, management capitalized a large part of the company's marketing expenses. In early 1988, deferred costs were almost 40 percent of the value of CUC's equity.

Information Discrepancy

Management did not want to make its market research and analysis available to competitors through public disclosure. Lacking this proprietary information, investors considered the company's policy of capitalizing membership acquisition costs unusual and were concerned that those capitalized assets might have to be written off as losses. Their fears were intensified by a recent, significant write-down of membership acquisition costs by Safeguard Services, Inc., a credit card registration company.

Agency Conflict

Investors' concerns about the potential profitability of new-product investments caused CUC's stock price to decline 35 percent relative to the market between October 1988 and March 1989. Management believed the company's stock price was undervalued, a serious problem because it was considering the use of CUC stock for an acquisition and believed that undervaluation made the company vulnerable to a hostile takeover by an informed investor. Healy and Palepu explained two possible reasons for the mismatch between managers' and investors' valuations: an information discrepancy and an agency conflict.

15

Financial Policy Changes

Between March 1989 and February 1990, CUC's management signaled its optimism about the value of marketing expenditures for new products in four ways:

1. It wrote off previously capitalized marketing expenses, reporting a loss for 1989, and discontinued the further capitalization of marketing expenses.

2. It implemented a leveraged recapitalization by paying a large special dividend financed by private debt. The special dividend represented 53 percent of the current stock price. The ratio of long-term debt to book assets increased from 7 percent to 82 percent. Projected quarterly debt payments for a five-year term ranged from 36 percent to 72 percent of free cash flow.

3. Management increased its ownership stake in the company.

4. Subsequently, CUC sent further signals to the market by using the company's excess cash flow to accelerate debt repayments and by repurchasing stock.

Finance theory suggests a leveraged recapitalization and an increase in management ownership can signal investors that managers believe their company is undervalued. A recapitalization funded by private debt can suggest that lenders with access to proprietary information are confident of the company's ability to repay its debt. The authors cite Michael Jensen, who says a leveraged recapitalization focuses management attention on cash generation, committing the company to use free cash flows to repay debtholders and limiting managers' ability to invest in unprofitable investments.

Market Response

The initial market response to the accounting change and the leveraged recapitalization was negative. Investors believed the write-down of marketing expenses validated their concerns and did not have detailed information about the leveraged recapitalization and how it would be financed. Then, as information was disclosed on a loan agreement with GE Capital and other aspects of the transaction, the market began to react more favorably. By the time the recapitalization was completed three months after the announcement, the 35-percent stock-price decline had been reversed.

Accelerated Payment

CUC announced both six months and nine months after the recapitalization that it was repaying GE Capital substantially more than the quarterly amounts required under the original credit agreement. Shortly thereafter, the company's board announced it had approved the repurchase of 9 percent of outstanding shares. The market reacted positively to these announcements as well. From the day after the repurchase announcement in June 1989 to December 1993, CUC's stock price increased 520 percent relative to the market. Marketing cash outlays, revenues, memberships, and operating cash flows continued to increase significantly during this period. Between 1991 and 1996, CUC's long-term debt decreased from 126 percent to 1.1 percent of capitalization. According to *The Wall Street Journal's Shareholder Scorecard,* in February 1997 CUC's average total shareholder return was 6.6 percent over the previous year, 14.9 percent per year over the past 3 years, and 36 percent per year over the past 10 years. As of May 1997, CUC's stock sold for 52 times recent earnings. Recently, CUC merged with HFS, Inc., owner of Avis, Inc., the car rental company, and Coldwell Banker and Century 21 Real Estate, both real-estate agent franchise companies, to form Cendant Corporation.

Healy and Palepu noted that the acceleration of debt repayments and the repurchase of shares communicated good news to investors because they confirmed the company's current cash-flow position was strong and because they supported management's contention that previous marketing outlays would generate strong cash flow in future years. The authors also noted that institutional shareholdings increased from an insignificant amount before the recapitalization to 88 percent of total shares outstanding three years after the recapitalization was completed. They concluded that CUC's strong long-term performance and stock-price increase validated management's judgment that its marketing investments would result in long-term profitability, but communicating such assurance to investors with credibility is a slow, complex process. They also observed that the accelerated debt repayments and the stock repurchases had a more immediate effect on the stock price than the recapitalization plan and that, contrary to traditional theory, CUC's stock price took 12 months to recover from its initial decline. The authors questioned whether such communication problems would have arisen in Germany or Japan, where large institutional owners often have more immediate access to inside information.

Leveraged Recap vs. LBO in Grocery Stores

On the basis of the experience of two similar companies, David J. Denis suggests some types of recapitalizations are more effective than others in creating economic and social benefits beyond those of the immediate transaction. He compares the HLTs undertaken by two large grocery store companies, Kroger Co. and Safeway Stores Inc.[13] Despite constant increases in earnings, both were underperforming their industry peers and threatened with hostile takeovers. For both, one of the reasons for poor performance was competition with regional, nonunionized chains.

In July 1986, the Dart Group, a firm controlled by the Haft family, announced a hostile tender offer for Safeway that represented a 33-percent premium over its common stock price 40 days before the offer. Ultimately, Safeway agreed to be taken private through an LBO by KKR and a group of Safeway managers for a premium of 58 percent over its price before the takeover contest began. As a result of the LBO, debt increased from 41 to 96 percent of the market value of the firm. KKR contributed 96 percent of the initial equity value. Safeway's top managers contributed the remaining 4 percent and increased their equity stake to 10 percent shortly after the transaction closed by taking advantage of a subscription agreement and options offered by KKR.

In September 1988, the Haft family attempted a takeover of Kroger, initially offering a 39 percent premium and later offering a 62-percent premium over Kroger's precontest stock price. Kroger's board rejected the bid in favor of its own leveraged recapitalization, even though analysts placed a higher value on Haft's offer. For each share of common stock held, investors received a special dividend, a junior subordinated debenture, and a stub share of Kroger common stock.

The Kroger payout was financed primarily through a $3 billion syndicated bank loan and the placement of $1 billion in increasing-rate notes. Shortly after the notes were issued, they were redeemed with the proceeds of a $625-million senior subordinated debenture and a $625 million subordinated debenture issue. The recapitalization increased total debt from 42 percent to 91 percent of the company's market value.

Stock held by Safeway's officers and directors increased from 0.7 percent before the buyout to 10 percent after the buyout. Stock held by Kroger's officers and directors increased from 1.4 percent of shares outstanding before the recapitalization to 3 percent after the recapitalization. Denis believes that a higher equity stake gave Safeway's management stronger incentives to increase efficiency and maximize the value of the company.

Board of Directors' Role

Before they were restructured, both Kroger and Safeway had large, stable boards of directors who held little equity in the companies. Kroger's board did not change as a result of its recapitalization. In contrast, Safeway's board was reduced from 18 to 5 after the buyout. Two members of Safeway's old board and management remained, and the remaining three seats were filled with KKR partners. Collectively, the board represented 93 percent of the company's equity. Denis concludes Safeway's new structure resulted in closer board monitoring of managerial performance. KKR partners are well known for their scrutiny of management and operations.

Executive Compensation

There was a low correlation between executive cash compensation and company performance at both Kroger and Safeway before their HLTs. After its leveraged recapitalization, Kroger did not change the structure of its executive compensation. Safeway did not increase the level of executive salaries after the buyout but raised the maximum bonus paid from 40 percent to 110 percent of base salary and tied bonus payments to performance measures more than before.

Asset Sales

Neither Kroger nor Safeway had sufficient EBITDA to service its debt after restructuring. Both therefore required operating improvements, asset sales, or a combination of the two to meet their debt obligations. Kroger's asset sales were moderate, netting $351 million; Safeway's asset sales were much higher, netting $2.3 billion. Kroger's recent ratio of capital expenditures to total assets has been about one-third below the level before recapitalization. Because Safeway sold more assets, it has been able to maintain its capital expenditures at the same percentage of assets as before the LBO. Denis believes Safeway's KKR-controlled board was responsible for its willingness to sell more assets.

Although both companies outperformed their industry and the stock market following their HLTs, Safeway's returns were higher. Denis believes Safeway's LBO was a more effective organizational form for increasing shareholder value, but he also believes Kroger's performance demonstrates that high leverage alone can bring about valuable operating improvements.

Well-Known LBO Defaults: Revco and Federated

The final case studies review two of the largest and best-known LBO bankruptcies. In both cases, cash flow was not sufficient to meet debt obligations because of the high price the buyout group paid, the amount of leverage employed, and poor business performance.

Revco: Inadequate Capital

Robert F. Bruner and Kenneth M. Eades show that the Revco Drug Stores LBO was inadequately capitalized and had a low probability of generating sufficient cash to meet its debt obligations.[14] When the $1.4-billion transaction closed in December 1986, it was one of the largest and most complex LBOs to date. The company filed for bankruptcy just 19 months later in July 1988. This was the first on a list of prominent LBO failures that would include Robert Campeau's Allied Stores and Federated Department Stores holdings, Integrated Resources, Ames Department Stores, Circle K, Hillsborough Holdings, and Greyhound.

Revco's 1986 LBO followed a period of takeover threats, internal fighting for control, and declining financial performance. Between 1979 and 1984, the company's sales grew at a compound annual rate of 19 percent, and earnings per share grew at 18 percent. Revco's stock price rose 60 percent, compared with 49 percent for the S&P 500 Index. In April 1984, the Food and Drug Administration (FDA) announced a possible link between E-Ferol, a vitamin product produced by one of Revco's subsidiaries, and infant deaths. Analysts estimated that Revco's liability could be $75 million, but the market value of the company's stock dropped by $160 million. Six days after the FDA announcement, Revco announced an agreement to buy Odd Lot Trading, a retailer of closeout goods, in exchange for stock. The acquisition, intended as an antitakeover measure, had unintended consequences. Odd Lot's two owners, who became officers with a 12-percent interest in Revco, attempted unsuccessfully to gain control of the company before they were fired in February 1985. Their 12-percent interest was repurchased in July 1985.

In March 1986, Revco CEO Sidney Dworkin proposed an LBO to Revco's board of directors in which shareholders would receive $33 in cash and $3 in exchangeable preferred stock, an 18-percent premium over the previous Friday's closing price on the New York Stock Exchange. After a dispute over the adequacy of the bid, Dworkin made a new offer of $38.50 in cash, which was accepted. Revco was taken private in December 1986 at a 48-percent premium over its stock price 12 months earlier and a 71-percent premium over the price at which it repurchased shares in July 1985. The plan for debt repayment was based primarily on asset sales and growth and secondarily on improvement in store profitability.

Revco's net income for the year ending May 31, 1986, was 18 percent less than the year before, and performance for the remainder of 1986 was considerably below plan. Nevertheless, a revised budget, used in the prospectus for the LBO's subordinated notes, the proxy statement to shareholders, and the solicitation statement for old debtholders, forecast a substantial improvement in performance. But just four days after the LBO closed, Revco's treasurer wrote an internal memorandum expressing serious concerns about the decline in the company's cash flows and stating that the company had no excess cash going forward. In March

1987, the lending banks were informed that Dworkin would step down as CEO, that progress on asset sales had been delayed, that operating income was running below budget, and that inventories were over plan. Because of cash-flow problems, the company was not able to stock its stores adequately for the December 1987 Christmas season. Revco's investment banking firm stopped making a market in its high-yield bonds in March 1988. After proposals were solicited from several firms, another investment banking firm was retained to devise a restructuring plan. Revco missed its first interest payment in June 1988 and filed for bankruptcy in July, after bondholders rejected its appeals for breathing room.

The financial press and the bankruptcy examiner alleged that the LBO left Revco inadequately capitalized, an assertion that Bruner and Eades confirmed by simulating Revco's financial performance using financial data from Revco and comparable companies publicly available at the time of the LBO. They observed that the forecast assumptions used by Revco's financial advisers were very optimistic in comparison with historical performance information for Revco and similar companies and concluded that Revco only had between a 5-percent and 30-percent probability of servicing its debt obligations during the critical first three years after the LBO.

The survival probabilities were relatively insensitive to assumptions about asset sales and sales growth, suggesting the company was brought down more by the capital structure of the LBO and the restructuring strategy than by management's failure to execute the strategy. The authors applied the same simulation technique to Eckerd Drugs, a competitor taken private at about the same time, and found a much higher probability of survival.

Bruner and Eades believe the primary implication of this study for finance practitioners is that capital adequacy has less to do with the amount and mix of various types of capital and more to do with the company's expected cash flows and the timing of debt-service obligations. They believe that this type of cash flow analysis is more appropriate than the discounted-cash-flow and other valuation methods used by the bankruptcy examiner to test whether the LBO left Revco inadequately capitalized.

Karen H. Wruck also highlighted key factors behind the Revco failure.[15] She noted the need for LBOs to have strong, predictable cash flows and, equally important, a strong management team, a proven business strategy, and an effective sponsor organization. At the time of the LBO, Revco's management team was in a state of constant turnover. The investment banking firm had never done an LBO before Revco, and the other buyout sponsors also were relatively inexperienced. After the LBO, only one nonmanagement director had a retailing background; all the others had financial-services backgrounds.

Furthermore, shortly after the buyout, a new CEO introduced weekly sales and promotions on selected merchandise, in place of the company's policy of everyday low prices, and expanded the product line to include high-ticket items such as TV sets, VCRs, and furniture. These changes required significant cash outlays when the company was already under pressure to increase cash flow.

Wruck pointed out that although the high level of fees paid to advisers for arranging the Revco transaction was subject to criticism, the real problem was a fee structure that encouraged managers and advisers to pay too much for the company. She explained that a high purchase price benefits advisers by increasing the likelihood that the deal will go through and also benefits managers who own stock before an LBO and do not roll it over. But then, after the transaction is closed, managers who have rolled over their stock and other shareholders have an incentive to maximize the value of the company and may be harmed by an excessive purchase price. In 124 LBOs between 1980 and 1989 studied by Steven Kaplan and Jeremy Stein,[16] managers reinvested an average of 46 percent of the value of their old investments; Revco's management reinvested only 26 percent, and Dworkin, Revco's CEO, reinvested only 5 percent. Two of the sponsors took out substantially more in fees than they invested.

When conglomerates with large equity bases pay too much for acquisitions, Wruck observed, they destroy shareholder value, but bondholders and other creditors are relatively unaffected. In Revco's case, overpayment financed with debt was a primary cause of financial distress. To assess whether the LBO investors overpaid, Wruck compared the Revco transaction with four other drugstore mergers and acquisitions during the same period. On the basis of the most similar transaction, the LBO of Jack Eckerd Corporation, she estimated the investor group paid between $200 million and $300 million too much for Revco.

High leverage forced Revco to renegotiate its contracts with creditors and address the problems that led to financial distress, as Jensen argued it would. However, the company went through a long, expensive workout process before emerging from bankruptcy. Conflicts among management, creditors, and other security holders complicated the reorganization process. They could not even be resolved by Drexel, which had helped reorganize many financially troubled companies earlier in the 1980s. Wruck believes that one way for companies to avoid such problems is to create the simplest possible financial structure and to align the interests of managers, shareholders, and creditors. She notes that "strip financing" techniques, in which a given party may hold both equity and debt, are one way to minimize potential workout conflicts.

Federated: Value Increase Despite Campeau

Steven N. Kaplan illustrated that an HLT can increase value even though the company is unable to meets its debt payments.[17] He also showed that the net costs of financial distress, and even bankruptcy, sometimes appear to be relatively small.

In December 1987, before Robert Campeau began an eventually successful hostile takeover quest, the market value of Federated's equity and debt was $4.25 billion. Campeau eventually paid $8.2 billion, including the price for common shares, the book value of assumed debt, and total fees. More than 97 percent of Campeau's purchase price was financed with debt.

Campeau was successful in selling assets and divisions but not in managing Federated's remaining assets. The company filed for Chapter 11 protection in January 1990. Just before the Chapter 11 petition, Campeau Corporation's board relieved Campeau of all operating responsibility. When Federated filed for Chapter 11, it was far from clear how costly the bankruptcy process would be. Some analysts questioned whether Federated would even survive, remembering the unsuccessful experience of another well-known retailer, B. Altman. (Allied Stores, which Campeau also purchased with high leverage, filed for Chapter 11 at the same time as Federated. Kaplan did not include Allied in the analysis described below.)

After declaring bankruptcy, Federated obtained **debtor-in-possession** financing and hired a new management team with strong retailing credentials. The CEO and COO were able to spend 90 percent of their time running the business, while the CFO managed negotiations with creditors and other aspects of the bankruptcy process. Improvements made by the new management team included a centralized data processing system, a new inventory management system, a team buying program, reduced reliance on promotions and sales to avoid price cutting, the sale or closing of unprofitable stores, centralization of back-office functions, and an emphasis on remodeling existing stores rather than opening new stores. Federated emerged from Chapter 11 in February 1992 as a better-run company than it had been before Campeau purchased it.

To determine whether value was created during this period, Kaplan compared the market value of Federated before the Campeau acquisition and after it emerged from bankruptcy. He calculated the post-bankruptcy value as the sum of asset sales, interim cash flows, direct bankruptcy costs, and the market value of the remaining Federated assets when the company went public again in February 1992. Market-adjusting each cash flow ahead to February 1992 at the rate of return on the S&P 500, Kaplan calculated the company's post-Campeau, post-bankruptcy market value to be $11.3 billion, significantly above the pre-Campeau market value of $8.2 billion but also significantly below the market-adjusted $14.9 billion that Campeau paid. He estimates the direct costs of bankruptcy to be a relatively minor $230 million.

Kaplan presented the Federated case as support for Wruck's argument that financial distress can provide benefits as well as impose costs.[18] Because of Federated's high debt load, financial distress occurred relatively soon after Campeau's acquisition. Chapter 11 provided breathing room for improving the company's operations by allowing Federated to obtain necessary funds through debtor-in-possession financing.

How HLTs Have Evolved in the 1990s

Recent studies show how HLTs have changed in recent years. Jay R. Allen recalls that smaller LBOs, in the $50-million to $150-million range, continued even through the 1990–91 recession, often funded just with senior debt.[19] Starting in 1991 and 1992, larger LBOs made a comeback. Their financial structures are more conservative than those employed in the late 1980s, with purchase prices five to six times EBITDA compared with seven to ten times in the 1980s, a minimum of two times interest coverage by trailing EBITDA, more senior debt, and equity of 20 percent or more. Lenders place strong emphasis on the reputation of the sponsors. There has been a shift away from public high-yield debt, particularly PIK and zero-coupon securities, toward private, senior debt provided by banks. Leading commercial banks and investment banks both compete and collaborate with each other in all phases of LBO financing, ranging from equity to senior debt. Some firms try to provide several forms of financing to a given company, perhaps helping to align bondholder and shareholder interests but also creating possible conflicts of interest. Increasing numbers of insurance companies, pension funds, and mutual funds have allocated portions of their portfolios to high-yield debt. But in the current high stock market, **financial buyers**, such as LBO sponsors, have difficulty competing for acquisitions with **strategic buyers**, such as large corporations making investments in selected industries with their own high-priced stock. Some financial buyers have become strategic buyers as they create **leveraged build-ups**, starting with one company and adding others in a consolidating industry. In recent years, more money has been available for investment than the stream of HLTs can absorb. Once again, there is a danger that eagerness to do deals will lead to HLTs of poor credit quality. Recently, however, the HLT default rate has been impressively low.

High-Yield Default Rates

Table 15.2 provides a history of high-yield, straight-debt default rates. The par value of high-yield defaults is shown as a percentage of the total par value of high-yield debt outstanding. Since 1971, the default rate has been above 5 percent for only two years: It was 10.1 percent in 1990 and 10.3 percent in 1991. The weighted-average default rate, based on par values of outstanding issues, was 2.6 percent for 1971 to 1996, 2.9 percent for 1978 to 1996, and 3.1 percent for 1985 to 1996. A recent report by the Salomon Brothers High Yield Research Group notes that the recent relatively low average default rate for high-yield debt has surprised most forecasters but can be explained by the continued bull stock market, low interest rates, easy availability of credit and refinancing capital, and the overall positive domestic U.S. economic climate in the seventh year of expansion.

Table 15.2
Default Rates for Straight, High-Yield Debt

Year	Par Value Outstanding (Millions of Dollars)	Par Value Defaults (Millions of Dollars)	Default Rate (Percentage)
1997*	296,000	2,446	0.826
1996	271,000	3,336	1.231
1995	240,000	4,551	1.896
1994	235,000	3,418	1.454
1993	206,907	2,287	1.105
1992	163,000	5,545	3.402
1991	183,600	18,862	10.273
1990	181,000	18,354	10.140
1989	189,258	8,110	4.285
1988	148,187	3,944	2.662
1987	129,557	7,486	5.778
1986	90,243	3,156	3.497
1985	58,088	992	1.708
1984	40,939	344	0.840
1983	27,492	301	1.095
1982	18,109	577	3.186
1981	17,115	27	0.158
1980	14,935	224	1.500
1979	10,356	20	0.193
1978	8,946	119	1.330
1977	8,157	381	4.671
1976	7,735	30	0.388
1975	7,471	204	2.731
1974	10,984	123	1.129
1973	7,824	49	0.626
1972	6,928	193	2.786
1971	6,602	82	1.242

* January through June 1997
Source: Salomon Brothers High-Yield Research Group

15

Conclusions

The HLTs described in this chapter, including LBOs and leveraged re-capitalizations, were undertaken for a variety of reasons, including an opportunity for management to buy a subsidiary from a large corporation; a perceived opportunity for an LBO sponsor organization to buy a company, take it private, improve its profitability, and take it public again at a profit; a defense against a hostile takeover attempt (sometimes by an LBO sponsor); a way to motivate management; and a way to send signals to the market concerning management's confidence in the company's future. The record appears to support the use of high leverage under the right circumstances: a company with strong, predictable cash flow; modest growth opportunities, implying a limited need for capital expenditures; and seasoned management. In the quadrant model used for the case-study companies, HLT candidates would tend to be more in the volatile-growth than the secular-growth category. They would also tend to have more fixed assets than intangible assets, because fixed assets provide more collateral for borrowing. The evidence that high leverage works for certain types of companies under the right circumstances is not intended to dispute the arguments for low leverage made by case-study companies in other circumstances.

The case studies of O.M. Scott and Safeway and other studies by Michael Jensen, Karen Wruck, and Steven Kaplan noted in this chapter show how the combination of management ownership and high leverage can provide both a carrot and a stick and result in superior financial performance for appropriate companies. Sealed Air and CUC are unusual examples of how a leveraged recapitalization can energize a company's management or send signals to the market about a company's future prospects. But the case studies earlier in this book and the HLTs described in this chapter show high leverage is often employed for only a short time. Three case-study companies—Home Depot, Paychex, and Sheplers—have used high leverage as a necessary tool for either starting or buying the company but then used strong operating cash flow to pay down their debt. Similarly, Sealed Air and CUC International reduced their debt after achieving the objectives they had sought with high leverage. Holthausen and Larcker showed in their study that many companies have gone public just a few years after being taken private in LBOs.

While the overall failure rate seems relatively low, a number of large, well-known defaults between 1989 and 1992 gave HLTs a bad reputation and caused the junk-bond market to dry up. The causes of those failures were often a combination of factors, including more leverage than underlying cash flows could service; a high amount of junk-bond financing, which at that time allowed less workout flexibility than bank debt or the earlier junk-bond market controlled by Drexel; and unfortunate timing. As the Denises pointed out in their study of leveraged recapitalizations that encountered financial distress, several events during this period—including the recession, the downfall of Drexel, and legislation restricting savings-bank investments in high-yield debt—had a compounded effect on the ability of highly leveraged companies to survive. Opler and Titman also showed that highly leveraged companies that depend on R&D—perhaps not suitable candidates for HLTs in the first place—and highly leveraged companies in concentrated industries often suffer competitively during a recession. Since 1992, HLTs have grown again in a prosperous economy. Although lessons have been learned about the boundary lines for sensible HLTs, history shows overheated markets usually result in at least a few excessively risky transactions.

Endnotes

1. Roden, Dianne M., and Wilbur G. Lewellen. "Corporate Capital Structure Decisions: Evidence from Leveraged Buyouts." *Financial Management* (Summer 1995): 76–87.

2. Jensen, Michael C. "The Eclipse of the Public Corporation." *Harvard Business Review* (September–October 1989): 61–74.

3. Kaplan, Steven N., and Jeremy C. Stein. "The Pricing and Financial Structure of Management Buyouts in the 1980s." University of Chicago Working Paper (January 25, 1991).

4. Wruck, Karen Hopper. "Financial Distress, Reorganization, and Organizational Efficiency." *Journal of Financial Economics* 27 (1990): 419–444.

5. Holthausen, Robert W., and David F. Larcker. "The Financial Performance of Reverse Leveraged Buyouts." *Journal of Financial Economics* 42 (1996): 293–322. Operating performance is measured in the study by two ratios: (1) operating earnings before depreciation, interest, and taxes divided by total assets and (2) operating cash flow before interest and taxes divided by total assets. Both measures are before taxes and interest to avoid the mechanical effects of leverage.

6. Palepu, Krishna G., and Karen H. Wruck. "Consequences of Leveraged Shareholder Payouts: Defensive versus Voluntary Recapitalizations." Harvard Business School Working Paper, 1992.

7. Opler, Tim C., and Sheridan Titman. "Financial Distress and Corporate Performance." *Journal of Finance* (July 1994): 1015–1040.

8. Denis, David J., and Diane K. Denis. "Causes of Financial Distress Following Leveraged Recapitalizations." *Journal of Financial Economics* 37 (1995): 129–157.

9. Evidence to support this hypothesis is presented in "The Evolution of Buyout Pricing and Financial Structure in the 1980s," by Steven Kaplan and Jeremy Stein, *Quarterly Journal of Economics* (May 1993): 313–357.

10. Baker, George P., and Karen H. Wruck. "Organizational Changes and Value Creation in Leveraged Buyouts: The Case of O.M. Scott & Sons Company." *Journal of Financial Economics* 25 (1989): 163–190.

11. Wruck, Karen H. "Financial Policy as a Catalyst for Organizational Change: Sealed Air's Leveraged Special Dividend." *Journal of Applied Corporate Finance* 7, no. 4 (Winter 1995): 20–37.

12. Healy, Paul M., and Krishna Palepu. "The Challenges of Investor Communication: The Case of CUC International, Inc." *Journal of Financial Economics* 38 (1995): 111–140.

13. Denis, David J. "The Benefits of High Leverage: Lessons from Kroger's Leveraged Recap and Safeway's LBO." *Journal of Applied Corporate Finance* 7, no. 4 (Winter 1995): 38–52.

14. Bruner, Robert F., and Kenneth M. Eades. "The Crash of the Revco Leveraged Buyout: The Hypothesis of Inadequate Capital." *Financial Management* (Spring 1992): 35–49.

15. Wruck, Karen H. "What Really Went Wrong at Revco." *Journal of Applied Corporate Finance* (Summer 1991): 79–92.

16. Kaplan, Steven N., and Jeremy C. Stein. "The Pricing and Financial Structure of Management Buyouts in the 1980s." University of Chicago Working Paper (January 25, 1991).

17. Kaplan, Steven N. "Campeau's Acquisition of Federated: Post-Bankruptcy Results." *Journal of Financial Economics* 25 (1994): 123–136.

18. Wruck, Karen Hopper. "Financial Distress, Reorganization, and Organizational Efficiency." *Journal of Financial Economics* 27 (1990): 419–444.

19. Allen, Jay R. "LBOs—the Evolution of Financial Structures and Strategies." *Journal of Applied Corporate Finance* (Winter 1996): 18–29.

Interview Protocol

I. Capital-Structure Policy

   A. What is your capital-structure policy?

      1. Do you prefer to use internally generated capital or external capital?

      2. Do you manage your capital structure via credit rating, coverage ratios, or debt-equity ratios? If you use debt-equity ratios, are they based on market or book values? To what extent do you use internal standards or external standards such as rating criteria and industry averages?

      3. What is your fixed- and floating-rate debt policy?

      4. What is your policy on the timing of equity and debt issues?

      5. How does your corporate tax position influence your capital-structure policy?

      6. How does your policy address flexibility, risk, income, control, and timing?

   B. To what degree do you consider your capital structure to be within your control, and to what degree is it determined by factors such as the nature of your company's assets, its performance, its perceived riskiness, industry norms, and market conditions?

   C. How widely has your capital structure varied in recent years? What are the reasons? How have changes in structure affected your company's cost of capital, its performance, its stock market value, and its financial flexibility?

   D. Does one capital structure apply to the entire company? Have you considered different structures or targeted stock for particular businesses or subsidiaries? Does your policy include separate financing at the subsidiary level?

II. Dividend Policy

    A. What is your dividend policy?

        1. How have factors such as investor expectations and reinvestment opportunities been considered and balanced?

        2. How have you taken corporate and investor tax considerations into account?

    B. Have you ever considered changing your dividend policy?

        1. How is dividend policy affected by expected market reactions?

        2. Have possible adverse market reactions ever prevented you from changing dividend policy?

III. Development and Approval of Policies

    A. How were your capital structure and dividend policies developed and approved?

    B. How frequently are these policies reviewed with other members of senior management and the board of directors? How important are these policies as top management issues?

    C. How do you evaluate the effectiveness of your capital structure and dividend policies?

IV. Instruments and Tactics

    A. What types of instruments have been most useful in maintaining or changing your capital structure and minimizing your cost of capital?

        1. Does your capital-structure policy include short-term debt and leases?

        2. To what extent have you used derivative financial instruments and other tactics such as asset securitization and overseas borrowing?

        3. How have you incorporated optionality into your capital structure through instruments such as convertibles, hydrids, warrants, puts, and calls?

B. Has your company bought back stock? If so, what were the reasons?

V. Communication with the Markets

A. How do anticipated market reactions affect your dividend and financing decisions?

B. Is your company's credit rating where you think it should be? Have you ever tried to change it?

C. What aspects of your capital-structure and dividend policy are investors, lenders, and analysts most interested in? How do they communicate their concerns?

D. What analytic tools, debt coverage ratios, and other ratios do you find most helpful in discussions with investors, analysts, and lenders?

E. Have you ever tried to appeal to a particular type of investor such as retail or institutional with a long-term outlook? Have you ever tried to change the mix of your investors?

VI. Related Issues

A. To what extent have your company's investment decisions been independent of the method of financing and to what extent have they been interrelated?

B. What do you consider to be the most appropriate method to value your company? How are your policies on capital structure and dividends related to your valuation method and your strategy to enhance shareholder value?

C. What sources of information, such as books, periodicals, and conferences, are most helpful to you as you think about capital structure?

APPENDIX B

Bibliography

Allen, Jay R. "LBOs—The Evolution of Financial Structures and Strategies." *Journal of Applied Corporate Finance* (Winter 1996):18–29.

Describes the evolution of highly leveraged transactions in the 1990s.

Baker, George P., and Karen H. Wruck. "Organizational Changes and Value Creation in Leveraged Buyouts: The Case of O.M. Scott & Sons Company." *Journal of Financial Economics* 25 (1989): 163–190.

In a detailed study of the effect on O.M. Scott & Sons Company of its sale to a group of managers and an outside LBO firm, the authors found that management equity ownership and the pressure of servicing a heavy debt load equity ownership can lead to improved management performance.

Barclay, Michael J., and Clifford W. Smith, Jr. "On Financial Architecture: Leverage, Maturity, and Priority." *Journal of Applied Corporate Finance* (Winter 1996):4–17.

The authors concluded in an earlier article that a firm's financial architecture is determined by its investment opportunities, and that high-growth firms tend to incur less debt than low-growth firms. In this article, they conclude that the debt incurred by high-growth companies tends to have shorter maturity and higher priority than the debt raised by more mature companies.

Barclay, Michael J., Clifford W. Smith, Jr., and Ross L. Watts. "The Determinants of Corporate Leverage and Dividend Policies." *Journal of Applied Corporate Finance* (Winter 1995):4–19.

A statistical survey of 6,700 companies over a 30-year period assesses the relative importance of factors such as taxes, contracting costs, and signaling effects on capital structure. The article concludes that for high-growth firms (firms with high market-to-book ratios), heavy debt can lead to underinvestment and dividends can lead to flotation costs for new financing, but for mature firms with limited growth opportunities (firms with low market-to-book ratios), high leverage and dividends can have substantial benefits in controlling the "free cash-flow" problem, the temptation of managers to overinvest in mature investments or make diversifying acquisitions.

Berle, Adolph A., and Gardiner C. Means. *The Modern Corporation and Private Property*. New York: Macmillan, 1932.

This book had a major impact on thinking when it was published because it suggested the managers of large corporations were sufficiently insulated from the capital markets that capital market discipline could not be applied. The implication was that the government should apply social and economic pressure. The rash of corporate takeovers, hostile proxy fights, and pension-fund activism that began in the 1970s raises questions about how well the premise of the study has held up. Its concerns have been reborn as agency theory issues.

Brealey, Richard A., and Stewart A. Myers. *Principles of Corporate Finance*, 4th ed. New York: McGraw-Hill, 1991.

One of the best current corporate finance textbooks, it has strong chapters on borrowing and dividend policies.

Brennan, Michael J. "Corporate Finance Over the Past 25 Years." *Financial Management* (Summer 1995):9–22.

This nontechnical article surveys the developments in corporate finance.

Bruner, Robert F., and Kenneth M. Eades. "The Crash of the Revco Leverage Buyout: The Hypothesis of Inadequate Capital." *Financial Management* (Spring 1992):35–49.

The authors show that the Revco Drug Stores LBO was inadequately capitalized and had a low probability of generating sufficient cash to meet its debt obligations.

Childs, John F. *Long-term Financing.* Englewood Cliffs, NJ: Prentice-Hall, 1961.

Childs was a vigorous supporter of the primacy of access to the capital markets as the key capital structure criterion. His view was that debt should be saved for emergencies.

Conroy, Robert M., and Robert S. Harris. "Stock Splits and Stock Prices in the U.S.: Why Do Share Prices Remain Constant?" Darden School Working Paper, Graduate School of Business Administration, University of Virginia, 1996.

The authors provide evidence that managers split stocks primarily based on some firm-specific price level, often the absolute level of the lagged split price, the price level after the prior split.

Denis, David J. "The Benefits of High Leverage: Lessons from Kroger's Leveraged Recap and Safeway's LBO." *Journal of Applied Corporate Finance* (Winter 1995):38–52.

The author compares Kroger's leveraged recapitalization with Safeway's LBO.

Denis, David J., and Diane K. Denis. "Causes of Financial Distress Following Leveraged Recapitalizations." *Journal of Financial Economics* 37 (1995):129–157.

The authors discuss possible reasons for the failures that befell nearly a third of the leveraged recapitalizations completed between 1985 and 1988.

Dewing, Arthur Stone. *The Financial Policy of Corporations.* New York: The Ronald Press, in various editions beginning in 1920 and ending in 1953.

This was a comprehensive study, which gave a good reporting of the historical developments of various techniques, but with a strong emphasis on the institutional frameworks and practices of the period, most of which are quite different in modern capital markets.

Donaldson, Gordon. "The Corporate Restructuring of the 1980s—and Its Import for the 1990s." *Journal of Applied Corporate Finance* (1994):55–67.

APPENDIX B

The article describes the way corporate management became insulated from the capital markets before the restructuring wave of the 1980s by accumulating large amounts of cash and diversifying into businesses that did not build shareholder value. It compares voluntary and involuntary restructuring and recommends measures for improved board oversight.

_____. *Corporate Debt Capacity*. Boston: Harvard Business School, 1961.

This is the most extensive field study that has been done on corporate capital-structure decisions. Although it is nearly 40 years old, many of the observations sound very contemporary. Donaldson describes a cash-flow approach to determining the amount of debt a company can manage. At the time, the computational requirements to use the analysis were significant drawbacks to its implementation, but the personal computer has overcome these problems.

Durand, David. "Costs of Debt and Equity Funds for Business: Trends and Problems of Measurement." *Conference on Research in Business Finance*, New York: National Bureau of Economic Research, 1952.

Durand lays out very clearly and simply the two schools of thought that have set the terms for the discussion of capital-structure criteria: Given an asset structure, does the corporate value depend solely on the earnings before interest and taxes, or do other factors come into play?

Fisher, Anne B. "Don't Be Afraid of the Big Bad Debt." *Fortune*, April 22, 1991.

The article notes that the number of triple-A-rated companies declined from 66 in 1980 to 40 in 1991, but that higher leverage has not made U.S. firms less competitive in the world economy.

Harris, Milton, and Arthur Raviv. "The Theory of Capital Structure." *Journal of Finance* (March 1991):297–355.

This article provides an excellent but somewhat technical comprehensive survey of capital-structure theory.

Harris, Robert S. "A Note on Elements of Capital-Structure Theory." Unpublished paper. The Darden Graduate School of Business Administration, University of Virginia, 1996.

This is a nontechnical review of the current state of capital-structure financial theory.

Healy, Paul M., and Krishna Palepu. "The Challenges of Investor Communication: The Case of CUC International, Inc." *Journal of Financial Economics* 38 (1995):111–140.

The authors show how a company used a leveraged recapitalization to send positive signals after the market showed concerns about the company's practice of capitalizing marketing expenses.

Holthausen, Robert W., and David F. Larcker. "The Financial Performance of Reverse Leveraged Buyouts." *Journal of Financial Economics* 42 (1996):293–322.

The authors examined the operating performance of a sample of 90 reverse LBOs. They found that these companies outperform their industries in the first few years after their IPOs.

Jensen, Michael C. "The Eclipse of the Public Corporation." *Harvard Business Review* (September–October 1989):61–74.

Jensen believes that new organizational forms, such as LBO associations with active investors, have created new models of general management and motivated gains in operating efficiency, employee productivity, and shareholder value.

Jensen, Michael C., and William H. Meckling. "Theory of the Firm: Managerial Behavior, Agency Costs and Ownership Structure." *Journal of Financial Economics* (October 1976):305–360.

This article represents a revival of concern about the uneconomic decisions made by managements that do not have the incentive to maximize shareholder value, now termed "moral hazard" or "agency costs." The latter term refers to the costs the shareholders incur by hiring agents in the form of professional managers to run the business on the shareholders' behalf.

Kahn, Sharon. "Deleveraging: America Fights Its Debt Habit." *Management Review* (February 1992):10–15.

This article describes a number of companies that took on substantial debt in the late 1980s and deleveraged in the early 1990s. In many cases, these companies are stronger and more focused than they were before they increased their debt.

Kaplan, Steven N. "Campeau's Acquisition of Federated: Post-Bankruptcy Results." *Journal of Financial Economics* 25 (1994): 123–136.

The author illustrates that an HLT can increase value even though the company is unable to meet its debt payments. He also shows that the net costs of financial distress, and even bankruptcy, need not be large.

Kaplan, Steven N., and Jeremy C. Stein. "The Pricing and Financial Structure of Management Buyouts in the 1980s." University of Chicago Working Paper (January 25, 1991).

The authors presented evidence to support the hypothesis that the market for highly leveraged transactions became overheated in the late 1980s, resulting in deals that were overpriced and poorly structured, and thus should not have been undertaken.

Lintner, John. "Distribution of Income of Corporations among Dividends, Retained Earnings, and Taxes." *American Economic Review* 46 (May 1956):97–113.

This model of how the dividend decision is made, based on an empirical study, has had great staying power. It says that the directors lag the increase in the dividend behind the increase in earnings and set a level they believe can be sustained in the face of whatever reasonable setbacks the company can face.

Logue, Dennis E., James K. Seward, and James P. Walsh. "Rearranging Residual Claims: A Case for Targeted Stock." *Financial Management* (Spring 1996):43–61.

The authors described targeted stock as a much weaker form of separating divisional businesses than other forms of equity reorganization, such as spin-offs and equity carve-outs, but they concluded from available empirical evidence that investors view it favorably.

Miller, Merton H. "Debt and Taxes." *Journal of Finance* (May 1977): 261–276.

Miller responds to the criticism that differential taxes among investors will permit the creation of an optimal debt-equity mix by suggesting that any value permitted by the tax differentials will be used up in the economy before all companies can take advantage of it. The first firms to do so will benefit, but none of the rest will.

Miller, Merton H., and Franco Modigliani. "Dividend Policy, Growth, and the Valuation of Shares." *Journal of Business* (October 1961): 411–433.

MM extended their proof that capital structure does not influence value to prove that dividends do not affect it either. Coverage of their analysis will also be found in any current financial text.

_____. "The Cost of Capital, Corporate Finance, and the Theory of Investment." *American Economic Review* (June 1958):261–297.

This is the initial MM article that laid the conceptual foundation for the value of a company being independent of its capital structure. Although it is of historic interest, a clearer explanation of their approach can be found in most finance texts. The empirical evidence they provided to validate the theory is generally ignored.

_____. "Corporate Income Tax Shields and the Cost of Capital: A Correction." *American Economic Review* (June 1963):433–443.

Following much criticism that their 1958 article did not properly allow for the effect of taxes on different layers of capital, MM revised their initial conclusion to indicate that if differential taxes exist, value will be maximized by the use of the capital that has the greatest tax cover.

Myers, Stewart C. "The Capital Structure Puzzle." *Journal of Finance* (July 1994):575–592.

As a Presidential Address to the American Finance Association, this article is much less mechanical than many appearing in the *Journal of Finance*. The puzzle to which Myers refers is how capital-structure decisions are made, which he suggests remains mysterious despite a generation of theoretical work. He proposes a "pecking-order" approach as the explanation for capital-structure decisions. Management first uses internal sources, then senior debt, then junior debt, and finally equity, somewhere along the line cutting off capital expenditures. One implication is that rather than using an average cost of capital, management uses a marginal one based on the security that is being raised to finance the marginal project.

Myers, Stewart C., and Nicholas S. Majluf. "Corporate Financing and Investment Decisions When Firms Have Information that Investors Do Not Have." *Journal of Financial Economics*, 13(1984):187–221.

This is an early investigation of the effects imperfect information might have on various parties to the capital-structure decision.

Opler, Tim C., and Sheridan Titman. "Financial Distress and Corporate Performance." *Journal of Finance* (July 1994):1015–1040.

The authors found that highly leveraged companies lose substantial market share to their more conservatively financed competitors in industry downturns.

Palepu, Krishna G., and Karen H. Wruck. "Consequences of Leveraged Shareholder Payouts: Defensive versus Voluntary Recapitalizations." Harvard Business School Working Paper.

The authors found that defensive recapitalizations have better stock price performance between the time of announcement and the payout, but that voluntary recapitalizations have better performance after the payout.

Roden, Diane M., and Wilbur Llewellen. "Corporate Capital Structure Decisions: Evidence from Leveraged Buyouts." *Financial Management* (Summer 1995):76–87.

The authors addressed the relationship between company characteristics and the financial structure of LBOs.

Ross, Stephen A. "The Determination of Financial Structure: The Incentive-Signaling Approach." *Bell Journal of Economics* (Spring 1977):23–40.

Given management compensation based on maximizing shareholder value, Ross develops a theoretical foundation that when management expects the firm to do well, it will lever the firm more highly. According to Ross, management has no incentives to give a false signal, and the market can interpret higher leverage as an insider's expectation of higher returns. This approach also challenges the perfect-markets concept that inside information does not exist for more than a very brief time, too brief for it to be of value.

Sihler, William W. "Framework for Financial Decisions." *Harvard Business Review* (March–April 1971):123–135.

This article offers a general review of the conceptual and practical aspects of corporate financing decisions but dates from before the capital asset pricing models.

Standard & Poor's. *Corporate Ratings Criteria*. New York: The McGraw-Hill Companies, 1996.

This is a description of the thought processes and methodologies employed in determining Standard & Poor's Ratings, including both quantitative and qualitative aspects of the analytical process.

Stern, Joel M., and Donald H. Chew, Jr., eds. *The Revolution in Corporate Finance*, 2nd ed. Cambridge, MA, and Oxford: Blackwell, 1992.

This compendium of articles by leading theorists is written from a less technical perspective.

Stiglitz, Joseph E. "Some Aspects of the Pure Theory of Corporate Finance: Bankruptcies and Take-overs." *Bell Journal of Economics and Managerial Science* (Autumn 1972):458–482.

This is an early attempt to show that the unsymmetrical incidence of bankruptcy costs can create the conditions for a capital structure that will maximize value.

Warner, Jerold B. "Bankruptcy Costs: Some Evidence." *Journal of Finance* (May 1977):337–347.

Warner challenged the possibility that bankruptcy costs can influence the cost of capital, because they are too small a portion of an ongoing company's value.

_____. "Financial Distress, Reorganization, and Organizational Efficiency." *Journal of Financial Economics* 27 (1990):419–444.

Wruck explained that financial distress is often accompanied by changes in management, governance, and organizational structure.

Wruck, Karen Hopper. "Financial Policy as a Catalyst for Organizational Change: Sealed Air's Leveraged Special Dividend." *Journal of Applied Corporate Finance* (Winter 1995):20–37.

The author described how a leveraged recapitalization can solve a free-cash-flow problem and restore a sense of urgency for a management lulled into complacency by corporate success.

_____. "What Really Went Wrong at Revco." *Journal of Applied Corporate Finance* (Summer 1991):79–92.

The author highlighted key factors behind the Revco failure. She noted the need for LBOs to have strong, predictable cash flows, and of equal importance, to have a strong management team, a proven business strategy, and an effective sponsor organization.

Glossary

Abnormal Returns Increases or decreases in returns in excess of the average of the risk-adjusted market return on a security. These returns are studied in connection with a specific event such as a takeover offer or the announcement of an acquisition, special dividend, or recapitalization.

Accretive Increasing in value.

Black-Scholes The original and best known Option Pricing Model. See Option Pricing Model.

C Corporation A corporation that operates under the rules of Subchapter C of the Internal Revenue Code. For a C corporation, income is taxed to the corporation as it is recognized. See S Corporation.

Call Option An option to buy an asset at a specified exercise price on or before a specified exercise date.

Call Provision A provision in a bond indenture that allows the issuer to buy bonds back from investors at a preset price during a specified time period.

Cash-Flow Adequacy Ratio A ratio developed by Fitch Investors' Service that compares net free cash flow (EBITDA minus cash taxes, cash interest, and capital expenditures) for a given year against average annual principal debt maturities over the next five years. This ratio is a useful indicator of whether a company with steady, predictable cash flows can bear the burden of high leverage.

Cash Flow Return on Investment Cash flow generated as a percentage of cash invested in the business. Cash flow generated is often considered to be free cash flow, the cash left from operating income before deducting noncash charges such as depreciation and amortization, but after deducting payment of taxes and incremental investment in equipment and working capital that are required to sustain the business. Cash invested in the business is often considered to be total assets minus current liabilities. A more specific proprietary model compares the cumulative cash invested in a business with the cash it is currently producing, recognizing that there is a finite life over which depreciating assets will produce cash and a residual value to nondepreciating assets such as working capital and land. When that model is used for valuation, assumptions are made about a growth in invested capital funded by free cash flow and a convergence of above-average returns toward market averages over time. This model is explained in detail in *Cash Flow and Performance Measurement: Managing for Value* (FERF 1996).

Company Registration An alternative proposed by the Securities and Exchange Commission (SEC) to the existing shelf registration procedure to ease paperwork requirements and expedite the issuance process. Seasoned issuers would be allowed to file a one-time registration form and then issue any amount or kind of securities indefinitely. Registration fees would be assessed on a pay-as-you-go basis. Company-update and transactional disclosures would be filed with the SEC in a Form 8-K at the time of the offering. The current shelf system, in contrast, requires registration of specific types of securities for a fixed period of time, with fees paid at registration. See Shelf Registration.

Convertible Security A bond or preferred stock that may be converted into another security, usually common stock, at the holder's option.

Costless Collar A method for taking a bullish view on a company's stock in which put warrants on the stock are sold and the proceeds are used to buy call options.

Credit Rating A rating agency's opinion of the general creditworthiness of an obligor with respect to a particular debt security or other financial obligation, based on an analysis of relevant business and financial risk factors. The analysis includes leverage, profitability, and cash-flow ratios as well as a qualitative assessment of industry characteristics and the company's management, competitive position, and financial policies.

Credit-Sensitive Notes Securities with an adjustable coupon that is based on the issuer's credit rating. In the event of a ratings upgrade, the coupon on the security is reduced. A ratings downgrade, by contrast, leads to an increase in the coupon. Credit-sensitive notes were first issued in 1989 by Enron Corporation. They were developed as a means to protect investors against event risk, the risk that a major structural change, such as an LBO or a leveraged recapitalization, will cause a ratings downgrade and a consequent loss for bondholders. Before credit-sensitive notes were introduced, the most frequent event-risk protection was in the form of "poison-put" provisions that allowed the investor to put the notes back to the issuer upon the occurrence of certain specified events that affected the credit rating. A potential disadvantage of a poison put is that investors might have to reinvest in a lower interest-rate environment after putting the bonds back to the issuer. Chrysler Financial's credit-sensitive notes issued in 1990 carried a one-time "put" for investors that could be exercised if Moody's Investors Service, which had Chrysler and Chrysler Financial under review at the time, lowered its ratings. The downside risk for the issuer of credit-sensitive notes tends to be greater than the upside potential because spreads tend to rise more when credit ratings fall below investment grade than they fall when ratings rise to higher investment-grade levels.

Debtor-In-Possession Financing Financing that is extended to a company in Chapter 11 proceedings and that is senior to all debt previously incurred by the company.

Dual Class Common Stock Dual class common stock is a method for concentrating majority ownership among insiders. With targeted stock, the relative voting rights generally are calculated every year based on the market capitalization of each business. In the event that the company sells the targeted business, there is sometimes a provision for proceeds to be paid to the shareholders of the targeted group, either in the form of a dividend or by exchange for stock of the selling corporation. Targeted stock is one of several alternative forms of equity reorganization, which include equity carve-outs and spin-offs. See Equity Carve-Out and Spin-Off.

Early Redemption (Put) Option A feature of some bonds that permits the holder to sell the bonds back to the issuer or to a third party at par or close to par in the event that interest rates rise and/or the quality of the issuer's credit declines. Bonds with these options are usually called Put Bonds, Puttable Notes, or Puttable Bonds.

Efficient Frontier The point at which taking on more debt starts to increase rather than decrease a company's cost of capital.

Employee Stock Option Program (ESOP) An employee benefit plan consisting of a tax-exempt trust (ESOT) established by the company. The trust must invest primarily in the company's stock, and it is permitted to borrow in order to acquire the stock. In an unleveraged ESOP, either the company can give cash to the trust with which to buy shares in the open market or it can issue new treasury shares to the trust. No debt is involved. In a leveraged ESOP, the funds used to purchase the company's stock are borrowed, by either the company or the ESOT.

When a company establishes a leveraged ESOP, it has two financing options. Either it can borrow money and relend the funds to the trust, or the trust can borrow directly from a lending institution. The trust uses the proceeds of the loan to purchase the company's stock, either from the company in the form of new treasury shares or on the open market. If the shares are bought on the open market, the proceeds go to previous shareholders, but if the shares are newly issued by the company, the proceeds go back to the company. The company then contributes cash and pays dividends on the stock held in the ESOP (and not yet allocated to employees) to allow the trust to service the debt. These contributions are generally tax deductible. The trust holds the shares in a "suspense account" and allocates them to the individual employees' accounts at a rate equal to the repayment of the loan.

Equity Carve-Out The sale of a portion of a wholly owned subsidiary's common stock to public investors. The shares in the subsidiary can be sold through a secondary offering by the parent company or through a primary offering by the subsidiary itself. Logue, Seward, and Walsh (1996) point out that the parent company generally retains a controlling interest in the subsidiary and often retains at least 80 percent of the voting rights to qualify for tax consolidation. Thus, tax and control considerations may limit the amount of equity capital raised in an equity carve-out.

Equity Put Warrant A warrant that contingently commits a company to buy a certain number of shares during a specified period for a defined price.

Financial Buyers Investors such as LBO sponsor firms that buy companies for purely financial objectives. The term "financial buyer" is used in contrast to the term "strategic buyer." See Strategic Buyer.

Forward Start Agreement A risk management agreement whose effective life does not start until a future date set by agreement or contingent on a specific event. All terms of the contract normally are set at the trade date.

Incentive Stock Options Incentive stock options do not create a tax event on the grant date for either the corporation or the employee. There are no tax implications on the exercise date for the corporation except for disqualifying dispositions, explained below. For the employee, the difference between the amount paid for the stock and its fair market value on the exercise date is recognized as compensation for alternative minimum tax purposes in the year in which the option is exercised. The compensation is considered an increase in the employee's basis in the stock. The basis is the purchase price for the purpose of calculating the subsequent capital gains or losses and its tax effect. There are no other tax implications for the employee for regular tax purposes. When the stock is sold, there are no tax implications for the company except in the case of a disqualifying disposition. The employee must recognize the difference between the sales price and the basis as a capital gain or loss.

A disqualifying disposition is the sale of stock within two years of grant or within one year of exercise. The excess of the fair market value over the option price on the exercise date or the sale date, whichever is less, is included in the employee's W-2 in the year the stock is sold. The employee's basis in the stock is the amount paid for the stock plus the compensation recognized. The corporation deducts as compensation expense the same amount the employee recognizes as compensation. See Nonqualified Stock Options.

Information Asymmetry Theory A theory that equity may be mispriced by the market if investors are not as well informed as management about the value of the company's assets. This theory holds that management, as the representative of existing shareholders, has a strong incentive to issue new equity when it believes the company is overvalued, and that shareholders typically mark down stock prices, recognizing their vulnerability to this process.

Interest-Rate Collar A combination of an interest-rate cap, which defines the maximum rate of interest the borrower will pay, and an interest-rate floor, which defines the minimum rate of interest the borrower will pay.

Interest-Rate Swap An agreement between two counterparties to exchange payments calculated as rates of interest on a defined principal amount known as the notional amount. The most common form of interest-rate swap is a fixed-floating swap, in which one counterparty pays at a defined fixed rate over the life of the swap and the other party pays at a defined floating rate such as the London Interbank Offer Rate (LIBOR).

Leveraged Buyout (LBO) A transaction in which existing shareholders are bought out and the company is recapitalized with thin equity and heavy debt.

Leveraged Build-Up An LBO in which one company is used as a foundation for the acquisition of other companies in the same business.

Leveraged ESOP See Employee Stock Option Program (ESOP).

Leveraged Recapitalization A change in financial structure in which leverage is increased substantially, often through a special dividend, but the ownership and management of the company are not changed.

Morris Trust A device prohibited by the Taxpayer Relief Act of 1997 for spinning off a subsidiary and selling it to another company tax free.

Net Operating Loss Carry-Forward For tax purposes, negative net income that can be carried forward to future years to offset taxable net income.

Nonqualified Stock Options Options that do not meet the requirements for incentive stock options. For nonqualified stock options, there are no tax implications for the corporation or the employee on the grant date but tax implications for both on the exercise date. The difference between the amount paid for the stock and the fair market value on the exercise date is included in the employee's W-2 in the year the option is exercised. The employee's basis in the stock is the amount paid for the stock plus the compensation recognized. The corporation deducts as compensation expense the same amount the employee recognizes as compensation. See Incentive Stock Options.

Option Pricing Model An equation for pricing a financial option on an underlying item (such as a currency amount, a security, or a futures contract) based on the spot price of the underlying, the strike price of the option, the interest rate, the time until option expiration, and the volatility of the underlying item.

Original Issue Discount The difference between par value of a bond and the actual issue price when that issue price is set at a level less than par to adjust the yield on the bond to current rates.

Overhang The number of shares of stock on which stock options have been granted but not exercised.

Payment-in-Kind (PIK) Securities Securities that allow the issuer to pay interest or dividends in the form of additional securities. The new securities may also be serviced by payments in kind.

Pecking-Order Theory A theory that management systematically prefers to fund investments with retained earnings rather than external financing and prefers debt to equity when financing is needed because information asymmetries may make the issuance of equity especially expensive. See Information Asymmetry Theory.

Performance Equity Redemption Cumulative Stock (PERCS) A form of mandatorily convertible preferred stock with a cap on the investor's upside opportunity.

Performance Equity-Linked Redemption Quarterly Paid Security (PERQS) Synthetic (dealer-issued) preferred equity redemption cumulative stock (PERCS). Also called synthetic high-income equity-linked debenture (SHIELD) or short-term appreciation and investment return trust (STAIR).

Pooling-of-Interest Accounting A method of accounting for a merger or an acquisition in which the financial statements of the two separate companies are added together to form the statements of the merged company as though they had been combined from their origins. The transaction may be required to be reported in different ways for financial reporting and taxation purposes. See Purchase Accounting.

Purchase Accounting A method of accounting for a merger or an acquisition in which the surviving company records the assets of the acquired company at the fair market value of those assets. The excess (or deficiency) of the purchase price over the adjusted value of the acquired company's assets is amortized as goodwill (or as negative goodwill, the value of assets in excess of the amount paid for them). The transaction may be required to be reported in different ways for financial reporting and taxation purposes.

Put Bonds and Put Notes Notes, also known as puttable bonds and puttable notes, that have embedded features called early redemption (put) options that permit the holders to sell the bonds back to the issuer or to a third party at par or close to par in the event that interest rates rise and/or the quality of the issuer's credit declines.

Put Warrant A security that gives the holder the right to sell the underlying or to receive a cash payment. The value of a put warrant increases as the value of the underlying declines. Put warrants, like their call warrant counterparts, generally have a term of more than one year.

(Source: *The Dictionary of Financial Risk Management*)

Reduced-Cash-Flow Securities Debt securities in which interest or principal payments are deferred from earlier to later years to reduce the cash-flow burden on the borrower during the earlier years.

Reset Bonds Bonds that initially pay relatively low interest rates (as in the case of HLTs) but on a specified later date require the rate to be set to the level that allows the bonds to trade at par in the market.

S Corporation A corporation that operates under the rules of Subchapter S of the Internal Revenue Code. While an election to operate under Subchapter S is in effect, the corporation is not subject to corporate income tax, the corporate alternative minimum tax, the accumulated earnings tax, or the personal holding company tax. The corporate income, whether or not distributed, is considered taxable income to the shareholders and is included, pro rata, in the shareholders' income tax calculations.

Sale and Leaseback The sale of an asset to an external party, often a financial institution, which in turn leases the asset back to the former owner.

Shelf Registration A procedure authorized by SEC Rule 415 in which a company registers, through one filing, all the securities it reasonably expects to sell over a subsequent two-year period. The purpose of shelf registration is to reduce the cost and facilitate the timing of new securities issuance. The SEC prohibited delayed security offerings prior to Rule 415 because of potential problems associated with certifying the issuing firm's financial position. A shelf registration gives management not only increased flexibility but also increased opportunity to exploit inside information by selling securities in a favorable market. Before shelf registration, most companies used the traditional fixed-price negotiated offering. Under this distribution method, the investment bank organizes an underwriting syndicate to buy the entire offering from the issuing firm at a negotiated price. Rule 415 initiated three new distribution methods: Dutch auction, bought deal, and the dribble out. The Dutch auction method has been used mainly for securities such as adjustable-rate preferred stock in which the rate of return is adjusted periodically. In a bought deal, the issuing firm sells its entire offering to one or two investment banking firms, which in turn try to resell the securities quickly to avoid market deterioration. With the dribble out, the issuer sells small amounts of securities authorized by the shelf registration as buyers appear. Past use of shelf registration has tended to be confined to the highest quality firms, with the bought deal the most frequent type of transaction.

Signaling A hypothesis that insiders know more about a company than outsiders and that changes in capital structure or dividend policy signify management's confidence in the company's future or lack thereof. For example, adding leverage voluntarily or increasing dividends communicates management's confidence.

Special Dividend A one-time dividend that is not intended to be repeated.

Spin-Off Division of the existing assets of a corporation into two or more parts. Current shareholders receive a pro rata distribution of equity claims on the assets of each new corporate entity.

Split-Coupon Bonds Bonds that stipulate low cash interest rates during their earlier years and predetermined higher interest rates during their later years.

Static Trade-Off Theory A theory that management consciously balances the tax advantages of additional debt against the expected costs of financial distress.

Stock Options Options to buy a company's stock granted to employees.

Stock Repurchase A company's purchase of its own stock on the open market.

Strategic Buyer A company that buys another company with strategic as well as financial objectives. The term "strategic buyer" is used in contrast to the term "financial buyer." See Financial Buyers.

Stub Shares Shares of stock that remain after a leveraged recapitalization, LBO, or similar transaction.

Sustainable Growth Rate A measure of a company's ability to grow without raising external capital based on the company's return on sales, asset turnover ratio, and the amount of earnings it retains after payment of dividends. The formula is:

Sustainable growth rate=[net income/sales][sales/assets] [1-(dividend payout rate/net income)]

Swaption An option to enter into a swap contract under specified terms.

Synthetic Convertible A combination of a straight debt issue and a warrant on the issuer's common stock, which is sold separately. Under certain circumstances, premium income from a warrant, subtracted from interest expense on straight debt, can result in lower borrowing cost than with a traditional convertible. Synthetics also offer the advantage of favorable U.S. accounting treatment. Whereas fully diluted earnings per share reflect the full number of shares underlying a traditional convertible from the day it is issued under a method known as "if-converted" accounting, synthetics are accounted for in component parts. Interest expense on the debt is recognized in the normal way. Warrants are accounted for by the treasury stock method, in which new stock issued is not recognized as long as the strike price on the call exceeds the stock price. For a potential issuer, there are several caveats. Companies with low stock-price volatility will receive less premium income from issuing warrants than companies with high stock-price volatility. The term for warrants does not normally exceed five years.

Targeted Stock A class of parent-company stock that tracks the performance of a specific business group within the company. The business group is not necessarily an individual legal subsidiary. Investors in targeted stocks have no claim on the underlying assets of the targeted business unit; they have the same claim on the assets of the parent company as they would with a single class of stock. The objective behind creation of targeted stock is to increase shareholder value by allowing different businesses within a corporation to be valued separately. However, keeping targeted businesses within one corporate structure may provide capital acquisition and tax benefits. Diversification may give the combined entity more borrowing capacity than individual units would have. Net operating losses from poorly performing businesses can be used to shield taxable income from other profitable business units. While targeted stock and dual-class common stock have some similar features, their purposes are different. Dual-class common stock is a method for concentrating majority ownership among insiders. With targeted stock, the relative voting rights generally are calculated every year based on the market capitalization of each business. In the event the company sells the targeted business, there is sometimes a provision for proceeds to be paid to the shareholders of the targeted group, either in the form of a dividend or by exchange for stock of the selling corporation. Targeted stock is one of several alternative forms of equity reorganization, which include equity carve-outs and spin-offs.

The following table shows several prominent issuers of targeted stock, the classes of targeted stock they have created, and the businesses represented by the targeted stock.

Company	Targeted Stock	Business
General Motors	Class E Shares	Electronic Data Systems (later spun off)
	Class H Shares	Hughes Electronics
Georgia-Pacific	Two separate classes of common stock	Timber Pulp, paper and building products
Pittston	Pittston Minerals Group Pittston Brink's Pittston Burlington	Coal and minerals Security Air courier
U S West	U S West Communications U S West Media Group	Telephone service Cellular telephone Cable TV International ventures
USX	U.S. Steel Group Marathon Group	Steel Oil

See Equity Carve-Out, Spin-Off, *and* Dual Class Common Stock.

Total Shareholder Return Change in price of a company's shares plus dividends reinvested. Dividends are assumed to be reinvested in the company to take earnings on dividends into account.

Yield Curve A graph illustrating the level of interest rates on a particular type of security as a function of time to maturity.

Zero-Coupon Bonds Bonds that promise a single payment of principal and interest at maturity.

Zero-Coupon Convertible Bond A bond that, like other zero-coupon bonds, sells at a deep discount to its face value, and, like convertible bonds, can be exchanged for a fixed amount of the issuing company's stock, allowing investors to benefit from a rise in the stock price. The issuer pays a lower rate on zero-coupon convertibles than on regular bonds in exchange for the conversion feature. Imputed interest is tax deductible each year even though the issuer does not pay it until maturity. If the bonds are later converted, the issuer retains the tax benefits already realized up to the time of conversion. The U.S. Department of the Treasury proposed changes in tax laws that would have prohibited the deduction of the imputed tax before it is paid, but those changes were not enacted in the Taxpayer Relief Act of 1997.

Comparison of Industry Financials

This appendix compares operating, leverage, and other financial ratios across 16 industries and across the four quadrants of the model used to categorize case-study companies for the research project. The analysis helps validate the characteristics used to specify the quadrants (fixed vs. intangible assets and secular vs. volatile revenue growth) by highlighting the differences among them. It also shows financial characteristics across a broader range of companies than represented in the case studies.

Table D.1 lists the 16 industries in this statistical analysis by quadrant. Tables D.2 through D.5 show averages of selected ratios for each of the 16 industries. The averages are calculated from year-end figures from 1980 to 1995 except for the following industries: Telephone industry figures start in 1984, after the AT&T breakup; biotechnology figures start in 1985; and computer software industry figures start in 1986. Because operating margins for the biotechnology industry were negative in earlier years and had high standard deviations, averages for the intangible-asset, secular-growth industries in table D.3 are shown both with and without biotechnology companies. Table D.6 is a comparison of average ratios across entire quadrants. The bilateral analysis in this table shows, for example, within the group of all companies with fixed assets, whether the average of a given ratio such as market to book is higher for companies with secular revenue growth or with volatile revenue growth. Tables D.7 through D.22 show selected ratios for each of the 16 industries in five-year intervals from 1980 to 1995 except for the telephone, biotechnology, and computer software industries, which are shown from 1985 to 1995.

The industry groups are drawn from the Standard & Poor's 500, MidCap 400, and SmallCap 600 lists. The industries were selected partly to coincide with the industries of the case-study companies and partly to illustrate salient financial characteristics of their quadrants. For example, the paper and forest-products industry is represented in the case studies and is also one of the best examples of operating volatility caused by economic cycles. The biotechnology and computer (software and services) industries are represented in the case studies and provide good examples of companies with rapid, "secular" growth, mostly intangible assets, low leverage, and low dividends. Airlines, shown in this analysis but not represented in the case studies, are a good example of operating volatility and high leverage associated with the financing of tangible assets. Food companies, also shown in this analysis but not represented in the case studies, are an example of relatively high leverage justified by strong, steady operating cash flow. As with the case studies, some industries are better illustrations than others of characteristics typical of their quadrants.

The comparative analysis is based on companies in the S&P 500 industry groups. For some industries, the MidCap 400 and the SmallCap 600 group are displayed as well in tables D.7 through D.22 to illustrate how financial characteristics vary by size within an industry. The financial ratios are based on weighted averages of company financial figures from COMPUSTAT.

Some trends over time can be seen for the 16-industry group as a whole. Consistent with the recent bull market, market-to-book ratios have increased across the board. Consistent with Department of Commerce figures for all U.S. manufacturing companies cited in Chapter 15, The Role of High Debt, leverage based on book values increased on average for 12 of the 16 industry groups from 1985 to 1990. But contrary to the Department of Commerce figures, book leverage also continued to increase for 10 of the 16 industry groups between 1990 and 1995.

Average leverage ratios based on market values show a different picture. On this basis, leverage increased for only 10 of the 16 industry groups between 1985 and 1990. Consistent with increasing market-to-book ratios, leverage decreased for 12 of the 16 industry groups based on market values between 1990 and 1995.

The market-to-book ratios are highest for companies in the intangible-asset, secular-growth quadrant. Biotechnology has the highest asset-growth rate in the 16-industry group. The market-value growth rate is higher for secular-revenue-growth than volatile-revenue-growth companies and higher for intangible-asset companies than fixed-asset companies. The ratio of the market-value growth rate to the asset growth rate is 2.0 for the secular-revenue-growth companies and 1.0 for the volatile-revenue-growth companies.

Both the gross margin and return on sales are higher for secular-revenue-growth than volatile-revenue-growth companies. They are also higher for intangible-asset companies than fixed-asset companies. This may be because companies in secular-growth and intangible-asset industries tend to have newer products and therefore relatively high pricing flexibility and few competitors. As expected, operating margins in secular-revenue-growth industries tend to have a lower standard deviation than those in volatile-revenue-growth industries.

The dividend-payout ratio is higher for volatile-revenue-growth than secular-revenue-growth companies, and higher for fixed-asset companies than intangible-asset companies. Debt as a percentage of total capitalization, based on both book and market values, also is higher for volatile-revenue-growth than secular-revenue-growth companies and is higher for fixed-asset companies than intangible-asset companies. This is consistent with the practices of the case-study companies in their respective quadrants, and also with the observations of Barclay, Smith, and Watts that high-growth firms tend to have low debt and pay low dividends or no dividends at all.[1]

The ratios of current and of noncurrent (fixed) assets to total assets are not completely as expected. Among secular-growth companies, intangible-asset companies have a higher average ratio of fixed assets to total assets than fixed-asset companies. Telephone companies have relatively low fixed assets, probably because those assets have been depreciated, and data-processing-service companies have relatively high fixed assets. Also, the secular-growth industries might have been expected to have newer, undepreciated assets and therefore relatively high percentages of fixed to total assets. However, three intangible-asset industries, data-processing services, lodging, and publishing, have relatively high fixed assets, and as mentioned above, the telephone industry lowers the average ratio of fixed to total assets for the fixed-asset group as a whole.

The ratio of cash to total book assets is highest for biotechnology and computer software, both intangible-asset, secular-growth industries, and for semiconductors, a fixed-asset, secular-growth industry. All three are research-intensive, high-growth, high-risk industries. Treasurers in these industries generally maintain generous cash reserves, in conjunction with low debt, for protection as well as for possible acquisitions. Comparing the quadrants, the ratio of cash to total book assets is higher for secular-revenue-growth than volatile-revenue-growth companies, and higher for intangible-asset companies than fixed-asset companies. Whereas volatile-revenue-growth companies need extra cash to see them through recessions, secular-revenue-growth companies apparently need even more to support continued expansion. The ratio of cash to total assets is lowest for the telephone, machinery, chemical, and forest-products industries. The telephone and chemical industries have relatively predictable revenues, and companies in all four industries apparently have sufficient borrowing power to supplement their cash reserves when necessary.

The following paragraphs discuss the salient characteristics of each quadrant in more detail.

Fixed Assets/Secular Growth

Secular growth is partly evidenced by sharply growing market-to-book ratios in all four industries. With the exception of the telephone industry, asset growth rates are relatively high. The telephone industry is considered a secular-growth industry because the "Baby Bells" and other telephone companies have been diversifying into a variety of newer telecommunications businesses. An increase in the market-to-book ratio from 1.4 in 1985 to 4.9 in 1995 shows that the market sees telephone companies as a growth industry. Consistent with other growth companies, the communications-equipment and the semiconductor industries have relatively low debt and low dividends. For the hospital industry, high debt coupled with high fixed assets reflects real estate that is mortgage financed.

Intangible Assets/Secular Growth

The biotechnology and computer software industries are particularly representative of fast-growing companies with mostly intangible assets; they have very low debt and dividend-payout ratios. The biotechnology industry has the highest market-value growth rate over 15 years. None of the S&P 500 biotechnology companies paid dividends during the period studied. The biotechnology companies show an interesting example of operating leverage. Operating margins increased from a negative 294 percent in 1985, before most of these companies had introduced their first products, to 44 percent in 1995, the highest of the 16 industry groups. Market-to-book ratios are highest in this quadrant, ranging in 1995 from 4.9 for data processing services to 9.7 for computer software and services.

Fixed Assets/Volatile Growth

The four industries in this quadrant show relatively high debt associated with high fixed assets and relatively high dividends associated with low- and moderate-growth companies. These industries also have low market-to-book ratios and volatile operating margins. The paper and forest-products industry has the lowest market-value growth rate over 15 years—approximately the GNP growth rate plus inflation. The machinery industry shows the highest standard deviation of operating margins within the 16-industry sample. For the machinery and chemical industries, debt as a percentage of capitalization increased substantially between 1985 and 1995. On a market-value basis, it increased more moderately for the machinery industry and declined for the chemical industry. In the paper and forest-products industry, the market-to-book ratios are higher in the MidCap 400 group and still higher in the SmallCap 600 group, a possible indication that the market pays a higher premium for specialty producers. Secured financing for airplanes is evidenced by relatively high debt and fixed assets in the airline industry. The 14.2 percent asset growth rate for this industry partly explains the overcapacity and financial losses it experiences in recessions. In 1990, the airline industry group's operating margin after depreciation was only 2.6 percent.

Intangible Assets/Volatile Growth

Both the food and the specialty-retail industries show relatively low operating margins. The publishing industry has the highest gross profit margins in the 16-industry group but average operating margins. The lodging industry group has high fixed assets and high debt because two companies in this group are in both the hotel ownership and the hotel management businesses. The other company in the group, Marriott International, a case-study company, is primarily in the hotel-service business and has relatively little real estate on its balance sheet. The specialty-retailing industry has the highest ratio of sales to total assets among the 16 industries, an indication of the high turnover required in retailing as well as the tendency of retailing companies to lease their premises.

Endnote

1. Barclay, Michael J., Clifford W. Smith, and Ross L. Watts. "The Determinants of Corporate Leverage and Dividend Policies," *Journal of Applied Corporate Finance* (Winter 1995):4–19.

Table D.1
Industries Listed by Quadrant

	Secular Growth	Volatile Growth
Fixed Assets	Telephone	Machinery
	Communications Equipment	Chemicals
	Semiconductors	Airlines
	Hospitals	Paper and Forest Products
Intangible Assets	Biotechnology	Lodging
	Computer Software and Services	Publishing
	Data Processing Services	Specialty Retailing
	Commercial and Consumer Services	Foods

Table D.2
Average Ratios (1980–1995)—Fixed Assets/Secular Growth

Industry	Telephone	Communi-cations Equipment	Semi-conductors	Hospitals	Average
Average Gross Profit Margin	51.1%	39.4%	47.1%	16.7%	38.6%
Average Operating Margin	23.1%	9.0%	13.9%	13.1%	14.8%
Standard Deviation of Average Operating Margin	1.86	1.68	9.65	0.94	3.53
Std Deviation of Avg Operating Margin/Average Operating Margin	8.05	18.64	69.26	7.14	25.77
Average Return on Sales	8.4%	5.2%	12.5%	4.9%	7.8%
Average Return on Assets	3.9%	6.0%	12.5%	4.5%	6.7%
Average Dividend Payout	91.8%	19.6%	5.7%	17.8%	33.7%
Average LT Debt/LT Debt + Equity (Book)	44.2%	17.0%	12.0%	52.0%	31.3%
Average Total Debt/Total Debt + Equity (Book)	48.3%	23.4%	16.9%	53.7%	35.6%
Average LT Debt/LT Debt + Market Capitalization	28.4%	8.7%	5.8%	33.5%	19.1%
Average Total Debt/Total Debt + Market Capitalization	31.7%	12.7%	8.2%	35.0%	21.9%
Average Current Assets/ Total Assets	68.3%	52.3%	53.4%	26.7%	50.2%
Average Noncurrent Assets/ Total Assets	31.7%	47.7%	46.6%	73.3%	49.8%
Average Cash to Total Assets (Book)	1.5%	5.5%	20.4%	3.0%	7.6%
Average Cash to Market Capitalization	1.9%	4.4%	11.6%	3.3%	5.3%
Average Sales to Total Assets	46.8%	116.1%	100.3%	91.0%	88.6%
Average Market to Book	2.3	2.4	2.7	2.3	2.4
15-Year Asset Growth Rate	4.6%	15.7%	17.4%	30.5%	17.0%
15-Year Market-Value Growth Rate	15.8%	24.3%	28.8%	57.3%	31.5%

Data Source for all tables: COMPUSTAT

313

A P P E N D I X   D

Table D.3
Average Ratios (1980–1995)—Intangible Assets/Secular Growth

Industry	Bio-technology	Computer Software	Data Processing Services	Commercial/Consumer Services	Average	Average w/o Biotech
Average Gross Profit Margin	28.2%	63.9%	47.4%	27.9%	41.8%	34.8%
Average Operating Margin	−26.3%	24.3%	13.9%	17.7%	7.4%	14.0%
Standard Deviation of Average Operating Margin	98.54	7.49	2.66	0.97	27.41	2.78
Std Deviation of Avg Operating Margin/Average Operating Margin	−375.09	30.80	19.19	5.49	−79.90	13.87
Average Return on Sales	23.3%	9.6%	5.4%	10.8%	12.3%	6.4%
Average Return on Assets	17.7%	9.1%	4.4%	10.0%	10.3%	5.9%
Average Dividend Payout	0.0%	10.6%	25.7%	61.1%	24.4%	24.4%
Average LT Debt/LT Debt + Equity (Book)	13.3%	17.2%	29.2%	7.6%	16.8%	13.5%
Average Total Debt/Total Debt + Equity (Book)	14.7%	20.9%	33.0%	12.5%	20.3%	16.6%
Average LT Debt/LT Debt + Market Capitalization	4.3%	10.8%	20.3%	8.0%	10.8%	9.8%
Average Total Debt/Total Debt + Market Capitalization	4.6%	12.3%	23.0%	9.2%	12.3%	11.1%
Average Current Assets/Total Assets	61.5%	54.4%	35.6%	44.3%	48.9%	33.6%
Average Noncurrent Assets/Total Assets	38.5%	45.6%	64.4%	55.7%	51.1%	41.4%
Average Cash to Total Assets (Book)	40.0%	17.4%	11.3%	12.2%	20.2%	10.2%
Average Cash to Market Capitalization	10.6%	5.3%	10.8%	6.3%	8.2%	5.6%
Average Sales to Total Assets	75.9%	95.6%	81.6%	92.8%	86.5%	67.5%
Average Market to Book	6.1	3.9	3.0	4.5	4.4	2.8
15-Year Asset Growth Rate	52.2%	9.6%	13.5%	14.9%	22.6%	9.5%
15-Year Market-Value Growth Rate	133.0%	38.0%	14.0%	14.0%	49.8%	16.5%

Table D.4
Average Ratios (1980–1995)—Fixed Assets/Volatile Growth

Industry	Machinery	Chemicals	Airlines	Paper and Forest Products	Average
Average Gross Profit Margin	27.2%	35.4%	14.2%	23.6%	25.1%
Average Operating Margin	7.3%	11.8%	5.6%	8.7%	8.3%
Standard Deviation of Average Operating Margin	3.28	2.29	2.80	3.29	2.92
Std Deviation of Avg Operating Margin/Average Operating Margin	45.16	19.44	50.32	37.83	38.19
Average Return on Sales	2.6%	4.8%	1.0%	4.1%	3.1%
Average Return on Assets	2.4%	4.8%	0.9%	3.6%	2.9%
Average Dividend Payout	52.2%	60.1%	23.0%	44.7%	45.0%
Average LT Debt/LT Debt + Equity (Book)	35.2%	30.7%	47.7%	38.6%	38.1%
Average Total Debt/Total Debt + Equity (Book)	43.9%	36.7%	50.3%	42.6%	43.4%
Average LT Debt/LT Debt + Market Capitalization	26.2%	22.1%	42.5%	33.4%	31.1%
Average Total Debt/Total Debt + Market Capitalization	33.9%	26.6%	45.1%	37.2%	35.7%
Average Current Assets/ Total Assets	49.5%	34.9%	22.4%	21.6%	32.1%
Average Noncurrent Assets/ Total Assets	50.5%	65.1%	77.6%	78.4%	67.9%
Average Cash to Total Assets (Book)	2.1%	2.9%	7.8%	1.9%	3.7%
Average Cash to Market Capitalization	2.8%	4.0%	22.3%	3.6%	8.2%
Average Sales to Total Assets	90.1%	101.4%	94.6%	87.5%	93.4%
Average Market to Book	1.8	2.0	1.4	1.3	1.6
15-Year Asset Growth Rate	14.1%	7.0%	14.7%	8.4%	11.0%
15-Year Market-Value Growth Rate	8.5%	12.3%	16.4%	7.9%	11.3%

Table D.5
Average Ratios (1980–1995)—Intangible Assets/Volatile Growth

Industry	Lodging	Publishing	Specialty Retailing	Foods	Average
Average Gross Profit Margin	25.5%	52.3%	32.7%	47.9%	31.7%
Average Operating Margin	18.1%	15.3%	9.3%	18.7%	12.3%
Standard Deviation of Average Operating Margin	3.12	2.63	1.53	5.18	2.49
Std Deviation of Avg Operating Margin/Average Operating Margin	17.28	17.19	16.36	27.64	15.69
Average Return on Sales	9.9%	8.5%	4.4%	4.8%	5.5%
Average Return on Assets	5.6%	7.8%	8.2%	8.0%	5.9%
Average Dividend Payout	42.2%	45.2%	18.8%	42.3%	29.7%
Average LT Debt/LT Debt + Equity (Book)	36.0%	27.0%	23.2%	39.9%	25.2%
Average Total Debt/Total Debt + Equity (Book)	37.9%	30.0%	25.9%	40.6%	26.9%
Average LT Debt/LT Debt + Market Capitalization	19.5%	12.2%	14.1%	24.9%	14.2%
Average Total Debt/Total Debt + Market Capitalization	20.7%	13.9%	15.7%	25.6%	15.2%
Average Current Assets/ Total Assets	24.3%	28.2%	50.6%	70.5%	34.7%
Average Noncurrent Assets/ Total Assets	75.7%	71.8%	49.4%	29.5%	45.3%
Average Cash to Total Assets (Book)	13.8%	2.1%	5.9%	6.8%	5.7%
Average Cash to Market Capitalization	12.7%	1.6%	3.5%	5.7%	4.7%
Average Sales to Total Assets	56.5%	91.2%	188.7%	165.2%	100.3%
Average Market to Book	2.5	3.1	3.7	4.0	2.7
15-Year Asset Growth Rate	19.5%	8.3%	6.7%	27.4%	12.4%
15-Year Market-Value Growth Rate	15.0%	9.3%	22.4%	17.6%	12.8%

Table D.6
Comparative Ratio Analysis

	Fixed Assets Secular vs. Volatile	Intangible Assets Secular vs. Volatile	Secular Growth Fixed Assets vs. Intangible	Volatile Growth Fixed Assets vs. Intangible
Average Gross Profit Margin	H	H	L	L
Average Operating Margin	H	H	H	L
Standard Deviation of Average Operating Margin				
Std Deviation of Avg Operating Margin/Average Operating Margin	L	L	H	H
Average Return on Sales	H	H	L	L
Average Return on Assets	H	S	L	L
Average Dividend Payout	L	L	H	H
Average LT Debt/LT Debt + Equity (Book)	L	L	H	H
Average Total Debt/ Total Debt + Equity (Book)	L	L	H	H
Average LT Debt/LT Debt + Market Capitalization	L	L	H	H
Average Total Debt/Total Debt + Market Capitalization	L	L	H	H
Average Current Assets/ Total Assets	H	L	H	L
Average Non-Current Assets/ Total Assets	L	H	L	H
Average Cash to Total Assets (Book)	H	H	L	L
Average Cash to Market Capitalization	L	H	L	H
Average Sales to Total Assets	L	L	H	L
Average Market to Book	H	H	L	L
15-Year Asset Growth Rate	H	L	H	L
15-Year Market-Value Growth Rate	H	H	L	L

H = Higher, L = Lower, S = Same

Table D.7
Telephone Industry Summary

	1995	S&P 500 1990	1985
Operating Summary			
Gross Profit Margin	54.9%	55.2%	46.3%
Operating Margin After Depreciation	24.1%	21.5%	25.4%
Dividend Payout	69.6%	71.1%	0.7%
Capitalization Summary			
LT Debt/LT Debt + Equity	50.1%	44.5%	41.5%
Total Debt/Total Debt + Equity	56.2%	49.2%	44.4%
Market to Book	4.9	2.1	1.4

Table D.8
Communications Equipment Industry Summary

	S&P 500 1995	1990	1985	1980	MidCap 400 1995	1990	1985	1980
Operating Summary								
Gross Profit Margin	40.4%	40.8%	41.7%	36.9%	54.8%	50.2%	47.6%	44.9%
Operating Margin After Depreciation	11.8%	8.8%	10.7%	10.9%	14.3%	11.6%	8.2%	14.8%
Dividend Payout	11.5%	18.7%	6.7%	22.8%	0.0%	0.0%	0.0%	0.0%
Capitalization Summary								
LT Debt/LT Debt + Equity	1.2%	18.9%	14.3%	20.4%	0.2%	4.1%	23.9%	28.5%
Total Debt/Total Debt + Equity	20.0%	29.9%	17.7%	23.2%	0.3%	4.4%	25.5%	29.8%
Market to Book	3.9	2.0	2.2	1.8	5.0	1.8	1.7	2.3

Table D.9
Electronics (Semiconductors) Industry Summary

	1995	1990	1985	1980
		S&P 500		
Operating Summary				
Gross Profit Margin	56.5%	47.7%	47.0%	42.3%
Operating Margin After Depreciation	30.7%	12.9%	14.7%	14.8%
Dividend Payout	4.1%	–19.3%	4.6%	13.3%
Capitalization Summary				
LT Debt/LT Debt + Equity	4.2%	12.3%	14.1%	1.9%
Total Debt/Total Debt + Equity	6.6%	16.9%	16.7%	15.8%
Market to Book	4.4	1.8	2.7	3.0

Table D.10
Health Care (Hospital Management) Industry Summary

	1995	1990	1985	1980
		S&P 500		
Operating Summary				
Gross Profit Margin	19.5%	16.4%	17.5%	15.0%
Operating Margin After Depreciation	14.7%	13.0%	14.0%	12.8%
Dividend Payout	4.4%	25.5%	24.2%	22.2%
Capitalization Summary				
LT Debt/LT Debt + Equity	50.7%	52.1%	56.9%	55.7%
Total Debt/Total Debt + Equity	51.6%	56.7%	57.6%	57.2%

Table D.11
Biotechnology Industry Summary

	1995	S&P 500 1990	1985
Operating Summary			
Gross Profit Margin	90.1%	66.8%	-261.4%
Operating Margin After Depreciation	44.1%	-6.9%	-294.2%
Dividend Payout	0.0%	0.0%	0.0%
Capitalization Summary			
LT Debt/LT Debt + Equity	12.6%	15.7%	11.0%
Total Debt/Total Debt + Equity	18.2%	16.6%	11.0%
Market to Book	6.1	4.3	1.4

Table D.12
Computers (Software and Services) Industry Summary

	1995	S&P 500 1990	1985
Operating Summary			
Gross Profit Margin	74.6%	72.2%	40.0%
Operating Margin After Depreciation	30.4%	26.9%	11.0%
Dividend Payout	-8.6%	2.2%	33.5%
Capitalization Summary			
LT Debt/LT Debt + Equity	10.6%	9.3%	24.1%
Total Debt/Total Debt + Equity	14.7%	13.4%	27.8%
Market to Book	9.7	6.7	2.5

Table D.13
Services (Data Processing) Industry Summary

| | S&P 500 | | | |
	1995	1990	1985	1980
Operating Summary				
Gross Profit Margin	46.1%	47.4%	49.9%	43.4%
Operating Margin After Depreciation	18.9%	13.4%	13.9%	10.4%
Dividend Payout	17.8%	24.3%	279.0%	15.0%
Capitalization Summary				
LT Debt/LT Debt + Equity	22.4%	23.7%	71.0%	21.3%
Total Debt/Total Debt + Equity	27.1%	25.8%	73.0%	28.5%
Market to Book	4.9	2.9	1.8	1.5

Table D.14
Services (Commercial and Consumer) Industry Summary

| | S&P 500 | | | | MidCap 400 | | | |
	1995	1990	1985	1980	1995	1990	1985	1980
Operating Summary								
Gross Profit Margin	50.4%	28.1%	22.5%	21.5%	30.6%	33.9%	23.3%	15.7%
Operating Margin After Depreciation	19.8%	18.8%	16.9%	19.0%	12.1%	12.9%	5.8%	6.8%
Dividend Payout	46.8%	56.8%	45.5%	51.4%	46.7%	44.6%	59.9%	44.1%
Capitalization Summary								
LT Debt/LT Debt + Equity	22.7%	12.7%	0.5%	0.4%	55.5%	60.0%	32.2%	28.9%
Total Debt/Total Debt + Equity	34.2%	19.4%	2.2%	0.9%	57.1%	62.0%	33.1%	34.3%
Market to Book	6.0	3.2	3.8	3.7	3.8	2.4	2.2	1.3

Table D.15
Machinery (Diversified) Industry Summary

| | S&P 500 | | | | MidCap 400 | | |
	1995	1990	1985	1980	1995	1990	1985
Operating Summary							
Gross Profit Margin	29.2%	28.5%	27.5%	26.8%	25.3%	23.7%	20.1%
Operating Margin After Depreciation	11.1%	92.7%	5.8%	11.3%	13.5%	12.0%	12.2%
Dividend Payout	25.6%	38.8%	44.8%	36.8%	15.1%	79.5%	33.2%
Capitalization Summary							
LT Debt/LT Debt + Equity	47.3%	35.4%	31.3%	23.0%	29.0%	4.8%	7.6%
Total Debt/Total Debt + Equity	61.0%	48.7%	36.1%	32.0%	40.1%	9.0%	7.7%
Market to Book	2.8	1.4	1.3	1.6	1.9	1.4	1.6

Table D.16
Chemicals Industry Summary

| | S&P 500 | | | | MidCap 400 | | | |
	1995	1990	1985	1980	1995	1990	1985	1980
Operating Summary								
Gross Profit Margin	39.6%	38.0%	32.9%	30.1%	32.5%	31.1%	30.6%	29.2%
Operating Margin After Depreciation	15.6%	13.0%	9.9%	10.5%	11.6%	13.5%	10.3%	12.9%
Dividend Payout	29.6%	45.0%	114.2%	44.1%	31.2%	48.6%	36.4%	31.2%
Capitalization Summary								
LT Debt/LT Debt + Equity	37.5%	29.1%	26.1%	30.6%	39.5%	38.4%	28.1%	21.6%
Total Debt/Total Debt + Equity	50.9%	38.4%	30.5%	35.0%	41.6%	40.3%	29.7%	24.1%
Market to Book	3.8	1.8	1.5	1.3	9.1	22.2	1.5	1.7

Table D.17
Airlines Industry Summary

	S&P 500				MidCap 400			
	1995	1990	1985	1980	1995	1990	1985	1980
Operating Summary								
Gross Profit Margin	14.5%	8.3%	15.3%	22.7%	38.9%	27.2%	22.1%	24.9%
Operating Margin After Depreciation	8.2%	2.6%	9.0%	6.6%	18.8%	11.3%	11.9%	3.9%
Dividend Payout	2.1%	13.5%	5.0%	14.3%	16.6%	22.8%	4.7%	0.0%
Capitalization Summary								
LT Debt/LT Debt + Equity	62.9%	42.6%	40.1%	33.5%	47.3%	46.8%	58.5%	70.3%
Total Debt/Total Debt + Equity	64.1%	48.6%	42.7%	36.2%	52.5%	51.4%	59.7%	72.4%
Market to Book	1.7	1.0	1.3	1.1	2.3	1.2	2.3	1.1

Table D.18
Paper and Forest-Products Industry Summary

	S&P 500				MidCap 400				SmallCap 600			
	1995	1990	1985	1980	1995	1990	1985	1980	1995	1990	1985	1980
Operating Summary												
Gross Profit Margin	29.1%	25.6%	20.6%	23.9%	32.1%	32.0%	31.1%	22.6%	27.3%	21.2%	22.7%	31.0%
Operating Margin After Depreciation	15.1%	10.6%	5.8%	9.1%	20.5%	18.2%	18.0%	10.2%	12.1%	9.9%	11.4%	19.8%
Dividend Payout	13.6%	46.3%	68.1%	44.4%	25.6%	42.5%	34.8%	389.0%	32.2%	53.9%	–386.0%	15.2%
Capitalization Summary												
LT Debt/LT Debt + Equity	45.2%	47.5%	31.5%	32.0%	30.8%	17.6%	24.1%	8.0%	44.5%	22.9%	34.1%	20.9%
Total Debt/Total Debt + Equity	50.2%	51.8%	33.4%	34.1%	32.6%	18.3%	25.5%	14.2%	46.4%	25.1%	36.2%	22.6%
Market to Book	1.5	1.0	1.1	1.1	1.9	1.7	1.9	1.5	3.7	1.6	1.5	1.0

Table D.19 Lodging Industry Summary

	1995	S&P 500 1990	1985
Operating Summary			
Gross Profit Margin	19.1%	25.2%	24.9%
Operating Margin After Depreciation	10.1%	17.3%	18.1%
Dividend Payout	12.0%	49.0%	44.5%
Capitalization Summary			
LT Debt/LT Debt + Equity	52.0%	36.3%	30.4%
Total Debt/Total Debt + Equity	53.9%	37.0%	30.7%
Market to Book	3.1	1.9	2.5

Table D.20
Publishing Industry Summary

	S&P 500				MidCap 400				SmallCap 600		
	1995	1990	1985	1980	1995	1990	1985	1980	1995	1990	1985	1980
Operating Summary												
Gross Profit Margin	53.5%	53.5%	52.4%	46.4%	55.6%	60.0%	56.6%	55.8%	49.4%	53.3%	54.1%	48.1%
Operating Margin After Depreciation	11.6%	12.6%	18.2%	15.5%	8.7%	7.7%	10.4%	10.4%	11.5%	23.8%	20.5%	14.9%
Dividend Payout	32.6%	12.8%	39.0%	39.8%	−74.1%	56.2%	32.2%	41.6%	−15.9%	165.2%	15.6%	29.7%
Capitalization Summary												
LT Debt/LT Debt + Equity	20.3%	33.7%	31.6%	26.0%	48.7%	20.2%	3.7%	11.3%	53.6%	48.7%	30.7%	32.3%
Total Debt/Total Debt + Equity	21.5%	36.7%	36.4%	27.5%	55.0%	23.6%	4.8%	18.5%	54.0%	48.9%	30.9%	32.3%
Market to Book	3.2	2.0	3.9	2.7	3.1	1.7	2.3	1.0	2.4	2.8	4.3	2.5

Table D.21 Specialty-Retailing Industry Summary

| | S&P 500 | | | |
	1995	1990	1985	1980
Operating Summary				
Gross Profit Margin	35.0%	33.4%	32.3%	30.5%
Operating Margin After Depreciation	10.4%	10.7%	9.8%	6.2%
Dividend Payout	28.2%	15.9%	14.6%	18.9%
Capitalization Summary				
LT Debt/LT Debt + Equity	17.1%	16.3%	21.2%	36.7%
Total Debt/Total Debt + Equity	20.8%	20.0%	23.3%	39.0%
Market to Book	3.0	3.8	4.1	1.0

Table D.22
Foods Industry Summary

| | S&P 500 | | | | MidCap 400 | | | |
	1995	1990	1985	1980	1995	1990	1985	1980
Operating Summary								
Gross Profit Margin	38.9%	42.8%	38.1%	28.6%	26.4%	26.5%	30.8%	21.6%
Operating Margin After Depreciation	13.0%	11.5%	10.1%	9.1%	6.8%	7.3%	7.8%	5.4%
Dividend Payout	51.3%	291.0%	45.3%	43.8%	−60.0%	25.4%	28.8%	36.5%
Capitalization Summary								
LT Debt/LT Debt + Equity	37.1%	38.4%	27.1%	23.0%	44.8%	43.1%	28.7%	31.7%
Total Debt/Total Debt + Equity	46.2%	48.0%	38.3%	33.0%	47.2%	50.0%	37.3%	38.0%
Market to Book	9.1	5.0	3.2	1.3	2.4	2.9	2.4	1.2

Henry A. Davis is a consultant and writer specializing in corporate finance and banking topics, and is a frequent contributor to *International Treasurer* and *Risk* magazines. He is director and secretary of the Madison Financial Group and has been a vice president of research and consulting at Ferguson & Co. Prior to that, he was director of research and treasurer at the Globecon Group, vice president at the Bank of Boston, and assistant vice president at Bankers Trust Company. He is the author of *Cash Flow and Performance Measurement: Managing for Value* (FERF, 1996), *Project Finance: Practical Case Studies* (Euromoney Books, 1996), and three other FERF studies. In addition, he is the co-author of the *Lender's Guide to the Knowledge Economy* (Amacom Books, 1996), *Foreign Exchange Risk Management: A Survey of Corporate Practices* (FERF, 1995), and *The Empowered Organization: Redefining the Roles and Practices of Finance* (FERF, 1994). Mr. Davis holds a bachelor's degree from Princeton University and an MBA from the Darden Graduate School of Business Administration, University of Virginia.

William W. Sihler currently holds the Ronald Edward Trzcinski Professorship in Business Administration at the Darden Graduate School, University of Virginia. He began his teaching career at the Harvard Business School in 1964, resigning in 1967 to accept an appointment as associate professor at the Darden Graduate School. From 1977 to 1991, he also held the position of executive director of the Center for International Banking Studies, which was located at the Darden Graduate School under the auspices of the Bankers' Association for Foreign Trade. Dr. Sihler co-authored *The Troubled Money Business* (HarperBusiness, 1991), *Financial Management: Text and Cases* (Allyn and Bacon, 1991), and *Financial Service Organizations: Cases in Strategic Management* (HarperCollinsCollege, 1993), and has authored many anthologized cases and a number of articles. He is president of Southeastern Consultants Group, Ltd., which provides educational and problem-solving consulting, and also serves on the board of the Curtiss-Wright Corporation. Dr. Sihler received his AB, MBA, and DBA from Harvard University.

ACKNOWLEDGMENTS

A research project of this nature is not completed without the kind help of many people. The authors would like to thank the entire FERF staff, Jim Lewis for his overall guidance, Gracie Hemphill for her help in managing every phase of the project, Bill Sinnett for his help in preparing and securing approval for the project proposal, and Janet Hastie and Rhona Ferling for their review and editorial guidance throughout the project. We would like to thank all of the participants from the case-study companies for their willingness to share ideas and to review numerous drafts to ensure those ideas were expressed correctly. We appreciate the assistance of the Advisory Committee and particularly Arthur Neis, chairman, for his help in defining the overall focus of the project, interpreting the results of the research, and reviewing and commenting on all parts of the manuscript. Finally, we would like to acknowledge Gordon Binder, chairman and CEO of Amgen Inc., for his help in arranging the Amgen case study; Bob Conroy, professor at the Darden Graduate School of Business Administration at the University of Virginia, for his guidance on using COMPUSTAT for the comparison of industry financials; Ed Emmer of Standard & Poor's for sharing information on the credit-rating process; Bill Fant, tax legislative adviser of the United States Department of the Treasury, for reviewing our summary of recent tax legislation; Libby Eshbach of the Darden Graduate School of Business Administration Library for her diligence and long hours in retrieving data from COMPUSTAT; Neal Goldman of Salomon Analytics Inc. for providing historical high-yield bond spreads; Andy Halula of Standard & Poor's/COMPUSTAT for securing approval to use COMPUSTAT data for the company financial summaries and comparison of industry financials; Bob Harris, professor at the Darden Graduate School, for sharing his survey of academic literature on corporate finance and for reviewing several sections of the manuscript; Jan Konstanty of Moody's for sharing information on the credit-rating process; Kenneth Langone, chairman and president, Invemed Associates, Inc., for his help in arranging the Home Depot case study; Mark Neagle, practice fellow at the Financial Accounting Standards Board, for his guidance on accounting and tax regulations related to stock options; Alice Peterson, treasurer of Sears Roebuck & Co., for her help with ideas on the proposal; Rawley Thomas, director of research, BCG/HOLT Planning Associates, for guidance on technical sources; Henry Wingate, head librarian of the Darden Graduate School, for helping make all the resources of the library available; and Karen Wruck, associate professor at the Harvard Business School, for her suggestions concerning case-study companies and previous studies of highly leveraged companies.